DK COLLECTOR'S GUIDES

ART DECO

Previous page: Green patinated bronze table lamp by Raymonde Guerbe in the form of a near-nude young woman in an Egyptian robe holding an orange, fan-shaped glass shade. *1920s. 20½ in (52 cm) high* **$2,000–3,000 HERR**

Circular bronze medallion decorated in relief with sun-ray and star motifs and a scantily clad young woman holding lightning bolts above the earth. *c. 1930 2¾ in (7 cm) wide* **$300–400 DD**

DK COLLECTOR'S GUIDES

ART DECO

JUDITH MILLER

with Nicholas M. Dawes

Photography by Graham Rae
with Andy Johnson, John McKenzie, and Heike Löwenstein

LONDON, NEW YORK,
MUNICH, MELBOURNE, DELHI

A joint production from **DK** and
THE PRICE GUIDE COMPANY

DORLING KINDERSLEY LIMITED
Senior Editor Paula Regan
Senior Art Editor Mandy Earey
Managing Editor Julie Oughton
Managing Art Editor Heather McCarry
Art Director Peter Luff
Publishing Director Jackie Douglas
Production Elizabeth Warman
DTP Designer Adam Walker
Picture Research Sarah Smithies
U.S. Editor Christine Heilman

Sands Publishing Solutions LLP
Editors David & Sylvia Tombesi-Walton
Art Editor Simon Murrell

THE PRICE GUIDE COMPANY LIMITED
Publishing Manager Julie Brooke
Managing Editor Claire Smith
Editorial Assistants Sandra Lange, Alexandra Barr
Digital Image Coordinator Ellen Sinclair
Consultant Keith Baker
Chief Contributor John Wainwright

First American Edition, 2005
Published in the United States by
DK Publishing, Inc.
375 Hudson Street
New York, New York 10014

The Price Guide Company (UK) Ltd
Studio 21, Waterside
44–48 Wharf Road, London N1 7UX, UK
info@thepriceguidecompany.com

05 06 07 08 09   10 9 8 7 6 5 4 3 2 1

Color reproduction by Colourscan, Singapore
Printed and bound in China by SNP Leefung

Discover more at
www.dk.com

Contents

Furniture 22

Epstein cocktail cabinet, p.58

Textiles 62

Clutch bag in the style of Delaunay, p.65

Glass 76

Daum cameo-glass vase, p.86

Platinum "duette" pin, p.171

Royal Winton Fan vase, p.138

English kettle and urn, p.184

How to use this book

DK Collector's Guides: Art Deco is divided into eight chapters: furniture; textiles; glass; ceramics; jewelry; silver and metalware; sculpture; and posters and graphics. Each chapter opens with an introductory overview that discusses the historical background of the medium and its place in Art Deco. Here you'll also find a list of key design points. This is followed by profiles of the most important Art Deco designers and factories from Great Britain, Europe, and the United States, as well as examples of their work. Sidebars provide an at-a-glance list of key facts for each designer or factory, and "A Closer Look" boxes highlight pieces of special interest. Every item is concisely described and provided with its measurements, an up-to-date price, and, when possible, a date of production.

Key Facts
Lists important dates in the history of each designer or factory, as well as particular characteristics of output.

Designer Information
Gives a fascinating insight into the career and history of an Art Deco designer or factory. Also highlights characteristics of their work and offers advice on what to look for when collecting.

The Caption
Describes the piece in detail, including the materials used, the date it was made, and its measurements.

The Price Guide
All prices are shown in ranges to give you a ballpark figure. If the piece is in a museum or has not been seen on the market for some time and no price is available, the letters NPA will be used.

The Source Code
With the exception of museum pieces, most items in the book were specially photographed at an auction house, dealer, antiques market, or private collection. Each source is credited here. See pp.230–34 for full listings.

Foreword

Standing in front of the Chrysler Building in New York and gazing up at its sculpted roof, you cannot help but be stunned by the beauty of its Art Deco style. The lines of the skyscraper sum up much of what Art Deco means to me—streamlined, elegant, and the first glimpse of the "modern" look that would define the 20th century.

In fact, the Art Deco period has become such an iconic era of the last 100 years that it is strange to think the movement was only given its name in the 1960s, when people wanted a blanket term for the many exciting new ideas that had emerged during the 1920s and 30s. Art Deco has come to mean everything from the exclusive, classical French designs of Jacques-Emile Ruhlmann to the revolutionary, clean Modernist lines of Le Corbusier and Ludwig Mies van der Rohe.

Its popularity at the time was aided by the post–World War I economy and technological developments that led to the rise of mass production. Many pieces, such as jewelry and radios, were made in the newly popularized plastic and were in the Art Deco style, but they were more affordable than much of the furniture, glass, silver, and ceramics being produced by most big-name designers.

New trade links and improved communications allowed the trend to spread worldwide. The obsession with speed and travel is reflected in the familiar streamlined designs of vivid posters featuring ships and trains.

What many people tend to forget is that this was also an age of female pioneers. At a time when women were only just winning the vote in Great Britain (1918) and the United States (1920), women such as Clarice Cliff were running their own businesses and marketing their own work. As Art Deco challenged old ideas, it allowed women new freedoms.

Art Deco's association with cocktail parties and the jazz scene makes it a seductive movement for collectors—one that rejected old-fashioned Victorian values and allowed flapper girls to revel in the liberation of dances such as the Charleston. I like to think that each time I buy a piece of Art Deco glass, I am bringing a little of that glamour back to life.

Judith Miller.

Lorenzl nude dancer statue, p.205

What is Art Deco?

When the musician Louis Armstrong was asked "What is jazz?", he replied: "If you have to ask, you will never know." He could justifiably have given the same reply about Art Deco, the movement that engulfed his own unique artistry as it raced through interwar culture at exhilarating speed.

Most protagonists of the Art Deco movement would not have been familiar with the term that came to define them, however. Unlike Art Nouveau, which was in common parlance by the 1890s, Art Deco is a relatively modern term. It was coined in 1966, when a museum exhibition held in the French capital presented a retrospective of the 1925 Paris Exposition. The term derives from the first syllables of the French for decorative arts (*arts décoratifs*), words that appeared in the full title of the seminal 1925 event: Exposition Internationale des Arts Décoratifs et Industriels Modernes. The exhibition

The Chrysler Building in New York is an impressive example of Art Deco architecture. In a celebration of the Age of Speed and the motor car, its tower's distinctive ornamentation was inspired by the hubcaps of Chrysler automobiles.

Goldscheider figure of a young female dancer cast in ceramic from a sculpture by Josef Lorenzl. The dynamic pose, slim figure, short dress, and bobbed hair with a skullcap are characteristic of fashionable young women of the 1920s and 30s and of Lorenzl's depiction of them. c. 1930. 17¼ in (44 cm) high **$7,000–9,000 JES**

featured contributions from 34 countries, and a host of individual designers, ranging in taste from traditional to outrageously avant-garde. Art Deco was intended as an umbrella term to define this extraordinary variety. For this reason, there is no such thing as an Art Deco style, but rather there are many versions, evolved over three decades, mostly in Europe and the United States.

The common theme is a clear intent to be "modern," a relatively new and daring concept for a generation whose parents had lived in the Victorian age. This modernity is the essential ingredient in all Art Deco production, whether it is the earliest, exotic taste inspired by the Ballets Russes in Paris before World War I, or the shiny glitz of an American diner from the 1940s.

Exposure to great Art Deco is seductive and intoxicating. Be aware of this if you choose to collect, but with a good eye, regular exposure, and passion, you will eventually feel the same way about this eclectic art movement as Louis Armstrong did about jazz music.

Mahogany secretaire by Jules Leleu inlaid with rosewood. It has two doors enclosing a fitted interior above an arched apron flanked by a pair of drawers. On tapering octagonal legs. *c. 1930 47¾ in (121 cm) wide* **$30,000–40,000 GYG**

Silver-plated tea set by Joseph Rodgers & Sons of Birmingham, England. The teapot, hot-water pot, V-form milk jug, and matching sugar bowl are of angular form, with Bakelite handles. *1935 Teapot: 7½ in (19 cm) high* **$7,000–9,000 JES**

Fantasque teapot by Clarice Cliff. Of conical form, it has a triangular spout and handle, and a Chinese hat lid, painted with a Broth Bubble pattern against a green, orange, blue, and black-banded ground. *c. 1930. 7 in (18 cm) high* **$900–1,200 ROS**

Globular vase by Charles Schneider, with an everted rim and a spreading foot in black glass. The latter contrasts with the red and orange intercalaire glass body etched with pairs of curved, straplike bands. *c. 1925. 9 in (22.75 cm) high* **$9,000–12,000 DD**

The 1925 Paris Exposition

Wrought-iron firescreen attributed to Edgar Brandt. At its center is a large cartouche of roses wrought in a stylized Cubist form. Like the rest of the piece, they have a hammered and polished finish. *1920s. 28½ in (72.25 cm) high* **$18,000–20,000 DD**

The concept of an international trade fair began in earnest in 1851, when Joseph Paxton's enormous Crystal Palace, in London's Hyde Park, housed the event still referred to as The Great Exhibition. Paris hosted several fairs, notably in 1889, under the Eiffel Tower, and the extraordinary Exposition Universelle in 1900. The organizers were naturally eager to repeat their success but were unable to stage a followup event until 1925, due largely to the disruption of World War I.

The 1925 Paris Exposition, held from April to October, was a remarkable achievement and an enormously successful event for the promotion of French industry and taste.

Thirty-four countries (not including the United States, which declined to participate, citing lack of commercial potential), presented pavilions and other exhibits, with scores of contributions from leading French *artistes décorateurs* and designers in all genres.

Wrought-iron console table by Raymond Subes. The top is on scrolling supports rising from a solid base and interspersed with stepped bars. Subes showed a nearly identical table at the 1925 Paris Exposition. *39½ in (100.5 cm) high* **$30,000–50,000 CALD**

The Parisian department store Galeries Lafayette's pavilion at the 1925 Paris Exposition had a bold Art Deco facade that, like the interior, was faced in a richly textured marble. Its entrance was dominated by a vast sunburst motif.

Elegant, concave-front commode by Jacques-Emile Ruhlmann. Now in the Musée du Louvre, it is in macassar ebony and features a stylized charioteer motif of inlaid ivory. Ruhlmann's furniture is widely considered the best of the Art Deco period. c. 1930. 88 in (224 cm) wide **NPA RMN**

Conical Montmorency vase by Lalique in opalescent glass. It is molded with four bands of cherries divided by ribbing and highlighted with blue staining, and it has the frosted finish found on many Lalique pieces. *1920s* *8 in (20.5 cm) high* **$10,000–15,000 AS&S**

Luminaries showed their work throughout the event. Jacques-Emile Ruhlmann had his own pavilion and contributed to several others, including the French Embassy building. René Lalique had two pavilions, contributed to the Sèvres pavilion and the Hall of Perfume, and displayed architectural glass in several places, notably an enormous illuminated fountain that greeted visitors at the main entrance. Edgar Brandt's wrought iron was used in the entrance gates and elsewhere, including his pavilion. Louis Süe and André Mare's architectural and interior designs were ubiquitous, mainly in a sumptuous, neo-Rococo form of Art Deco identified by rich gilding and detail such as stylized fruits. This taste is commonly referred to as "1925 style."

More than 50 million visitors passed through Edgar Brandt's gates, many of them foreigners of wealth and influence. Within a few years, modern French style was internationally popular, particularly in the United States. Anyone who visits the Chrysler Building in New York, designed by William Van Alen (1883–1954), will see 1925 Paris preserved in the magnificent lobby.

Carlton Ware luster bowl printed and hand painted with a polychrome-enamel Tutankhamun pattern over a cobalt-blue ground. Its jewel-like appearance is produced by a high-gloss pearlized glaze. *1920s. 5½ in (14 cm) wide* **$400–700 WW**

Hexagonal gray stoneware vase made by the Faïencerie de Longwy and decorated with an Egyptianesque pattern in gilt and blue, yellow, and red enamels over a craquelure glazed ground. *c. 1925. 7 in (18 cm) high* **$1,500–2,000 QU**

Ovoid vase by Jean Mayodon, decorated with images of Adam, Eve, and the serpent in the Garden of Eden. Mayodon often drew on Biblical and Classical imagery for inspiration. *1930s 22½ in (57 cm) high* **$30,000–50,000 CUV**

Origins and influences

Influences on Art Deco are as varied as the movement itself. The Ballets Russes is widely considered to be the spark that ignited Art Deco in Paris, fueled by a colorful *Arabian Nights* theme. Early Art Deco includes exotic fashion by the Ballets' designer Paul Poiret or furnishings by his protégé Paul Iribe that were made before World War I. Indeed, Poiret maintained his influence throughout the period, as witnessed by his magnificent display from a barge floating on the Seine at the 1925 Paris Exposition.

World War I devastated northern Europe, but the aftermath saw a gradual growth in the new taste for adventure, leisure, and luxury. This Age of Elegance (peaking at the Exposition Coloniale in Paris in 1931) introduced colonial

influence, evident in the use of exotic materials such as sharkskin, ivory, and macassar ebony. African themes were popularized, too, by black American Jazz Age performers, first and foremost the dancer Josephine Baker, who, for the French, embodied the combination of African and American cultures. Increased communications revived the taste for Asian design and created a style devoted to luxury travel; this can be seen in cars, ocean liners, train car interiors, and grand hotels. Unique for its short life span as an exotic influence on Art Deco is Egyptian styling, which emerged with the discovery of Tutankhamun's tomb in 1922 and all but disappeared by the late 1920s.

The geometric approach seen in a lot of Art Deco is rooted in neoclassicism and restrained ornament, which was a reaction to Victorian excesses. The most popular stylized image may be the frozen fountain—also the title of a 1931 design book by Claude Bragdon. Much post-1930s Art Deco is also influenced by the Depression and forced austerity; this is most visible in American streamlined style and the use of inexpensive materials.

Unsigned andiron (one of a pair) in aluminum and bronze in the form of a stylized water fountain. The latter was boosted in popularity as a decorative motif by Lalique's glass fountain at the 1925 Paris Exposition. c. 1930. 20¼ in (51.5 cm) high **$10,000–12,000 (the pair) DD**

Large *cloisonné* platter with a jungle landscape and female nudes in shades of blue. Inspired by the African art of Picasso, it was designed by the Primavera Design Studio of the French department store Au Printemps and made by the Faïencerie de Longwy. 1920s. 14½ in (36.75 cm) wide **$5,000–6,000 DD**

Stained-ivory and tortoiseshell box in shades of brown and orange and engraved with Asian-style plant-form imagery. The latter is flanked by silver bands that, like the silver clasp, are set with small diamonds. c. 1920s 3¼ in (8.25 cm) wide **$3,000–4,000 NBLM**

Iconography

The desire to be modern led designers to numerous themes, some deeply rooted in their own cultures, but many entirely new. Among the most apparent innovations in Art Deco was the new approach to graphic layout and typefaces. This was developed by pioneers in this area at the Wiener Werkstätte, the Bauhaus, and beyond, including French poster artists and Edward Johnston's perennially popular London Underground typeface of 1916. Most Art Deco typefaces use geometric stylization, a technique evident throughout the movement from about 1925 and found in all forms of Art Deco, from jewelry to architecture. Pure geometry, sometimes expressed in design drawings as mathematical formulae, is best seen in the work of silversmith Jean Puiforcat (1897–1945).

In many designs, the geometric pattern is an interpretation of Aztec, Inca, or other native American iconography, which had a strong influence on French taste in the mid-1920s due in part to increased travel opportunities to the Americas. The most popular icon related to this cultural trend is the sunburst, but many zigzag

Watercolor design for a French "Soldes" (sale) poster. The uncluttered typeface and clear layout, enhanced by the contrast of a pale tint and a dark shade of brown, typify the boldness of Art Deco poster design. *20½ in (52 cm) wide* **$3,000–4,000 JES**

Parachute lamp with a stitched vellum shade and a bronze and ivory base with a chryselephantine figure of a fairylike female dancer from a sculpture by Richard W. Lange of Rosenthal und Maeder. *1925* *34 in (86 cm)* **$18,000–20,000 JES**

14

Platinum ring by F. Folgert in Machine Age style with a row of coglike forms of graduated size. It is channel-set with alternate rows of round-cut diamonds and square-cut rubies. *1940s. ¾ in (2 cm) long* **$3,000–5,000 MACK**

Circular silver compact enameled in black, red, and cream. Probably of German origin, it features an asymmetrical geometric pattern resonating with speed and dynamism. *1930s 3½ in (9 cm) wide* **$300–500 JES**

Bottle-shaped stoneware (grès) vase designed by Charles Catteau for Boch Frères Keramis with a segmented pattern of stylized, sun-ray-like forms enameled in green, yellow, and blue beneath bands of blue and yellow under the rim. *c. 1925. 12½ in (32 cm) high* **$1,800–2,500 MOD**

designs are also native American in origin. The sun culture, a consequence of post–World War I leisure-seeking, also brought images of the flora and fauna of the colonial world to Paris. Several animals came to symbolize Art Deco feminine elegance, just as the lily had symbolized languid female beauty in the Art Nouveau period. *Biches* (deer), pumas and other big cats, and the chic borzoi hounds became the iconic subjects of the style.

There is no substitute for the female form itself, of course, and Art Deco designers delighted in depicting sleek, slim bodies with cropped hairstyles dressed in costumes suitable for Les Folies Bergères, the latest fashions, or undressed in seductive poses.

Modern technology became another fashion accessory, with planes, automobiles, and even parachutes featuring in uniquely Art Deco designs.

Patinated bronze figure of a recumbent deer with impressive wooden antlers, cast from a sculpture by Karl Hagenauer. The figure combines flowing curves, clean angles, and elongated, tapering limbs. *c. 1930. 11½ in (29.5 cm) long* **$1,500–2,200 QU**

New lifestyles

The history of culture is punctuated by cataclysmic events, and few rival World War I in terms of influence or contrast between before and after. It is impossible to understand the Art Deco movement without considering the Great War. Prior to 1914, life in much of the western world was conservative and predictable, with well-established social conditions governing the roles of men, women, and class. The modern age, considered by many the true beginning of the 20th century, began in 1918 with a burst of energy that is the essence of the Art Deco movement. It was the first roar of the 1920s.

The effects and manifestations of this new era are both obvious and subtle. New roles for women during the war years, combined with a dramatic reduction

Breakfront cocktail cabinet by Harry and Lou Epstein veneered in mirror-cut walnut. The upper cabinet has two hinged double doors enclosing a mirrored and illuminated interior. *1929 61¾ in (157 cm) high* **$9,000–10,000 JAZ**

Bee Jackson photographed in the early 1920s, when she was world champion of the Charleston, the dance craze that swept across the United States during the Jazz Age.

Hinged Philadelphia bracelet in yellow bakelite with, at the opening, two opposing rows of bakelite triangles in red, yellow, green, and black. *1930s. 1½ in (3.5 cm) wide* **$2,000–3,000 JES**

English silver cigarette case decorated with the stylized figures of a fashionably dressed young couple polychrome enameled on a black enameled ground. *1931. 2¾ in (7 cm) long* **$4,000–5,000 JES**

Queen Mary **ashtray** of geometric form, made for the luxury cruise liner in pink on black urea-formaldehyde plastic by The British Buttner Pipe Company Ltd. *1930s 4½ in (11.5 cm) long* **$300–400 JES**

Issue of *Vogue* magazine (one of 13) for the year 1934. This is the "Winter Travel" edition; other subjects include spring and fall fashions from Paris and London. *1934 13 in (33 cm) long* **$500–600 (the set) ON**

in the numbers of young men (France, Germany, and Great Britain all lost about one in 20 of their male population in the conflict), led to postwar female prominence in all fields, from recreation and sports to politics and business. Female liberation was evident in the fashion for short hair and pants and in a new consumerism aimed at women. Simple but radical new trends included "flapper" women smoking, drinking, and generally enjoying themselves in domains previously open only to men.

The general wave of liberation that spread through Europe in the 1920s created the cocktail bar (especially popular with Americans in Europe during Prohibition), making any cocktail accessory of the period delightfully Art Deco. Youth culture gained respect, due in part to the heroic role played by young people in the war, resulting in even the most traditional members of society trying to act "modern." The most influential vehicle in spreading the modern word, including all things American, was radio, common in most western homes by the 1930s. Just looking at a period radio evokes the strains of jazz or a big band, the theme music of the Art Deco movement.

Sparton Model 557 radio, design influenced by Walter Dorwin Teague, with a blue mirrored cover, black sleigh base, and chrome fins. *c. 1935. 17 in (43.25 cm) wide* **$1,800–6,000 EG**

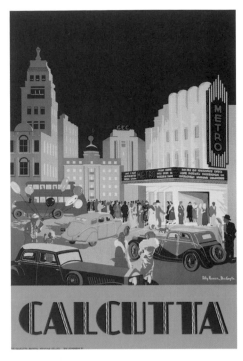

Polychrome Calcutta advertising poster designed by Philip Kumar Das Gupta, promoting a night out at the new Metro Cinema. Owned by MGM and boasting a fashionable Art Deco facade, it was the first real movie theater in Calcutta. *1938. 39 in (99 cm) high* **$2,500–3,000 SWA**

A worldwide style

Globalization is commonly considered a modern phenomenon, but Art Deco had touched much of the world by the 1930s, uniting diverse cultures in the pursuit of modernity. Although Paris is the movement's undisputed birthplace, Art Deco spread far and wide, due to trade routes between France and other European countries and to colonial ties, notably those linking Great Britain with India, the Netherlands with Southeast Asia, and France and Belgium with several African countries. Certain Asian cities, notably Shanghai, became thriving centers of international trade, and well-preserved Art Deco interiors may be found there today; so, too, in South America, a haven for Germans and other wealthy Europeans in the interwar years.

Japanese Art Deco is not related to colonial ties, but arose from a general desire in interwar Japan to emulate Western fashions. The wealthiest Japanese visited France, bringing back modern artifacts. Among this elite was the thoroughly modern Prince Asahi, who commissioned

Tourism poster designed by P. Irwin Brown for the Japanese Government Railways. Printed in muted shades of green, blue, yellow, and black, it is a simple but evocative image of a peaceful Japanese evening tableau. *1934 37¼ in (94.5 cm) high* **$1,000–1,800 SWA**

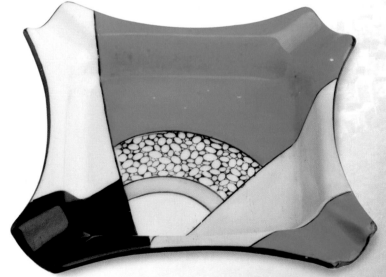

Japanese porcelain ashtray designed and made by Noritake. Its curvaceous streamlined form is hand-painted in green, black, and yellow enamels, with an asymmetric pattern that includes a band of faux crushed eggshell. *1930s. 4½ in (11.5 cm) wide* **$120–180 BAD**

Henri Rapin to design a remarkable private residence in the heart of Tokyo in the late 1920s, furnished by leading *artistes décorateurs* and lit with Lalique fixtures. The house is beautifully preserved and open to the public as the Teien Art Museum.

The best Art Deco architecture in the world is in the United States. Enclaves of low-rise architecture still exist, mainly in California and Florida. Miami Beach, a hugely popular resort for New Yorkers and Midwesterners in the 1930s, boasts an entire Art Deco District of preserved housing, hotels, and shopping facilities, much of it lit by night in spectacular colored neon. For sheer power and inspiration, though, nothing rivals the great American skyscrapers, found mostly in Manhattan, where the Rockefeller Center, the Chrysler Building, and the Empire State Building stand proudly as symbols of Art Deco.

Miami's Art Deco Historic District was built from the late 1920s to around 1940. Initially inspired by the architecture of the 1925 Paris Exposition, the buildings display angular, clean lines and strong vertical accenting. Decorative forms include geometric patterns, industrial symbols, traditional Egyptian, American Indian, and Mayan motifs, and, in some areas, nautical imagery.

Statue of Christ the Redeemer on the Corcovado peak overlooking Rio de Janeiro, Brazil. With its bold, flowing lines, smooth surface, and stylized features, Paul Landowski's monument is Art Deco sculpture on the grandest scale. An inherently traditional symbol of Latin American Catholicism, it also embraces modernity, in both style and construction. *1924-31. 125 ft (38 m) high*

The beginnings of Modernism

The Swiss architect Le Corbusier (1887–1965) remarked during an interview at the 1925 Paris Exposition that the event represented "the end of an era of antique-lovers and the beginning of a modern age." The "antique-lovers" he referred to were designers such as Süe et Mare or Jacques-Emile Ruhlmann. Their work, although unmistakably modern, was nevertheless rooted in the 18th century, as was evident in the use of traditional materials, forms, and methods of cabinetry. Le Corbusier's contribution to the Exposition was the avant-garde Pavillon de l'Esprit Nouveau (Pavilion of the New Spirit), furnished with modular units and tubular-steel furniture of his own or Bauhaus design and decorated with little color beyond the paintings of Fernand Léger.

Le Corbusier was proved right, of course. The lasting legacy of 1925 is almost entirely derived from his small and controversial pavilion, which at the event received little recognition or critical praise. Le Corbusier could not have predicted the Depression, which gave inexpensive, mass-produced furnishings a new relevance in society, or the modern respect given to progressive designers such as Ludwig Mies van der Rohe (1886–1969) or his Bauhaus

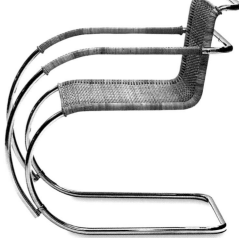

Tecta reissue of a cantilevered, chromed tubular-steel–framed armchair originally designed c. 1927 by Ludwig Mies van der Rohe. This example has a cane seat and back. *2004 31 in (79 cm) high* **$1,200–1,500 TEC**

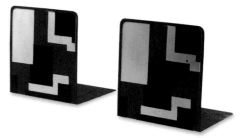

Pair of L-shaped bookends designed by Marianne Brandt in sheet metal with a geometrical pattern in red, black, and gray lacquering. *c. 1930. 5¾ in (14.5 cm) high* **$500–700 HERR**

Knoll International reissue of a Barcelona MR90 chair designed in 1929 by Ludwig Mies van der Rohe with a chromed-steel X-frame and buttoned leather cushions. *1980s. 29½ in (75 cm) wide* **$1,000–1,500 L&T**

Bauhaus architectural and design study of cubic and rectangular forms, utilizing brass and sheet copper with red- and blue-tinted window glass. *c. 1920. 14 in (35.5 cm) high* **$25,000–35,000 QU**

colleagues Walter Gropius (1883–1969) and Marcel Breuer (1902–81). However, he did accurately predict the longevity of the style we now call Modernism, once included under the umbrella of Art Deco.

Modernism did not begin in 1925. Early trends toward simplicity in form, design for industrial manufacture, and the influence of architects can be traced to the pre–World War I years, notably the Dutch De Stijl movement led by Gerrit Rietveld (1888–1964). An overwhelming influence, however, stemmed from the German Bauhaus, a school of architecture and design founded in Weimar in 1919. Tubular-steel furniture, the bread and butter of the Modern movement, was introduced at the Bauhaus about 1925.

From classical Art Deco to Modernist designs, the desire was to create a stylish, modern look to suit the new era. A revival in the mid-1960s contributed to the style's enduring popularity.

Thonet reissue of a nest of tables originally designed in 1925 by Marcel Breuer with chrome-plated tubular-steel frames and painted wooden tops. 2004. Largest: 23¼ in (60 cm) high **$800–1,000 TEC**

Cassina reissue of chaise-longue LC-4 originally designed by Le Corbusier, Charlotte Perriand, and Pierre Jeanneret in 1928. In chrome-plated tubular steel, matt black base, and black leather upholstery. c. 2000. 63 in (160 cm) long **$1,200–1,800 QU**

Furniture

Art Deco furniture is as varied as the culture of the period and ranges in standard of manufacture from craftsmanship and materials worthy of an 18th-century French *ébéniste* to inexpensive, mass-produced items. Most formal French pieces reflect contemporary trends, notably the taste for Louis XVI style, and arguably only the most progressive designs transcend historic interpretation.

The best Art Deco furniture was made in France by French and immigrant designers drawn to the cutting edge of modern taste celebrated at the 1925 Paris Exposition. French designers achieved international prestige and patronage, particularly among wealthy Americans, who traveled regularly to Paris in search of the latest fashions and entertainment.

Outside France, indigenous styles of Art Deco furniture struggled for survival. A sleek style of Art Deco using birch wood appeared briefly in Scandinavia before evolving into the familiar postwar Danish Modern, while a severe, dark-wood architectural brand of Art Deco with strong neoclassical overtones was popular in Germany and Austria in the 1930s, though it is considered an extension of Biedermeier. Architect Albert Speer designed extreme versions of this furniture.

ADAPTING FRENCH STYLE

Few British Art Deco furniture makers attempted innovative, indigenous styles, preferring conservative interpretations of formal French taste. Most furniture of the London School, including the work of the Epstein brothers (*see p.58*) and Ray Hille (*see p.59*), represents this movement in walnut and veneers.

Following the 1925 Paris Exposition, several large American furniture-makers, including Heywood-Wakefield, made interpretations of French formal style using mahogany, palisander, macassar ebony, and ivory. The furniture of Jacques-Emile Ruhlmann (*see pp.26–27*) achieved great prestige and popularity in New York after it was promoted by the B. Altman department store and was a prime target for reproduction.

Pair of American Skyscraper-style bedside cabinets made in black lacquered and silvered wood, raised on nickel plant-form and ball feet, and with a glass top to the lower tier. *1930s. 40 in (101.5 cm) high* **$9,000–12,000 HSD**

THE RISE OF THE *ARTISTE DÉCORATEUR*

By the late 1920s, many leading French Art Deco furniture designers, led by Ruhlmann, grew into the exalted position of *artiste décorateur*, offering entire interior schemes of their own conception. Most of the period's visionaries were also architects, notably Eileen Gray (1879–1976), who came to Paris from her native Ireland and developed a modern style of lacquered wood and tubular-steel furniture sold through her own Galerie Jean Desert from 1922 until about 1930. Pierre Chareau (1883–1950) was another architect and furniture designer, best known for his Parisian Maison de Verre, built largely in glass between 1929 and 1931. The pieces of Pierre Legrain (1889–1929) combined bold African imagery with fashionable French taste, while

Armand-Albert Rateau (1882–1938) used Egyptian and exotic motifs in furniture often cast in bronze. Jean-Michel Frank (1895–1941) championed the use of luxurious materials such as soft leathers, parchment, sharkskin, vellum (used on walls and furniture), and mellow, blond woods. Frank's simple, elegant style has led to a vast number of modern copies, as well as legitimate reproductions.

A UNIQUELY BRITISH TASTE

British furniture designers who broke from the French tradition include Gordon Russell (*see p.57*), whose work is architecturally elegant, Betty Joel (*see p.56*), whose sensuous, feminine, and curvaceous lines evoke the Hollywood spirit found in American Decorator pieces, and Gerald Summers (1899–1967), who favored plywood, reflecting Scandinavian influence.

Older firms, such as Gillows of Lancaster (est. 1727), which employed Paul Follot (*see p.28*) in the 1930s, and Heal & Son of London (est. 1800), made fine but reserved Art Deco in French taste, including some pieces in limed oak. This furniture has been largely ignored by modern collectors but is rarely disappointing. Other English firms include the Birmingham-based PEL (Practical Equipment Ltd.), founded in 1931 as a maker of Bauhaus-style tubular-steel furniture.

AMERICAN ART DECO STYLES

Beyond copies of French style, two principal schools evolved in American Art Deco furniture: Decorator and American Modern. Decorator furniture implies a custom-made, unique style, often designed to satisfy a particular patron. This category is exemplified by the designs of English-

Transat chair designed by Eileen Gray and named after the French cruise-liner company Transatlantique. It has an unlacquered wooden frame with chrome hardware, a sling seat, and an adjustable back rest upholstered in brown leather. Alternative versions had lacquered frames and/or black leather upholstery. *1925–30. 42 in (106.5 cm) deep*
$25,000–35,000 ($2,500–4,000 for a modern reproduction) JES

KEY POINTS

Art Deco furniture is characterized by the bold precision of its shapes and forms. The degree to which decoration is determined by theories of functionalism and/or minimalism varies, but decorative details are rarely superfluous add-ons. Indeed, decoration is often limited to the aesthetic properties intrinsic to favored materials. In addition to plate mirror glass, chromed tubular steel, and patinated bronze, these include high-gloss lacquer, ivory, mother-of-pearl, and woods such as sycamore, burr walnut, Amboina, and macassar ebony.

Heal's English-made sideboard comprising three recessed central drawers flanked by two cupboards, all raised on turned tapered and fluted legs. The front and sides are veneered in boldly figured macassar ebony and bordered top and bottom by ebony and ivory banding. Ivory is also employed for the pulls and feet. *1929–30 35 in (89 cm) high* **NPA MAL**

Design for a small salon by Jacques-Emile Ruhlmann. The opulent materials and the interplay of detail and color draw on pre-20th century French decoration, yet the room is unmistakably modern.

Warren McArthur (1885–1961), and Norman Bel Geddes (*see p.190*), who all worked in innovative materials and geometric style. Gilbert Rohde (*see pp.50–51*) designed functional wood furniture, mostly for Herman Miller and Heywood-Wakefield, while Kem Weber (1889–1963) brought the modern style to California in the 1930s. The most innovative designer of the period was Frank Lloyd Wright (1867–1959), the greatest US architect. He is unquestionably the leading influence on American Art Deco style, beginning with extraordinary rectilinear metal furniture designed for the Larkin Office Building in Buffalo, New York, as early as 1904. His work is widely reproduced and copied.

born T. H. Robsjohn-Gibbins (1905–76), who worked mostly in the US from the 1930s to the 1950s in exaggerated neoclassical taste, claiming the Greek rooms at the Victoria & Albert Museum as his main source of inspiration. His most celebrated client was the hotelier Conrad Hilton.

The best American Art Deco was designed by Europe-inspired members of the Modern movement from about 1930. They include Donald Deskey (*see p.48*), Paul T. Frankl (*see pp.46–47*),

French walnut-veneered pedestal table by an unrecorded designer and maker. Raised on a columnar pedestal of circular section, its circular top has a plain apron rimmed with quadrant beading and mirrors the smaller diameter base supported, in turn, on X-frame feet with chamfered edges. *1930s. Top: 24¼ in (61.5 cm) wide* **$5,000–7,000 LM**

Twin-door cabinet by Jean-Michel Frank and Adolphe Chanaux. It has a sycamore-wood carcass and is veneered with squares of parchment. The use of the latter, and of materials such as vellum, shagreen, and leather, is typical of Frank's designs. *c. 1930. 43¼ in (110 cm) wide* **$150,000+ GYG**

Barrel chair by Frank Lloyd Wright. Conceived in 1904, it preempted Art Deco style by almost two decades, and has been consistently reproduced with minor modifications to this day. *1937. 32 in (81 cm) high* **$30,000–40,000 ($1,000–1,800 for a modern reproduction) WRI**

Jacques-Emile Ruhlmann took over management of the family decorating firm on the death of his father, François Ruhlmann, in 1907.

He first exhibited furniture designs at the Salon d'Automne in 1913.

The firm of Ruhlmann et Laurent was founded in 1919.

The 1920s were Ruhlmann's decade of achievement, highlighted by a spectacular display at the 1925 Paris Exposition.

Ruhlmann was seriously affected by the Depression years and business declined between 1929 and his death in 1933.

Jacques-Emile Ruhlmann

The French luxury taste in Art Deco furnishings is embodied by Jacques-Emile Ruhlmann. His creations are considered national treasures in France and fought over by international museums and collectors.

Jacques-Emile Ruhlmann (1879–1933) grew up surrounded by the elegant, high-quality wallpapers, paintings, and mirrors available at his father's Parisian interior-design firm, Societé Ruhlmann, and he began working there after military service in 1901. He showed early talent as a designer and draftsman, and produced thousands of sketches and working drawings throughout his career. These offer a glimpse into his design process and are rare and highly prized today.

Ruhlmann's style changed relatively little throughout his productive period and is thus easily identified. His furniture is characterized by elegant lines, complementary to the French Gôut Grec or Louis XVI style, the use of exotic materials, and exceptionally high standards of craftsmanship, comparable to the work of royal *ébénistes* in the 18th century.

In 1919 Ruhlmann went into partnership with Pierre Laurent, a builder and remodeler, to found REL (Ruhlmann et Laurent), the biggest firm of its type in Paris, employing more than 600 people. REL thrived through the 1920s and Ruhlmann enjoyed the elegant lifestyle he designed for. An avid fly-fisherman, he designed and used a tackle box made from macassar ebony and furnished his showroom with beloved antiques mixed with his own creations.

Following his death, Ruhlmann furniture designs were made under the direction of his nephew, Alfred Porteneuve.

Above: Black lacquered stool-frame table with slender, tapering legs and a rectangular frosted-glass top. *c. 1935. 31½ in (80 cm) wide* **$60,000–80,000 CALD**

METICULOUS DESIGN

Many of Ruhlmann's furniture designs have been reproduced, but the standard of detail is never replicated. Look for careful choice of woods and precisely executed inlays of ivory, mother-of-pearl, or metal. Carved detail, found mostly on earlier furniture, is always subtle and of the highest standard. Ruhlmann also paid close attention to hardware: keys and escutcheons tend to match, and original keys will increase value.

Ruhlmann was also renowned for his interior-design work and created critically acclaimed living spaces for wealthy clients.

Variant of a Napoleon-model armchair with an upholstered oval back, hexagonal seat, and curved arms. The tapering legs appear to be outside rather than underneath the chair. *1920 38½ in (98 cm) high* **$25,000–35,000 CALD**

RUHLMANN-
DESIGNED INTERIOR

Brown leather-upholstered armchair with a rounded back and white-piped "elephant ear" arms, all raised on macassar ebony feet. Introduced for the 1931 Exposition Coloniale Paris.

38 in (96.5 cm) wide

NPA   **DEL**

Brown velvet-upholstered armchair with a burr Amboina-wood frame with ebony details and gilt-metal sabots, originally commissioned for the family of Marcel Coard. *c. 1910*

39½ in (100.5 cm) high

NPA   **DEL**

Nickel-plated and hammered-bronze ceiling lamp made in the style of Ruhlmann, with two graduated shades composed of hanging strings of Egyptian-style pearls. *1920s*

27½ in (70 cm) wide

$3,000–4,000   **CSB**

Low fireside table with a rotating circular top, stepped pedestal, and arched base veneered in Amboina. Has the highly desirable "Ruhlmann Atelier A" signature. *c. 1930*

29¼ in (74.5 cm) wide

NPA   **DEL**

Ola Ola reading desk with an adjustable and foldable top and a wheeled frame, all made in macassar ebony. It bears the "Ruhlmann Atelier B" signature. *c. 1920*

31½ in (80 cm) wide

NPA   **DEL**

A CLOSER LOOK

Rosewood-veneered and ivory-inlaid cabinet of demi-lune form raised on fluted spindle legs with two cupboards flanking a central slide, shelved recess, and drawer. It carries the very desirable "Ruhlmann Atelier A" signature. *c. 1920. 50¾ in (129 cm) wide* **NPA DEL**

FLORAL SWAG AND TAILS CARVED IN DEEP RELIEF

Understated inlay work is used to contrast with hardwood veneers. Ruhlmann's favorite materials included tortoiseshell, mother-of-pearl, bronze, and, as here, ivory

Ruhlmann usually employed figured hardwood veneers such as macassar ebony, Amboina, and, as here, rosewood. He also sometimes used shagreen (sharkskin) as a veneer

Prior to 1925, when his pieces became more Cubist, Ruhlmann was inspired by neoclassical forms and motifs, as exemplified by this floral swag-and-tails carving

Slim, tapering legs, sometimes embellished, as here, with fluting, are a recurring feature of Ruhlmann's neoclassical-inspired furniture

Paul Follot was a member of the Societé des Artistes Décorateurs from 1901.

He was associated with Pomone, the interior-design store with Bon Marché, from 1923.

The Pomone stand at the 1925 Paris Exposition was designed by Follot.

Neo-Rococo style applies to Follot's designs of the mid-1920s.

His style continually evolved, beginning as Art Nouveau and becoming Cubist by the late 1920s, and entirely Modernist by 1930.

Paul Follot remained active until the mid-1930s.

Paul Follot

One of the main protagonists of the Art Deco movement, Paul Follot exercised a massive influence well beyond his native France. His style was often copied, and the term "Follot style" is still in widespread use.

Paul Follot (1877–1941) began his career in Paris before 1900 and was soon recognized as a progressive designer by La Maison Moderne. This was the short-lived gallery of modern design founded in Paris in 1899 by the German dealer Julius Meier-Graefe, a rival to Siegfried Bing and his better-known gallery Maison de L'Art Nouveau.

Follot's colleagues at La Maison Moderne included Maurice Dufrène (*see p.33*) and Clement Mere, who enjoyed careers parallel to Follot's in success and standard of design.

Today, Follot is best known as an Art Deco furniture designer, although he was active as an interior designer for most of his career. He also worked in a wide range of categories, including metalwork, jewelry, ceramics, textiles, and carpets. His work was regularly exhibited at Parisian salons and is best identified by documentation from exhibitions, since few pieces are signed.

By 1920, Follot developed an elegant, luxurious furniture design evoking early Louis XVI in style. Like his 18th-century forebears, he used exotic woods, expensive materials, and complex cabinetry. This style was copied throughout France and abroad and is commonly presented today as "in the manner of Follot."

Above: Giltwood-framed footstool of rectangular form, raised on turned and reeded feet. Its brightly colored upholstery is typical of early Follot. *c. 1920. 25 in (63.5 cm) wide* **$8,000–12,000 CALD**

Amboina-wood cabinet raised on turned and reeded feet and comprising a large central cupboard enclosed behind curved doors and flanked by five tiers of drawers. The highly figured Indonesian wood is contrasted with ivory handles. *c. 1925*
60¼ in (153 cm) high

$18,000–22,000   **TDG**

Rare bergère chair (one of a pair) with ribbed upholstery supported on a stained and polished hardwood frame. The latter features a U-shaped seat rail that extends up to scrolled arm terminals and is raised at the back on saber legs and at the front on fluted and tapered ebonized legs. *c. 1920*
32 in (81.5 cm) high

$15,000–22,000 (the pair)   **CALD**

Süe et Mare

The design team of Louis Süe and André Mare was responsible for establishing the unique Art Deco style referred to as "1925 style." Their furniture ranges from simple elegance to outright flamboyance.

The style of 18th-century France, evolving from Louis XV Rococo to "Le Goût Grecque" of Louis XVI, was highly popular in 1920s interior design and architecture. Many designers, notably Paul Follot (*see opposite*), Louis Süe (1875–1968), and André Mare (1887–1932), successfully interpreted this taste into modern Art Deco, learning many lessons from the past.

By 1912, both Süe and Mare were established in Paris—the former as an architect, the latter as a Cubist painter. At the end of World War I (in which they both fought), they began to collaborate, designing a war memorial together in 1919. Later that year, they formed their interior design firm, the Compagnie des Artistes Français.

In the 1920s, Süe et Mare achieved rapid but short-lived success, peaking at the 1925 Paris Exposition, for which they designed several buildings and interiors. By this time their style featured sweeping curves, often highlighted with gilding, rendered in mahogany or pale woods, with inlays of mother-of-pearl or ivory. Much of their furniture was manufactured by the established firm of Fontaine, which took over Süe et Mare in 1928 when the partnership experienced financial difficulties.

Above: Large mahogany commode with an overhanging top, two doors with wreathlike handles, square corner posts raised on tapering feet, and bead-molding decoration. *c. 1920* *45 in (114.5 cm) wide* **$12,000–18,000 LM**

Demi-lune side table made in bird's-eye maple and mahogany. Raised on elegant, flattened cabriole legs with stylized hoof feet, the table has a large single frieze drawer set beneath a broad cross-banded top with a thumb-molded edge. *c. 1925*

48 in (122 cm) wide

$30,000–40,000   **CALD**

Rosewood side chair with an arched, upholstered back, a stuffed-over seat, a characteristically curvaceous and undulating carved seat rail, and cabriole legs terminating in tightly scrolled and padded feet. *c. 1925*

39 in (99 cm) high

Overmantel giltwood mirror produced in the style of Süe et Mare by an anonymous maker. The frame's S-scrolls and faux drapery motifs, together with its undulating arched-top mirror glass, display the Baroque-like extravagance characteristic of many Süe et Mare pieces. *c. 1925*

34¼ in (87 cm) high

$2,000–3,000   **CSB**

$12,000–18,000   **CALD**

Jules Leleu

During the interwar years, Jules Leleu prospered in Paris as a furniture designer. His Art Deco creations were produced in large numbers, sometimes for commercial patrons, and his pieces are characterized by simple, elegant lines.

Jules Leleu (1883–1961) successfully turned his training as a sculptor into a career as a furniture designer and interior decorator after World War I. Mastery of line is evident in much of his work. Unlike Follot (*see p.28*) or Süe et Mare (*see p.29*), Leleu rarely ventured toward the exotic in style or materials, preferring an unadorned elegance in his later work more evocative of the French Directoire than the excesses of Louis XV or Louis XVI styles. His earlier furniture may be unsigned but is often attributable through contemporary catalogs or interior-scheme photographs. It is typically in dark woods with little flourish and may be mounted in brass, either plain or nickel-plated. This practical style appealed to commercial clients, and much Leleu furniture consists of chairs, desks, and side tables suitable for offices, hotels, or ocean liners. Cabinetry is rare.

In the late 1920s, Leleu embraced architectural Modernism and used more metal in his designs. Generally, his work compares to that of his better-known contemporary Jacques-Emile Ruhlmann (*see pp.26–27*) and is sometimes unfairly referred to as "poor man's Ruhlmann."

Above: Small pedestal table with a round top under mirror glass, a smaller round base in brass, and a central column set in a sleeve of sycamore. *1930s.* Top: 15¼ in (39 cm) wide **$3,000–4,000 CSB**

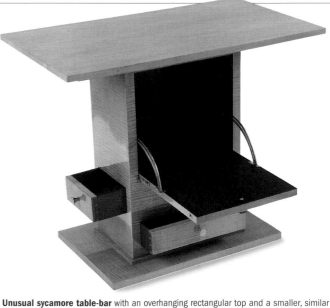

Unusual sycamore table-bar with an overhanging rectangular top and a smaller, similar base. The fall-front bar between them has a drawer to the front and to the side, and its interior is veneered in contrasting dark-brown mahogany. *c. 1930*

24 in (61 cm) high

$20,000–30,000   **CALD**

Mahogany side chair (one of a pair) with a stuffed-over seat and a padded back. The latter has an inverted-heart bottom rail, the flattened arms have distinctive stepped scroll terminals, and the tapering legs terminate in gilt-bronze sabots. *Early 1940s*

29 in (73.5 cm) high

$18,000–22,000 (the pair)   **CALD**

Léon and Maurice Jallot

This father-and-son team designed and manufactured Art Deco furniture of high quality but mostly conservative taste. By the 1930s, their work became comparable to Ruhlmann's in style.

Léon Jallot (1874–1967) was an accomplished furniture designer and craftsman by the time he began collaborating with his son Maurice (1900–71). He had also worked in fabrics, interior design, and architecture. Léon's earlier style relied on natural wood, often with carved details in the manner of late 18th-century French provincial furniture. He produced large, ambitious pieces, including complex cabinetry, a tradition he continued in Art Deco taste between the wars. Typical Jallot furniture made before the mid-1920s is of oak or veneered in sycamore or fruitwood.

Maurice Jallot studied furniture design at the Ecole Boulle in Paris. He introduced more refined techniques, including the use of shagreen, leather, and parchment applied to furniture surfaces.

After 1925, the father-and-son team adopted a more modernistic style in keeping with current trends, and their 1930s furniture is sleek-lined, with metal or even plastic elements.

Above: Ebonized hardwood dining chair by Léon and Maurice Jallot. It has chrome mounts and side rails, and an upholstered seat and back refinished in green leather. *1930. 33 in (84 cm) high*
$8,000–12,000 CALD

Hexagonal-top occasional table by Léon Jallot, raised on six slender, square-section tapering legs united by a radial stretcher. Finished in lacquer, it is decorated with stylized floral bouquets and leaves. *c. 1920*
29½ in (75 cm) high

$18,000–22,000   CALD

Rosewood and ebonized secretaire by Maurice Jallot. Of slightly serpentine form, it houses a glazed shelf and a fall-front writing desk above six drawers. On splayed feet with gilt-bronze sabots. *Mid-1940s*
59¼ in (150.5 cm) high

$30,000–40,000   CALD

Exceptional rosewood and mahogany-veneer secretaire by Léon Jallot. Subtly bow-fronted and with mirror-cut mahogany crotch veneers to the exterior, this piece was exhibited at the 1925 Paris Exposition. *c. 1925*
34¾ in (88 cm) wide

$40,000–60,000   CALD

De Coene Frères was established in Kortrijk, Flanders, in 1895 by brothers Jozef and Adolf De Coene. It is known in Flemish as Kortrijk Kunstwerkstede Gebroeders De Coene.

Traditional furniture was De Coene Frères' staple until the late 1920s.

High-quality Art Deco furniture was produced during the 1930s.

A variety of products is still produced by the company, including architectural elements.

De Coene Frères

Flourishing in Belgium throughout the 1900s, De Coene Frères is little known outside of northern Europe. However, this firm's best furniture rivals French Art Deco of the highest order in standards of both design and manufacture.

De Coene Frères began in the late 19th century as a modest company manufacturing furniture of honest simplicity, in the provincial manner. This tradition continued into the 1920s, by which time De Coene had become Belgium's largest furniture-maker.

The firm exhibited at the 1925 Paris Exposition as part of the "Section Belge," but De Coene's displayed furniture was mostly in the traditional style, certainly compared to the Modernist examples by Belgian designers Marcel Baugniet and Victor Servranckx. Inspired by the commercial success of modern styles in 1925, De Coene began actively copying the French taste.

De Coene's Art Deco furniture is of high quality, often made in exotic materials such as macassar ebony and lacquer, and it resembles the work of Léon and Maurice Jallot (*see p.31*). Pieces may be signed, with a label or ink stamp. Individual designers for De Coene are not recorded, but the recent success of other Belgian Deco furniture, notably the work of Maison Franck of Antwerp, shows this market is developing a new respect.

De Coene Frères remained Belgium's largest and most prestigious furniture company until the late 1970s and is still in operation today.

Above: Lyre or U-shaped console raised on a matching shallow-arched base, all veneered in French-polished mahogany. *1930s* 29½ in (75 cm) high **$3,000–5,000 LM**

Neoclassical-style open-arm desk chair and black lacquered desk. The chair's black lacquered frame accommodates a green-leather upholstered back and seat pads. Its tapered front legs end in nickel-clad feet, echoing chrome bands at the junction of the legs and seat rails. The desk is raised on corner posts of tapering circular section, and its rectangular top spans two pairs of drawers flanking a broad kneehole. The nickel handles and feet are matched by bands of nickel stringing around the perimeter. *c. 1940*

Chair: 34¾ in (88 cm) high
Desk: 68 in (172.5 cm) wide

Bridge chair (one of a pair) with a padded backrest and a drop-in seat pad covered with a two-tone red checker-pattern fabric. The mahogany frame features gently bowed arms, arm supports, and seat rails. *c. 1930*

32¼ in (82 cm) high

$4,000–6,000 (the pair)   LM

$12,000–20,000 (the set)   LM

Maurice Dufrène

By the early 1920s, Maurice Dufrène was mainly an interior designer, or *artiste décorateur*, who operated at the highest level of his profession. His style is more mature and conservative than that of younger designers of the period.

Several leading Parisian department stores—notably Galeries Lafayette and Au Printemps—played an essential role in the promotion of Art Deco taste within and beyond Paris. In these shops, fashionable clients could shop for couture and accessories on one floor and be presented with the latest interior concepts by leading designers on another, all arranged in tempting room settings.

The Parisian designer Maurice Dufrène (1876–1955) was already well established and respected in his field by the time he assumed responsibility for La Maîtrise studio at Galeries Lafayette in 1921. Best known for his furniture, he also designed fabrics, metalwork, pottery, rugs, and interiors. Early in his career, Dufrène developed an austere, neoclassical style of furniture design that was sympathetic to the perennially popular Louis XVI taste. His pieces were typically made in dark mahogany or, occasionally, exotic woods, sometimes with ebonized detail.

Unlike the work of Süe et Mare (*see p.29*) or Paul Follot (*see p.28*), Dufrène's furniture has little carved ornament; by the 1930s his style became angular and even simpler. His pieces may be signed with a "La Maîtrise" label.

Above: Mahogany-frame desk chair with an arched-tub padded back descending to boldly scrolled arm terminals, and with a padded squab above scrolled and tapering legs. *c. 1920*
28 in (71 cm) high **$8,000–12,000 CALD**

KEY FACTS

Dufrène began designing in 1899 and worked in the Art Nouveau style before World War I.

Furniture design was Dufrène's specialty in the 1920s. He taught at the Ecole Boulle in Paris 1912–23.

La Maîtrise interior design showrooms at the Galeries Lafayette were managed by Dufrène from 1921.

Dufrène designed La Maîtrise pavilion at the 1925 Paris Exposition.

Mahogany dressing table with marquetry decoration and selective ebonizing. Its beveled oval-mirror triptych stands above a central tabouret enclosing a welled interior flanked by four tear-shaped drawers. *1921–22*
52¾ in (134 cm) wide

$18,000–22,000   **CALD**

Mahogany chair (one of a set of four plus matching footstool) designed for La Maîtrise. It has distinctive stepped "falling water" legs, and the original fabric on the upholstered seat and back features a Niagara pattern. *1920s*
37 in (94 cm) high

$18,000–22,000 (the set) CALD

French and Belgian Furniture

Stylish Art Deco furniture from France and the more derivative work from Belgium are relatively plentiful in today's marketplace. Most is made to the high standards of French tradition, and value depends largely on attribution. Many items, including most upholstered pieces, where condition plays a key role, are impossible to connect to a designer. Despite few signatures, however, extensive archives of period photographs make attribution possible in many cases. Retailer signatures do not count as attribution, but they help identify designers. In general, elegant, exotic woods and detail such as inlay suggest a date prior to the mid-1930s and are preferable. Many later pieces tend to be larger and simpler in concept. Better names include Dominique, active from 1922, René Herbst, who worked in distinctive style and founded the Union des Artistes Modernes in 1930, and the Modernist Francisque Chaleyssin.

French blond-wood cheval mirror on a single-drawer bedside cabinet, with striped and chevron-pattern veneering. *c. 1930*

65 in (165 cm) high

$900–1,200   JAZ

Exceptional French secretaire in mahogany and palisander (a Brazilian rosewood) on splayed bronze feet. With glass pulls. *1930s*

50½ in (128.5 cm) high

$30,000–50,000   SWT

Three-part French oak armoire by Maxime Old, raised on block pedestal feet and with wrought-iron pulls. This piece was exhibited at the Salon des Artistes Décorateurs in 1945.

77 in (195.5 cm) wide

$80,000–120,000   LM

French satinwood buffet made by Desny of Paris. A central display cabinet with sliding glass doors, beneath a black-glass insert, is flanked by a pair of cabinets with chrome handles. *1930s*

83 in (211 cm) wide

$9,000–15,000   SDR

Rosewood and mahogany side table designed by Lucie Renaudot. Its circular top is edged with dentil-pattern ivory inlay and raised on four stepped and gently tapered legs of square section, the latter united by a square undershelf. *1925*

23½ in (59.5 cm) wide

$20,000–30,000   CALD

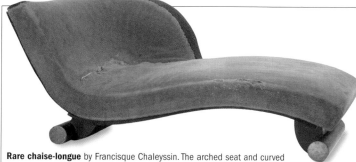

Rare chaise-longue by Francisque Chaleyssin. The arched seat and curved back are upholstered in the original raised-pile fabric and rest on two splayed supports terminating in transverse roller feet. These are lacquered red and gilded by André Ducaroy. *1930s*

63 in (160 cm) long

$7,000–9,000   CSB

French mahogany-framed armchair (one of a pair) with hooped back rails and fluted and tapering spindle legs. *c. 1925*

37 in (94 cm) high

$9,000–12,000 (the pair)   MOD

Cherry-wood game chair (one of a pair) by Dominique. The seat, back, and arm rolls are in their original red Aubusson fabric. *1945*

31 in (78.5 cm) high

$12,000–18,000 (the pair)   CALD

French club chair (one of a pair) upholstered largely in its original tobacco-colored water-buffalo hide (the seat covers are replacements). Its curved arms and sides are modeled in the "streamline" style associated with the profiles of fast sports cars of the period. *1930s*

37½ in (95.25 cm) long

$9,000–12,000 (the pair)   DD

French folding screen or room divider. Each of its four hinged sections is faced on either side with different geometric-pattern marquetry work executed on various light, dark, and reddish-brown woods, including some fruitwoods. *1930s*

73 in (185 cm) high

$4,000–6,000   CSB

Eric Bagge

Born in provincial France in 1890, Eric Bagge trained in architecture and worked mainly in interior and textile design during the Art Deco years. His pieces, made by Parisian furniture shops, are of high standard in design and manufacture. Bagge's early furniture was sold through the showrooms of Saddier, Mercier Frères, or La Maîtrise at Galeries Lafayette, which Bagge managed in the late 1920s; they may bear the retailer label. In 1930 Bagge opened his own Paris retail outlet. His furniture is architectural and geometric in style and compares with the work of Pierre Chareau (1883–1950). Bagge is well known for his contributions to the 1925 Paris Exposition, for which he designed the Hall of Jewelry and various interior furnishings. He died in 1978.

Eric Bagge–designed two-tier coffee table with a circular top and undershelf veneered in walnut, as is the central columnar support. The latter is trimmed with a chrome collar around its base and internally illuminated beneath a frosted-glass insert. *c. 1930*

35 in (89 cm) wide

$15,000–20,000

LM

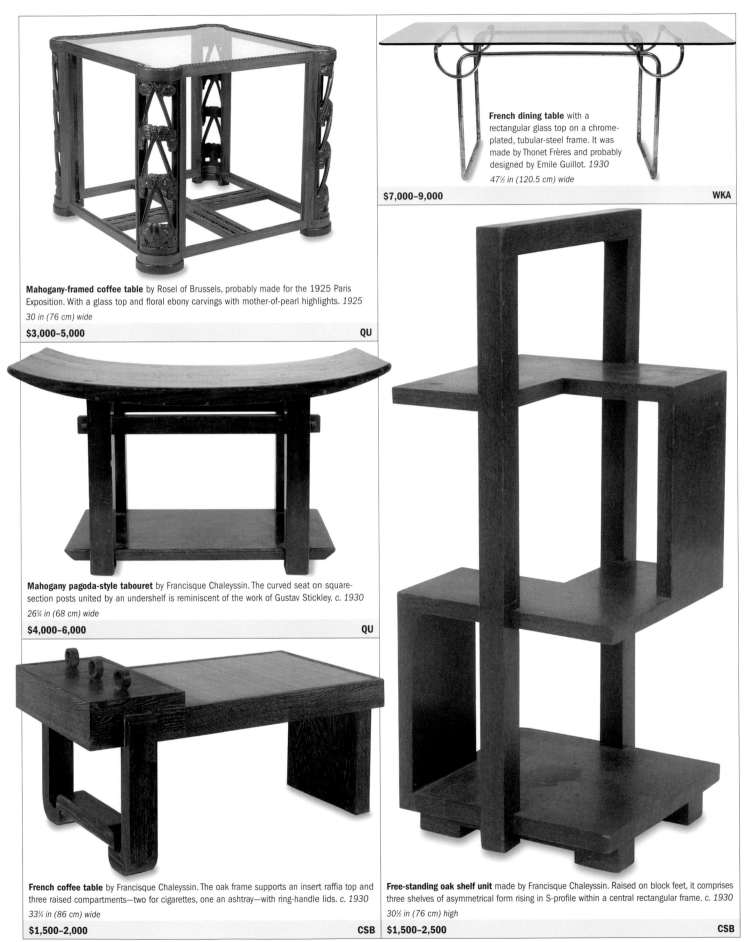

Mahogany-framed coffee table by Rosel of Brussels, probably made for the 1925 Paris Exposition. With a glass top and floral ebony carvings with mother-of-pearl highlights. *1925*
30 in (76 cm) wide

$3,000–5,000 QU

French dining table with a rectangular glass top on a chrome-plated, tubular-steel frame. It was made by Thonet Frères and probably designed by Emile Guillot. *1930*
47½ in (120.5 cm) wide

$7,000–9,000 WKA

Mahogany pagoda-style tabouret by Francisque Chaleyssin. The curved seat on square-section posts united by an undershelf is reminiscent of the work of Gustav Stickley. *c. 1930*
26¾ in (68 cm) wide

$4,000–6,000 QU

French coffee table by Francisque Chaleyssin. The oak frame supports an insert raffia top and three raised compartments—two for cigarettes, one an ashtray—with ring-handle lids. *c. 1930*
33¾ in (86 cm) wide

$1,500–2,000 CSB

Free-standing oak shelf unit made by Francisque Chaleyssin. Raised on block feet, it comprises three shelves of asymmetrical form rising in S-profile within a central rectangular frame. *c. 1930*
30½ in (76 cm) high

$1,500–2,500 CSB

Sandows chair by René Herbst with a nickel-plated tubular-steel frame and its original blue-gray elastic seat and back straps. *1930s*

32 in (81.25 cm) high

$5,000–7,000   **BONBAY**

Wooden and chrome-plated steel armchair by Pol Buthion, with a deep seat and a canted back rest in a dark-maroon fabric. *1930s*

33 in (84 cm) high

$3,000–5,000   **CSB**

French armchair (one of a pair) with an angular frame made of a hardwood finished in a high-gloss black "piano" lacquer. It is also gilded along the tops of the arms. The upholstery is white Alcantara, a synthetic, suedelike fabric. *c. 1930*

35 in (89 cm) long

$7,000–9,000 (the pair)   **SWT**

French side table with a rectangular top on open lyre supports and an arched X-frame base. Finished in a high-gloss, black lacquer contrasted with a chrome band above the base. *1930s*

36 in (91.5 cm) wide

$1,800–2,500   **SWT**

Unsigned French side table with an octagonal top, with a white plastic insert, above a pair of black lacquered, intersected U-shape wooden supports and X-frame feet. *1930s*

34 in (86.5 cm) wide

$1,800–2,500   **SWT**

Lighting

The interwar years have been termed the Age of Elegance. Much of this elegance was achieved by paying attention to innovative concepts in interior lighting design. As a result, today's collectors can enjoy a varied legacy.

From the tiniest desk lamp to enormous hanging fixtures designed to be used in hotels or on ocean liners, Art Deco lighting is a rewarding field to explore. Most common are desk or table lamps in chrome, made from about 1920 well into the postwar years in both Europe and the United States. Many combine chrome with wood, Bakelite, or other synthetics, and although they may have a high standard of Modernist design, they remain affordable.

Signed or attributable examples by French designers are the most sought-after. Reproductions exist. Early industrial design is often inexpensive but of high quality. Floor lamps, also known as torchères, were designed from about 1925 to provide indirect (upward) light. These are often of large scale and most attractive when found in pairs.

Lamps in wrought iron signed by leading designers such as Edgar Brandt or Paul Kiss are among the most valuable Art Deco lighting pieces. Many have alabaster shades, which may be replaced with modern copies. This does not drastically reduce value. Figural Art Deco lamps are often metal, ceramic, or glass sculpture mounted as table lamps, and they may be more valuable without the mounting. Anything by Ruhlmann is highly prized.

Bauhaus table lamp by Christian Dell with a multirotational green-glass shade. *1920s 17 in (43 cm) high* **$2,000–3,000 LM**

Chromed-metal desk lamp by Marc Erol with three frosted-glass shades and a stepped rectangular green-glass base. *c. 1925 20¾ in (53 cm) wide* **$4,000–6,000 MOD**

Machine Age table lamp with fluting to the conical base and a domed shade that clips to the bulb. *1930s. 11 in (28 cm) high* **$800–1,200 DETC**

Contemporary copy of a nickel-plated table lamp designed by Donald Deskey. *c. 1935 12 in (30.5 cm) high* **$800–1,200 DETC**

French stained-glass lamp of geometric form made from leaded panels of gray, blue, and white stained glass. *c. 1930 26½ in (67 cm) high* **$2,000–3,000 CSB**

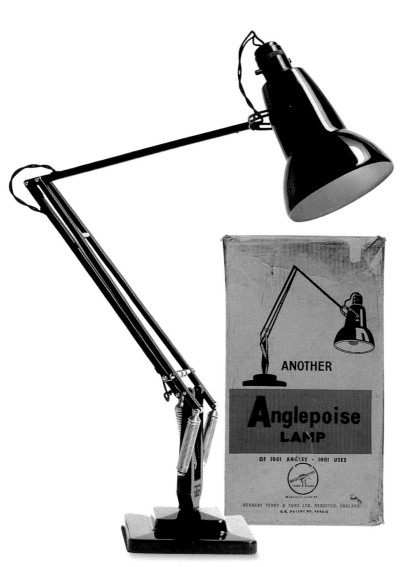

Figural alabaster table lamp in the form of a nude female holding a drape. *1930 17 in (43 cm) high* **$500–900 DETC**

French wall sconce (one of a pair) with gilt-bronze and glass-bead shade. *1930s. 17¾ in (45 cm) high* **$1,200–2,000 (the pair) CSB**

Black lacquered Anglepoise lamp designed in 1932 by George Carwardine and reissued by Tecta in 2004. *35½ in (90 cm) high (max)* **$300–500 TEC**

American wood-and-metal table lamp with birds-in-flight and foliage decoration to the medallion section of the base. *c. 1940 23¼ in (59 cm) high* **$1,200–2,000 MOD**

French table lamp with a wrought iron-and-bronze rectangular shade pierced with a flower-and-foliage pattern. *c. 1925 17 in (43 cm) high* **$3,000–5,000 MOD**

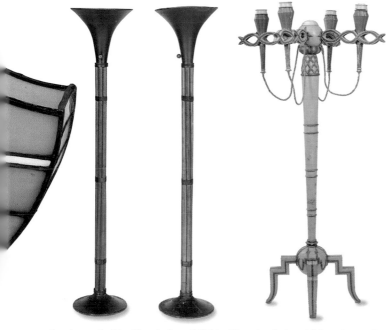

American pair of torchères by Russel Wright with ribbed bamboo shafts. *1930s. 25¾ in (65.5 cm) high* **$2,500–4,000 SDR**

Floor-standing candelabrum in carved softwood, designed by Otto Prutscher. *1924 63½ in (161 cm) high* **$6,000–9,000 DOR**

American table lamp with chrome and black enameled shade and base. Unsigned. *1930s 18 in (46 cm) high* **$800–1,200 DETC**

Electrolier chrome table lamp with graduated ball shaft and enameled base. *1930s. 15½ in (39.5 cm) high* **$1,000–1,500 DETC**

KEY FACTS

Hungarian-born Marcel Breuer joined the Bauhaus in 1920.

Furniture design was Breuer's specialty and he became a Master of Interiors by 1926.

The Bauhaus School cabinet-making workshops were headed by Breuer 1924–29.

Breuer is best known for the cantilever chair in tubular steel, manufactured from 1925.

The Whitney Museum, completed in 1966, is one of Breuer's New York projects.

The Bauhaus closed in 1933.

Marcel Breuer

The style of Marcel Breuer was considered radical even in 1925 Paris, where comparable works were displayed in Le Corbusier's Pavillon de l'Esprit Nouveau (Pavilion of the New Spirit) to little critical acclaim.

"Is it Art Deco?" is a question sometimes posed about Bauhaus in general and the works of Marcel Breuer (1902–81) in particular. However, if one's definition of Art Deco includes all styles shown at the 1925 Paris Exposition, then the creations of this highly innovative architectural designer certainly fall under the Deco umbrella.

Breuer had a unique opportunity to alter the course of 20th-century design at the revolutionary Weimar-based Bauhaus School of Architecture and Design, where he worked in the mid- to late 1920s alongside luminaries such as Ludwig Mies van der Rohe. Unlike Mies, Breuer used nonreinforced steel tubing—a concept he allegedly drew from bicycle frames—to create inexpensive, springy

cantilever chairs and a variety of other simple furnishings, many made by the Austrian firm Thonet. He also designed laminated-wood furniture, some made by the company Isokon during his period in Great Britain in the mid-1930s. In 1937, Breuer moved to the United States. From 1946, he lived in New York, where he practiced as an architect and industrial designer.

Reproductions of Breuer's work abound, but original pieces will command higher prices.

Above: Upholstered chaise-longue made by London's Isokon Furniture Co., with a broad, cantilevered birch-wood frame. It has been reupholstered in a black fabric. *c. 1935. 51¼ in (130 cm) long* **$5,000–7,000 WKA**

Chair No. 301 with a cantilevered aluminum frame and a lacquered, form-hugging birch-plywood seat and curved back rest. These aluminum frames were produced in both shiny and dull silver finishes. *c. 1935*

29½ in (75 cm) high

$2,000–3,000 **CSB**

Tecta reissue (D4) of folding armchair Model B4 with a nickel-plated tubular-steel frame and red leather strap seat, arms, and back rest. Designed in 1927, this model was originally made by Standard-Mobel Lengyel & Co. of Berlin. *2004*

28 in (71 cm) high

$800–1,200 **TEC**

Tecta reissue of a black-stained ask desk and integral lacquered-steel cabinet with four drawers. Also with a chromed leg and a swivel pad, it was originally designed in 1932 for the Werkbund Exhibition in Neubühl. *2004*

63 in (160 cm) wide

$1,800–2,200 **TEC**

Alvar Aalto

The most famous Finnish architect in 20th-century design, Alvar Aalto manufactured and marketed furniture that proved internationally popular and is widely copied.

KEY FACTS

Hugo Alvar Henrik Aalto graduated from the Helsinki University of Technology in 1921, practicing as an architect.

Artek was founded in Helsinki in 1930 by Aalto. His furniture was marketed in Britain by Finmar Ltd. from 1934.

An "organic Modernist" style applies to most of Aalto's furniture made during the late 1930s and after World War II.

Important design contributions to the 1937 Paris Exposition and the New York World's Fair of 1939 earned Aalto international recognition.

The technique of laminating plywood and bending it by a steaming process was not entirely new when the Finn Alvar Aalto (1898–1976) founded his company Artek in 1930. The method relied on design principles pioneered at the Bauhaus School by a generation of architects that influenced Aalto extensively during both his studies and his professional career.

Aalto's rare early designs were in tubular steel, and all his Art Deco furniture was designed during the 1930s, much of it in combination with his architect wife, Aino Marsio, whom he married in 1924. It is made almost exclusively in laminated birch, a wood that is indigenous to Scandinavia, and widely admired for its clean lines and practical economy of design. These aspects led to extensive use of Aalto's style for institutional furniture, including school chairs, stacking stools, and tables.

Aalto was especially popular in the United States, where he lived during the 1940s. Many of his pre–World War II designs are still manufactured by Artek and by the American firm Herman Miller, which began reproducing them in 2002. Collectors should look for pieces that show age and have early labels.

Above: Trädgardbord No. 330 table made of birch. Its circular top is assembled in a radiating pattern around a circular metallic insert. *c. 1940. Top: 31½ in (80 cm) wide* **$7,000–10,000 BK**

Lounge chair No. 37 produced by Artek with broad, cantilevered, one-piece arms, legs, and feet in birch. The upholstered seat and back are covered in a putty-colored fabric with coordinated piping. *1935–36*

34 in (86 cm) wide

$2,000–3,000 FRE

Table-desk and chest of drawers made in birch wood by Artek. The rectangular table is raised on turned legs of circular section. The chest, model number 296, is on four wooden casters. *1930*

Table: 28¼ in (71.5 cm) high

$4,000–6,000 QU

Armchair No. 31 made by Huonekalu-ja Rakennustyötehdas Oy of Finland with cantilevered one-piece arms, legs, and feet in birch. The undulating birch-plywood seat is stained black. *c. 1930*

31 in (79 cm) long

$5,000–7,000 WKA

European Furniture

Art Deco furniture made in continental Europe beyond France was not widely exported and is therefore fairly uncommon outside its country of origin. Most pieces are unsigned and difficult to attribute, but a good eye and the willingness to pore through period publications in foreign languages can be highly rewarding.

Most high-style pieces reflect national culture. German and Austrian interwar furniture, for example, tends to be severe, often in dark or stained woods and sharply outlined. Most Austrian pieces evolved from the Wiener Werkstätte style but remain unattributed. Works from the later (Weimar) Bauhaus are gaining in popularity. Eastern European furniture tends to include references to folk art in color or ornament, while Italian pieces, made in larger quantities and exported mainly to the United States, are usually large and extravagant, loosely inspired by French Art Deco in line and use of exotic woods, ivory, and parchment. This area is also gaining in respect, especially the work of Giò Ponti.

Czechoslovakian hall stand comprising a chromed tubular-steel frame with a tall, rectangular mirror above a seat-and-drawer unit finished in a pale-blue lacquer. *c. 1930*

70¾ in (180 cm) high

$2,000–3,000　　　　　**DOR**

Viennese Cactus hall stand in lacquered oak. It comprises a broad post with asymmetrical shelving supported on stepped brackets above a green enameled-metal base. *c. 1925*

56 in (142 cm) high

$1,800–2,200　　　　　**DOR**

Limited-edition easy chair (No. 2 of 25) by Dutch designer Hein Stolle, in dowel-jointed pine with canted and slatted seat and back and H-form armrests. *c. 1930*

36 in (91.5 cm) high

$1,200–2,000　　　　　**BONBAY**

Bauhaus upholstered armchair designed by Peter Keler. It has a brass-jointed pearwood frame supporting an upholstered seat and back covered in a woolen fabric. *1925*

27¼ in (69 cm) high

$6,000–9,000　　　　　**WKA**

Tubular-steel chaise-longue slung with a linen-and-cotton fabric and convertible into a rocking chair. Designed by Battista and Gino Giudici, it was made by Fratelli Giudici of Locarno, Switzerland. *c. 1935*

44½ in (113 cm) long

$8,000–12,000　　　　　**WKA**

Stained and highly polished beechwood armchair designed by the Hungarian Lajos Kozma, with curved arms, supports, back slat, and top rail, and a bentwood stretcher. *1920s*

36 in (91.5 cm) high

$1,200–1,800　　　　　**HERR**

Beechwood armchair designed by the German Erich Dieckmann, with a slatted seat, an adjustable canted and curved plywood back rest, and stretchered back legs. *c. 1930*

32 in (81.5 cm) high

$4,000–6,000　　　　　**WKA**

Italian burr-walnut-veneered buffet with a mirror-augmented splashback and an asymmetrical shelf above, respectively, a two-door cabinet and a drawer unit, all on an ebonized plinth. *1930s*

70 in (177.5 cm) wide

$3,000–4,000　　　　　**FRE**

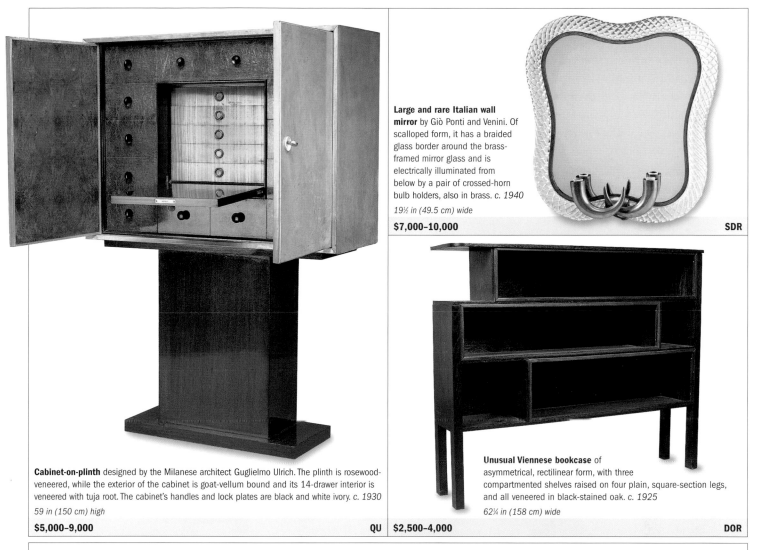

Large and rare Italian wall mirror by Giò Ponti and Venini. Of scalloped form, it has a braided glass border around the brass-framed mirror glass and is electrically illuminated from below by a pair of crossed-horn bulb holders, also in brass. *c. 1940*

19½ in (49.5 cm) wide

$7,000–10,000　　　　　　　　**SDR**

Cabinet-on-plinth designed by the Milanese architect Guglielmo Ulrich. The plinth is rosewood-veneered, while the exterior of the cabinet is goat-vellum bound and its 14-drawer interior is veneered with tuja root. The cabinet's handles and lock plates are black and white ivory. *c. 1930*

59 in (150 cm) high

$5,000–9,000　　　　　　　　**QU**

Unusual Viennese bookcase of asymmetrical, rectilinear form, with three compartmented shelves raised on four plain, square-section legs, and all veneered in black-stained oak. *c. 1925*

62¼ in (158 cm) wide

$2,500–4,000　　　　　　　　**DOR**

Josef Frank

The Austrian architect Josef Frank (1885–1967) began his career before World War I and flourished in 1920s Vienna under Bauhaus influence, designing homes with all furnishings in an economical, modern style. Frank's early furniture was mostly designed for upper-middle-class bourgeois homes and made to high standards by Thonet. He was forced to leave Vienna in 1933 under pressure from anti-Semitic regulations restricting Jewish ownership of businesses.

Frank relocated to Sweden and became principal designer for the Stockholm-based firm of Svenskt Tenn. During World War II, he lived and worked in the United States, but he returned to Sweden at the end of his career. In addition to furniture, Frank designed a wide range of textiles, most of which were produced in Sweden from the mid-1930s. Frank was relegated to relative obscurity until 1996, when a retrospective of his work at the Bard Graduate Center in New York City gave him wide recognition and respect.

Josef Frank circular-topped occasional table made by Thonet in beechwood with a plain apron, three curved supports, and a circular undershelf. The top has a beige felt cover under a glass plate, and the piece retains its original Thonet paper label. *c. 1925*

26¾ in (68 cm) wide

$4,000–6,000　　　　　　　　**WKA**

Swedish Furniture

Swedish Art Deco furniture owes its origins partly to post–World War I changes in Swedish society, mainly to the establishment of a Social Democratic government in 1932. Prior to this period, most Swedish furniture was conventional and historical, more in line with the Biedermeier style it evolved from than the sleek Modernism it would eventually become (think IKEA).

The 1930 Stockholm International Exhibition brought a breath of fresh Modernist air, largely in the form of Danish designer Kaare Klint and the Finnish Alvar Aalto, both of whom inspired Swedish design. The three principal names in 1930s Swedish furniture are Axel Larsson, Sven Markelius, and Bruno Mathsson. Swedish furniture was not widely exported until after World War II but is fairly plentiful and inexpensive in Scandinavia. Almost all of it is in birch or other blond woods, sometimes with minimal inlay or ebonizing, in Biedermeier fashion. With a high manufacture quality, most pieces are appealing and practical, allowing good value.

Birchwood dresser with open shelves flanked by cupboards, raised above a pot-shelf on baluster legs. Decorative details include sunburst patterns in the birch. c. 1930

59 in (150 cm) wide

$5,000–9,000   **LANE**

Birchwood side table raised on bracket feet with a central partition between open shelving and two drawers. The latter have ebonized handles, and the rectangular top has a black glass insert. c. 1930

26 in (66 cm) wide

$2,000–3,000   **LANE**

Birchwood dressing table/desk raised on bracket feet. It has three drawers with ebonized handles. The rectangular top is piano-hinged at the back and lifts to access further storage space. *Early 1920s*

35¾ in (91 cm) wide

$2,500–4,000   **LANE**

Birchwood-frame club chair with arms and legs of square section. Its leather upholstery is secured with rows of decorative brass rivets. *Early 1930s*

25¾ in (65.5 cm) high

$2,500–4,000   **LANE**

Birchwood-frame club chair with curved arms descending to elongated block feet, and with generously padded black leather upholstery to the back, seat, and sides. *Early 1930s*

25¼ in (64 cm) high

$2,500–4,000   **LANE**

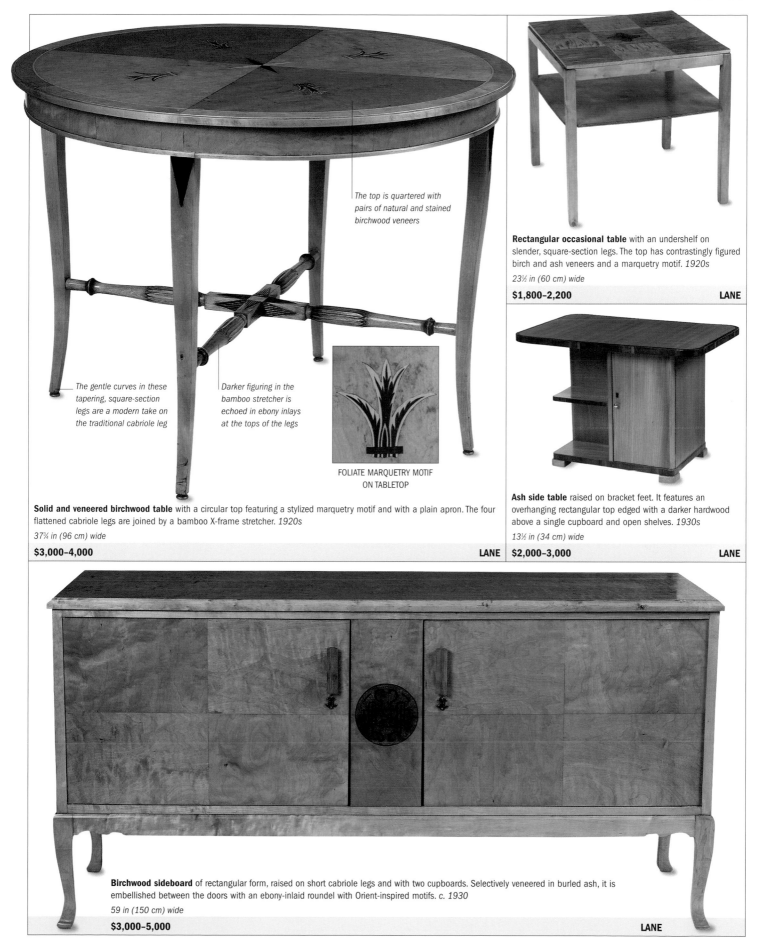

The top is quartered with pairs of natural and stained birchwood veneers

The gentle curves in these tapering, square-section legs are a modern take on the traditional cabriole leg

Darker figuring in the bamboo stretcher is echoed in ebony inlays at the tops of the legs

FOLIATE MARQUETRY MOTIF ON TABLETOP

Solid and veneered birchwood table with a circular top featuring a stylized marquetry motif and with a plain apron. The four flattened cabriole legs are joined by a bamboo X-frame stretcher. *1920s*

37¾ in (96 cm) wide

$3,000–4,000   **LANE**

Rectangular occasional table with an undershelf on slender, square-section legs. The top has contrastingly figured birch and ash veneers and a marquetry motif. *1920s*

23½ in (60 cm) wide

$1,800–2,200   **LANE**

Ash side table raised on bracket feet. It features an overhanging rectangular top edged with a darker hardwood above a single cupboard and open shelves. *1930s*

13½ in (34 cm) wide

$2,000–3,000   **LANE**

Birchwood sideboard of rectangular form, raised on short cabriole legs and with two cupboards. Selectively veneered in burled ash, it is embellished between the doors with an ebony-inlaid roundel with Orient-inspired motifs. *c. 1930*

59 in (150 cm) wide

$3,000–5,000   **LANE**

Paul Frankl

Rarely found outside the United States, Paul Frankl furniture embodies American Modernism. Frankl's pieces, designed for Manhattan apartments, are inseparable from the architecture and culture of New York.

The work of the Czech-born designer Paul Frankl (1886–1958) exemplifies a New World tradition—that of immigrant workers using skills learned in their country of origin to create something uniquely American.

A sophisticated architect, Frankl arrived in the United States in 1914 and fell in love with New York City and the "modern living" it offered. He became a key member of the New York Modern Movement, together with the Viennese architect Josef Urban (1872–1933) and Donald Deskey (*see p.48*). Frankl designed buildings and furniture, concentrating on the latter from the mid-1920s. In 1922 he established Frankl Galleries in Midtown Manhattan; four years later he introduced the signature line Skyscraper Furniture. Skyscrapers already dominated the Manhattan skyline in 1926, although the biggest ones were still under construction. They represented optimism and progress for a modern world, a concept evident in Frankl's design philosophy and expressed in his publication *New Dimensions*. Although Skyscraper Furniture appears inexpensively made, built from California redwood and nickel-plated steel, with crudely lacquered surfaces normally in red and black, it is among the most sought-after of all American Art Deco furniture.

In the 1920s Frankl also designed lacquered furniture in Chinese taste, which is not as popular, and from about 1930 he made mostly metal furniture. He continued working after World War II, designing furniture for manufacturers such as Johnson Furniture and Brown & Saltzman, as well as Barker Brothers retailers of Los Angeles.

Above: Nickel-plated steel-frame console table with a black lacquered top and a stepped, black lacquered-wood base. *1930s 27 in (68.5 cm) wide* **$15,000–20,000 AMO**

Skyscraper Furniture dressing table made in black lacquered wood with chromed-steel pulls, trim, and stretchers, and a mirror-glass oval back and rectangular top. *c. 1925 44 in (112 cm) wide* **NPA DEL**

SKYSCRAPER FURNITURE

The great skyscrapers of the Manhattan skyline, made possible by the New York Zoning Act of 1916, are symbols of optimism and a society's faith in modern industry. Paul Frankl once remarked that the 1925 Paris Exposition would have been a lot different if America had exhibited a skyscraper or two. He chose the stepped building form as commercial inspiration for his Skyscraper line, introduced in 1926 and designed exclusively for New York apartment living, the quintessential modern lifestyle.

SKYSCRAPER
FURNITURE LOGO

Black-painted wooden dining table with a white plastic insert top, raised on twin rectangular supports and extendable with the addition of a pair of D-shaped console tables (not shown). *1930s*

95½ in (242.5 cm) long

NPA   **DEL**

La Jolla Commission coffee table with black lacquered top and legs. The trim around the top, like the undershelf, is finished in red lacquer. *c. 1940*

30½ in (77.5 cm) square

$7,000–10,000   **MSM**

Skyscraper Furniture gentleman's valet commissioned by the Texas King Ranch. Its mirror is raised and flanked by, respectively, a blond-wood plinth and pairs of drawers. *1928*

42½ in (108 cm) wide

$10,000–12,000   **MSM**

Skyscraper Furniture chest in Californian redwood. It has asymmetrically configured drawers, single cupboard, and slide. The interior of the cupboard is lacquered red. *Late 1920s*

56 in (142.25 cm) high

$10,000–15,000   **SDR**

Black lacquered wooden-framed chair (one of a pair). Its black vinyl upholstery has red vinyl piping. Very similar to a pair illustrated in a Frankl article in *Art and Decoration*. *c. 1925*

24 in (61 cm) wide

$8,000–12,000 (the pair)   **MSM**

Rare Streamline sofa with matching end tables. The latter are lacquered black, and the sofa is upholstered in black leather. The triple speed-band trim inset around their bases is nickel-plated steel. *1930s*

88 in (223.5 cm) wide

$15,000–20,000 (the set)   **MSM**

Donald Deskey

A close encounter with Donald Deskey's furniture is like stepping into a classic 1930s movie set in New York City. It is quintessentially Art Deco, representing a culture and lifestyle that existed all too briefly.

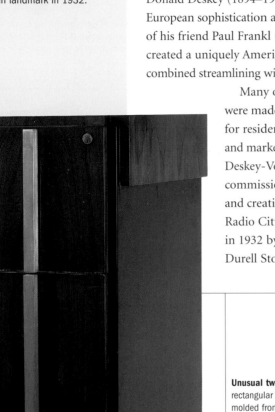

Donald Deskey (1894–1989) may have lacked the European sophistication and architectural training of his friend Paul Frankl (*see pp.46–47*), but he created a uniquely American modern style that combined streamlining with French Art Deco taste.

Many of Deskey's early designs were made as private commissions for residences or corporate offices and marketed under the trademark Deskey-Vollmer. His greatest commission was for furnishing and creating the interior design of Radio City Music Hall, completed in 1932 by architect Edward Durell Stone as a cornerstone of the Rockefeller Center in Manhattan. Radio City was sympathetically restored in 1999, when a few original pieces were sold and replaced. However, this Art Deco landmark has changed remarkably little and visitors can still admire Deskey's work.

From about 1930 to 1934 Deskey produced hundreds of economical furniture designs for mass production using aluminum, Bakelite, cork, and steel. This work is growing in popularity and may bear the label of several furniture companies, including John Widdicomb, S. Karpen of Chicago, or Ypsilanti Reed.

Above: Radio City Music Hall sofa from the Rockefeller Center, with a rosewood frame upholstered in brown vinyl and orange fabric. *c. 1930 72 in (183 cm) wide* **$20,000–25,000 MSM**

Unusual two-tier coffee table with a rectangular top and a smaller undershelf molded from black Bakelite. Both are supported on four one-piece legs and feet fashioned from square-section, chromium-plated steel tubing. *c. 1925*

28 in (71 cm) long

$10,000–15,000   **MSM**

Filing cabinet (one of a pair) with a black lacquered carcass and four drawer fronts in boldly figured rosewood, like the overhanging top. The large, barlike drawer pulls are in nickel-bronze. *c. 1935*

55½ in (141 cm) high

$25,000–35,000 (the pair)   **AMO**

D-shaped knee-hole desk with a black lacquered top, frieze, and plinth; rosewood-veneered sides and drawers; and chrome-plated banding. *c. 1935*

50 in (127 cm) wide

$20,000–30,000   **HSD**

Eugene Schoen

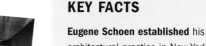

Heavily influenced by (and sometimes mistaken for) French style, Eugene Schoen's furniture is among the highest-quality American Art Deco work in standards of manufacture and design.

Only the wealthy elite could afford to patronize the design studio of Eugene Schoen (1880–1957) by the time he offered Art Deco furniture, after the Depression. Most of Schoen's furniture was made and retailed by Schmieg & Kotzian (also trading as Schmieg, Hungate & Kotzian in the 1930s). Established in 1897 and active until 1994, this fashionable New York furniture firm was renowned for making mostly high-quality reproductions of 18th-century formal furniture with traditional handcraftsmanship.

Schmieg & Kotzian's access to the finest materials and standards of manufacture suited Schoen, who designed in the French taste. Many of his pieces use wood veneer patterns

as ornament. Materials include a variety of dark exotic woods used in veneer or parquetry. Seat furniture is elegant, with subtle carved detail, and comparable to Ruhlmann (see pp.26–27) in style. In the late 1930s Schoen also designed avant-garde furniture using nickel and glass.

Eugene Schoen designed furniture up until the mid-1940s. His work is highly sought-after, extremely scarce, and rarely found outside the United States. Pieces are not always signed.

Above: Pair of one-drawer end tables made by Schmieg, Hungate & Kotzian of New York. They are veneered in East Indian rosewood. *1930s. 20 in (50.75 cm) high*
$10,000–15,000 MSM

Two-seater settee made by Schmieg, Hungate & Kotzian with a rosewood-veneered frame, splayed, tapering legs, and an arched and channeled back. The seat, back, and sides are upholstered in white linen. *1929*
49½ in (125.75 cm) wide
$10,000–15,000

SDR

Five-drawer chest made by Schmieg, Hungate & Kotzian with a mid-brown mahogany carcass and plinth, bleached mahogany drawer fronts, and dark-brown drawer pulls configured together into a square. *c. 1935*
41½ in (105.5 cm) wide
$15,000–20,000

AMO

Chest-on-stand made by Schmieg, Hungate & Kotzian. The carcass and the splayed leg stand are solid and veneered mahogany. The drawer fronts are cross-hatched mahogany parquetry and the circular pulls have faux pearl centers. *c. 1935*
45 in (114.5 cm) wide
$15,000–20,000

AMO

Mahogany-top chest of drawers with black enameled sides and base, four mahogany drawers set slightly off-center, and long sycamore drawer pulls.
c. 1935. 43 in (109 cm) wide
$10,000–15,000 HSD

Gilbert Rohde

Some of the most practical and stylish furniture ever made in the US was designed by Gilbert Rohde. His solid, heavy, and reliable work can still be found across the country, from dining rooms to office buildings.

When Gilbert Rohde (1894–1944) founded his New York design studio in 1927, he was flush with avant-garde ideas he had learned while traveling through Germany. His lines are distinctly late Bauhaus, as are many of his concepts, notably Walter Gropius–style modular and sectional furniture, which Rohde is credited with popularizing in the United States.

Rohde liked natural materials, with American maple and exotic hardwoods as veneers and wood or sparse metal hardware. His characteristic wooden drawer pulls of mushroom shape with incised wavy lines are easily recognizable.

The overwhelming majority of Rohde's work was designed for corporate manufacturers, notably the Herman Miller Furniture Co., for which he also created clocks and light fixtures. Rohde was responsible for starting Herman Miller's association with modern design and for steering the firm toward industrial office furniture, a field in which it is a world leader today.

In addition to Herman Miller, Rohde also created several designs for Heywood-Wakefield in Massachusetts, John Widdicomb, Kroehler Manufacturing, and Troy Sunshade Co. of Ohio. For Kroehler, Rohde designed a line of innovative children's furniture, while his work for Troy Sunshade, which dates from 1933, is mostly chromed tubular-steel seat furniture in Bauhaus style. It includes the widely reproduced Z bar stool, which bends one piece of tubular steel into the support and seat.

Gilbert Rohde furniture is often marked or identifiable through period catalogs, many of which have been reprinted. His custom and limited-edition furniture may also bear a paper label with a signature.

Above: Three-door sideboard veneered in East India laurel wood, with chrome and black enameled pulls and a black enameled plinth. *1930s. 19 in (48 cm) wide* **$6,000–9,000 SDR**

HERMAN MILLER FURNITURE CO. METAL TAG, INCLUDING GILBERT ROHDE'S SIGNATURE

HERMAN MILLER FURNITURE CO.

In 1930 Gilbert Rohde traveled to the furniture-making center of Grand Rapids, Michigan, looking for new clients. At the time, the Herman Miller Furniture Co., founded in 1923, was close to bankruptcy. Its main product was reproduction Chippendale, but owner D.J. DePree took a chance on Rohde and began making "modern" furniture. By 1941 the partnership was thriving and hundreds of designs were in production, mostly cabinet furniture. Many pieces bear the original metal or foil tag, and can include a four-digit code, the first two indicating the year of introduction.

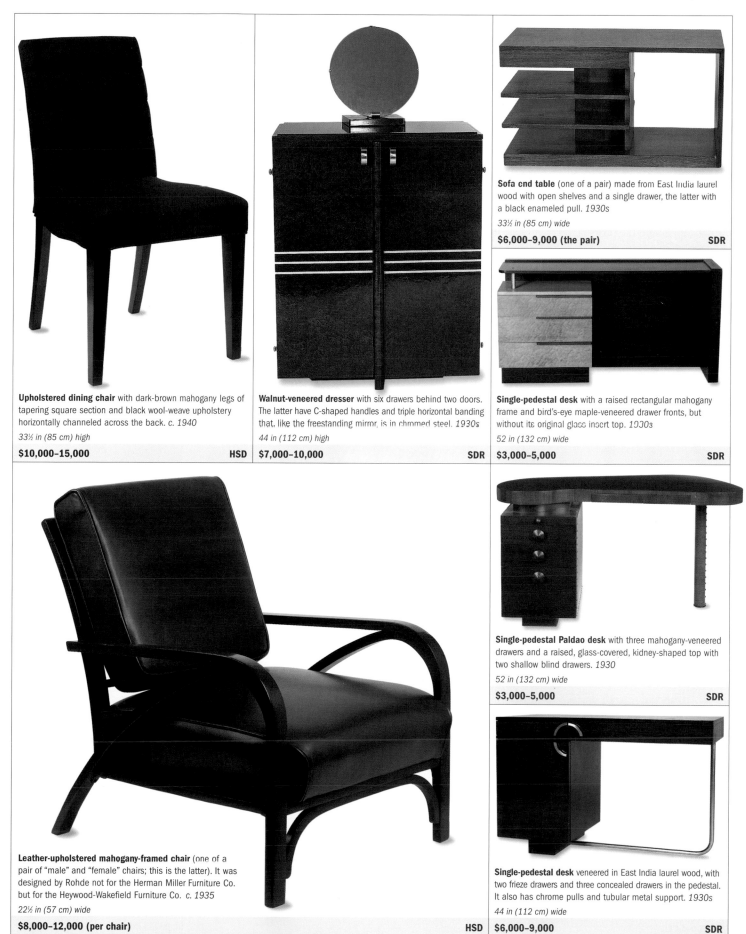

Upholstered dining chair with dark-brown mahogany legs of tapering square section and black wool-weave upholstery horizontally channeled across the back. *c. 1940*

33½ in (85 cm) high

$10,000–15,000   HSD

Walnut-veneered dresser with six drawers behind two doors. The latter have C-shaped handles and triple horizontal banding that, like the freestanding mirror, is in chromed steel. *1930s*

44 in (112 cm) high

$7,000–10,000   SDR

Sofa end table (one of a pair) made from East India laurel wood with open shelves and a single drawer, the latter with a black enameled pull. *1930s*

33½ in (85 cm) wide

$6,000–9,000 (the pair)   SDR

Single-pedestal desk with a raised rectangular mahogany frame and bird's-eye maple-veneered drawer fronts, but without its original glass insert top. *1930s*

52 in (132 cm) wide

$3,000–5,000   SDR

Leather-upholstered mahogany-framed chair (one of a pair of "male" and "female" chairs; this is the latter). It was designed by Rohde not for the Herman Miller Furniture Co. but for the Heywood-Wakefield Furniture Co. *c. 1935*

22½ in (57 cm) wide

$8,000–12,000 (per chair)   HSD

Single-pedestal Paldao desk with three mahogany-veneered drawers and a raised, glass-covered, kidney-shaped top with two shallow blind drawers. *1930*

52 in (132 cm) wide

$3,000–5,000   SDR

Single-pedestal desk veneered in East India laurel wood, with two frieze drawers and three concealed drawers in the pedestal. It also has chrome pulls and tubular metal support. *1930s*

44 in (112 cm) wide

$6,000–9,000   SDR

American Furniture

The overwhelming majority of American Art Deco furniture is unsigned, relatively affordable, and loosely based on French Art Deco or the Bauhaus. However, several unique design strands exist. These include a glitzy Hollywood style incorporating mirrored surfaces and blue glass, and a powerful streamlined style, popular from the early 1930s until after World War II. This latter style is well represented in many American diners and a wide range of industrial design products beyond furniture, including the work of Warren McArthur, Russel Wright, and others who steered the United States into the postwar years. A common but reliable label is Modernage Furniture, a retailer that began in 1920s New York and still operates in Miami, where it moved in the 1940s. Among the most valuable American Art Deco furniture are room screens. These were highly popular in interior design from the late 1920s and a specialty of Donald Deskey, among others. Most room screens are clearly signed.

Gray suede-upholstered lounge chair with a loose seat squab and ebonized block feet, made by Modernage Furniture of New York. *1930s*

28 in (71 cm) wide

$400–700 SDR

Two unmarked occasional tables raised on tapering square-section legs and finished all over with panels of mirror glass. One has a circular top and apron; the other a rectangular top with a single drawer. *1930s*

Rectangular table: 25½ in (64.75 cm) high

$800–1,200 (for both) SDR

Unmarked club chair (one of a pair) raised on rectangular block hardwood feet and reupholstered in black leather. *1930s*

31 in (78.75 cm) wide

$2,000–3,000 (the pair) SDR

Square club chair (one of a pair) by Modernage with its original bias-cut maroon upholstery but a new cushion cover. *1930s*

34 in (86.5 cm) wide

$600–900 (the pair) SDR

Single-pedestal desk made by Warren McArthur Industries. Its three-drawer pedestal is finished in a black laminate and suspended in a tubular aluminum frame that incorporates the desk top, the end support, and a raised, square shelf. The mushroom-shaped drawer pulls are in aluminum. *1930s*

49 in (124.5 cm) wide

$2,500–4,000 SDR

Tubular aluminum-framed side chair by Warren McArthur Industries. It has "hockey puck" feet and the original burgundy-colored oilcloth seat and back support. *1930s*

34½ in (87.5 cm) high

$1,800–3,000 SDR

Tall dresser-chest finished in mahogany parquetry work and banding, with pyramidal amber Bakelite drawer pulls. It is marked "Made in Grand Rapids, Michigan." *1920s*

60½ in (153.5 cm) high

$1,500–2,000 SDR

Large hardwood dresser by Modernage, with three open shelves above three frieze drawers and two cupboards with sliding doors. *1930s*

72 in (183 cm) wide

$1,200–1,800 SDR

Fine and rare end table designed by Russel Wright for Heywood-Wakefield. Its open shelves and two drawers are finished in contrasting veneers. *c. 1935*

28½ in (72.5 cm) wide

$12,000–15,000 SDR

Three-panel screen painted by Robert Winthrop Chanler with two zebras in black and tan on an ivory ground (the reverse has diagonal stripes in black and silver foil). *1928*

78 in (198 cm) high

$12,000–18,000 SDR

Eliel Saarinen

Eliel Saarinen (1873–1950) was born in Finland and studied architecture in Helsinki. He became successful designing for the Finnish pavilion at the 1900 Paris Exposition Universelle and was well established when he arrived in the United States in 1922. Saarinen is best known as the director of the Cranbrook Academy, near Detroit, Michigan, where he worked from its establishment (1922) until his death. Cranbrook still operates as a progressive art school and is considered a training ground for postwar American Modernists, notably Charles Eames, who worked with Saarinen's son Eero. Exquisite Art Deco furnishings designed by Saarinen for Cranbrook or for private commissions are exceptionally rare. However, his commercial designs for Johnson Furniture from the late 1930s may be found at a reasonable price.

Eliel Saarinen–designed four-drawer maple-wood chest made by the Johnson Furniture Co. It has maple and chrome pulls and a dark-brown plinth. With Johnson Furniture Co. decals and metal tags. *c. 1940*

48 in (122 cm) wide

$1,200–1,800 SDR

Eliel Saarinen–designed nightstand (one of a pair), made, like the chest shown on the left, by the Johnson Furniture Co. for its FHA (Flexible Home Arrangements) line. *c. 1940*

30 in (76.25 cm) high

$1,200–1,800 (the pair) SDR

Unusual unmarked mantelpiece of asymmetrical form with a deep wood-veneered mantelshelf with a black lacquered top, supported by a rectangular and a curved pedestal in, respectively, wood veneer and black lacquer. *1930s*

59½ in (151 cm) wide

$1,200–1,800　　　　　　　　　　SDR

Rare asymmetric server designed by Russel Wright and made by Heywood-Wakefield. It features a single drawer and a two-door cupboard finished in burlwood and black lacquer. *Early 1930s*

45 in (114.5 cm) wide

$3,000–5,000　　　　　　　　　　SDR

Tubular-frame day bed designed by Kem Weber and made by the Lloyd Manufacturing Co. with a chrome and selective green enamel finish and brown vinyl upholstery. *c. 1935*

74 in (188 cm) long

$500–900　　　　　　　　　　SDR

Unmarked Skyscraper-style vanity unit of asymmetrical form comprising a single drawer, shelves, two cupboards, and a large rectangular mirror. It is finished in bird's-eye maple veneer with a black enameled trim. *1930s*

61½ in (156.25 cm) wide

$700–900　　　　　　　　　　SDR

Wolfgang Hoffmann

Wolfgang Hoffmann was born in Vienna, Austria, in 1900 and died in America in 1969. The son of Josef Hoffmann, founder of the Wiener Werkstätte, he was already well schooled in modern design when he began working in the United States around 1930. Hoffmann's style is European Modernist, using tubular and bent plated steel, lacquered wood, and glass. Most of his pieces were designed for the Howell Furniture Co. of Illinois and may be labeled. Similar work was done in California by the German immigrant Kem Weber (1889–1963), who also worked in laminated wood.

Wolfgang Hoffmann three-piece sectional davenport for the Howell Furniture Co. It has a tubular "Chromsteel" frame supporting side, back, and seat cushions upholstered in slinkskin and black leather. *1936*

79½ in (202 cm) long

$4,000–7,000　　　　　　　　　　SDR

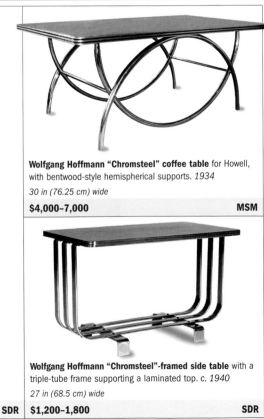

Wolfgang Hoffmann "Chromsteel" coffee table for Howell, with bentwood-style hemispherical supports. *1934*

30 in (76.25 cm) wide

$4,000–7,000　　　　　　　　　　MSM

Wolfgang Hoffmann "Chromsteel"-framed side table with a triple-tube frame supporting a laminated top. *c. 1940*

27 in (68.5 cm) wide

$1,200–1,800　　　　　　　　　　SDR

Unmarked cocktail bar with an illuminated and mirror-lined center cabinet behind fluted, black lacquered doors, flanked by a pair of cabinets with blond wood-veneered doors. Raised on a veneered and lacquered U-shaped base. *Late 1920s*

55¼ in (140.25 cm) wide

$5,000–7,000 SDR

Unmarked two-drawer commode veneered in highly figured, book-matched Amboina-wood. The drawers have pyramidal bronze pulls and butt-jointed, hemispherical bronze discs. *c. 1930*

31½ in (80 cm) wide

$2,500–4,000 S&K

Green-and-white lacquered side table (one of a pair) made by Grosfeld House. The single drawers have brass pulls. *c. 1940*

19½ in (49.5 cm) wide

$12,000–15,000 (the pair) HSD

Four-drawer metal dresser by Norman Bel Geddes. It is finished in two-tone pink and beige enamel, with chrome button pulls. *1930s*

41 in (104 cm) high

$700–900 SDR

Black leather-upholstered armchair designed by Kem Weber for the Lloyd Manufacturing Co. It has a sprung seat and back and triple-tube, D-shaped sides in chromed steel. *1937*

27½ in (70 cm) wide

$5,000–7,000 MSM

Black lacquered-wood side table designed by Charles Hardy. With one flat J support and two tubular supports in nickeled steel. *1936*

20 in (51 cm) wide

$4,000–6,000 HSD

Betty Joel was born Mary Stuart Lockhart in Hong Kong.

She married David Joel in 1918, and founded Betty Joel Ltd. the following year.

A traditional, historical style is characteristic of her early furniture.

Her Art Deco contributions date mostly from the 1930s.

Joel's peak of popularity and refinement came at the 1935 British Art & Industry Exhibition, held in London.

Betty Joel designed furniture for several film sets, notably for Alfred Junge, art director at MGM in England in the 1930s.

Betty Joel

A consummate society designer, Betty Joel created modern furniture in refined English taste for an equally refined English patronage, including members of the royal family. Her work is little known outside Britain.

Betty Joel (1896–1985) was a prominent member of a select group of London-based designers catering to the British social elite. The group included designers Alistair Maynard and Sir Ambrose Heal, as well as decorator Syrie Maugham. Joel's early furniture, made immediately after World War I and sold through her studio on Sloane Street, is almost Edwardian conservative, evoking the English Regency or the style of Thomas Sheraton.

Betty Joel Art Deco furniture was mostly made in the 1930s, by which time she had moved to Knightsbridge. She favored British woods, including sycamore used in veneer, and exotic colonial woods. Forms are fundamentally neoclassical, with a tendency to be geometrically modern in the early 1930s. Many examples were made by N. R. Hamilton of Portsmouth Road, London, and may bear the firm's "Token" furniture trademark. By the mid-1930s, some Joel furniture, including beds and sofas, took on a Hollywood glamour and was characterized by sweeping outlines.

Betty Joel work is found almost exclusively in Great Britain and includes designs for several commercial interiors, notably the Savoy Hotel.

Above: Three-tiered drum table made in solid and veneered oak. It is without a "Token Works" paper label, but it is in the style of Betty Joel. *c. 1935. Top: 24 in (61 cm) wide* **$1,000–2,000 TDG**

Mahogany center table with a stepped-edge, canted rectangular top above a single side drawer, and end posts of fluted rectangular section, with the latter rising from stepped and fluted trestle ends. *1929*

48¼ in (122.5 cm) wide

$1,200–1,800	**L&T**

Asymmetrical bookcase (one of a pair) with open shelving and two cupboards, and raised on fluted block feet. Typically, decoration is confined to the strident figuring of the Australian oak doors. *1932*

36¼ in (92 cm) wide

$4,000–7,000 (the pair)	**L&T**

Gordon Russell Ltd.

While Betty Joel could have achieved success only in fashionable London, Sir Gordon Russell moved to the rural Cotswolds, where he created a uniquely British blend of Art Deco and Arts and Crafts.

Sir Gordon Russell (1892–1980) and his brother Dick (1903–81) were members of the Cotswold School, a legacy of centuries of Arts and Crafts tradition in the region that continues to the present day. Russell's Cotswold contemporaries—including Sidney Barnsley, Peter Waals, and Robert "Mouseman" Thompson—tended to work in a traditional style, making handcraftsmanship deliberately evident in their work.

Russell's furniture was aimed at a larger audience. Made from local woods such as oak, cherry, and walnut, his creations vary from early, neo-Tudor pieces in the style of Lutyens to starkly geometric, highly functional cabinetry produced from the early 1930s until after World War II.

He also ventured into modern design of French influence, working with macassar ebony, ivory inlay, and marquetry veneers, and produced a selection of Bauhaus-inspired tubular-steel furniture in the mid-1930s. This, however, met with only limited success in conservative Britain. Much of Russell's work is clearly labeled.

Above: Large corner desk No. 705 designed by Gordon Russell and made by R. France in cherrywood and English walnut. *1930* 45¾ in (116 cm) wide **$3,000–5,000 L&T**

Oak and laburnum-wood highboy designed by Gordon Russell with a twin-door cupboard above four drawers and its carcass raised on bracket feet. *1926*
67 in (170 cm) high
$5,000–9,000 **BRI**

Ilmington cherrywood dressing table with a hinged triptych mirror resting on a rectangular top above twin, semi-bowed pedestals. The latter are raised on plinths and have three graduated, oak-lined drawers with inset handles. *c. 1935*
54 in (137 cm) wide
$1,500–2,500 **L&T**

Harry and Lou Epstein

Harry and Lou Epstein were from a family of six brothers in the furniture business. They began production in the 1930s and can be credited with popularizing the uniquely British Art Deco taste in suite furniture.

With few exceptions, British Art Deco furniture tended to follow the trend established abroad, rather than setting innovative styles. Most of the Epsteins' work confirms this perception. Exhibiting high quality of craftsmanship, most pieces by the London-based firm were custom-made in veneers of burr maple, sycamore, or walnut. Reproductions of 18th-century French and English styles are common, but a conservative Art Deco style became the trademark by World War II.

Dining-room suites—typically consisting of extension table, up to eight chairs, sideboard, small server, and bar cabinet—were a specialty; they are an attractive collecting opportunity.

After World War II, Epstein worked mainly in bleached walnut, making Art Deco–style furniture into the 1950s. The firm began signing about 1960; later pieces may be labeled "H. & L. Epstein" or "Epstein & Goldman."

Above: Quartetto nest of tables veneered in burr maple, with serpentine-cut rims to the undershelves and tops. The latter also have ebony stringing. *c.1930. Top: 30 in (76 cm) wide* **$1,800–2,200 JAZ**

Semicircular, two-tiered cocktail cabinet finished in mirror-cut walnut veneer. Both pairs of convex doors open to mirror-backed, glass-shelved bars with internal strip lighting. The lower half stands on splayed legs ending in hoof feet, and it incorporates a drawer-shelf at frieze level. *1930s*

64 in (162.5 cm) high

$3,000–4,000   **JAZ**

Dining table and carver (from a set of six chairs and two carvers). The table is veneered in burr maple and edged with maple, its top secured to a U-shaped support with a concave-sided base. The chair's splayed legs are of gently tapered square section and of solid walnut, while its back and side panels are veneered in burr walnut. With padded internal back and sides. *1932*

Table: 78 in (198 cm) long
Chair: 35 in (89 cm) high

$10,000–15,000 (the set)   **JAZ**

Ray Hille

The Art Deco furniture made by Hille (pronounced Hilly) combines elegant sophistication with British conservatism. This was thanks to Ray Hille, who was heavily influenced by contemporary French taste.

The London-based firm of Hille was established in 1906 and operated closely in parallel with Epstein (*see opposite*). Both companies were founded by Jewish immigrants and relied on family members for design and management; both produced mainly reproductions of 18th-century furniture and custom-made creations.

It was Ray Hille, the daughter of the founder, who introduced modern taste to the firm. She was dismayed by the poor showing and critical reviews of British furniture at the 1925 Paris Exposition and saw the commercial potential in modern design. Unlike the Epsteins, Ray Hille traveled extensively to Paris and was heavily influenced by French fashions. Some of her designs are little more than interpretations of the work of Paul Follot (*see p.28*) and other designers, made in blond wood or exotic veneers.

The firm is best known today for innovative postwar designs for commercial interiors, notably the work of Robin and Lucienne Day, whose careers echo those of Charles and Ray Eames in the United States. Among Hille's best-known designs are the Hillestak chair of 1950 and the often copied Polyprop stacking chair of 1963, both designed by Robin Day.

Above: Maple and sycamore desk-dresser of classic Art Deco rectangular and curved form, with two drawers, a cupboard, and contrasting ebony plinth and door handle. *1928* *35¾ in (91 cm) wide* **$3,000–4,000 JAZ**

KEY FACTS

Art Deco designs in French taste were produced by Ray Hille until World War II. She had begun designing in the mid-1920s.

Art Deco Hille furniture carries no maker's marks.

Innovative design blossomed at Hille after World War II thanks to the efforts of Ray Hille.

Office furnishings have been the specialty of the firm since the early 1950s.

The work of British Modernist Robin Day (b. 1915) has been produced by Hille.

Hille Furniture still operates today (now based in Darwen, Lancashire). It remains under family ownership.

Nest of three tables fashioned from Amboina-wood and satinwood and supported on cabriole legs. The elongated ovoid tops are cut with rippling pie-crust rims and aprons. The Amboina-and-satinwood parquetry work is configured in a radiating geometric pattern. *1925* *Largest: 31 in (79 cm) wide* **$2,500–4,000** **JAZ**

Armchair from a three-piece suite with a U-shaped frame veneered with walnut and raised on an ebonized stepped plinth. The reclining back pad, seat pad, interior sides, and sprung base are upholstered in cream leather with a brown-leather piping trim. *1928* *72½ in (184 cm) wide* **$7,000–10,000 (the set)** **JAZ**

British Furniture

British Art Deco furniture, made mostly in London but also provincially, was mainly designed for middle-income families with relatively limited space and budget. There is a little of the elegant detail evident in French furniture and great attention to economy of design and manufacture. Many pieces are extremely practical and consist of simple box-shaped chests or cabinets. The lesser of these date from the late 1930s or 1940s and are in plywood.

Pieces worthy of more attention are distinctively British, such as the delightful baby-grand pianos made by John Strohmenger of London, usually in sycamore with ebonized details; the tasteful work marketed through the Rowley Gallery; aluminum furniture from the war years; and anything by Lloyd Loom. British furniture copying French Art Deco tends to be less successful, although the innovative designs of PEL (Practical Equipment Limited) made in Birmingham in the 1930s in Marcel Breuer style are justifiably gaining in popularity.

English chest of drawers of rectilinear form with two half- over three full-width drawers. The carcass and drawer fronts are veneered with walnut and, respectively, edged and divided by black lacquer banding. The latter is also applied to the plinth. *1930s*

48½ in (123 cm) wide

$1,200–1,800   JAZ

The neoclassical influence is evident in the stepped bases and fluted columns of the ebonized pilasters

Burr-maple veneers, cut from diseased maple branches, display a desirable tightly scrolled figuring and grain

Baby-grand piano made by John Strohmenger & Sons of London. The carcass, veneered with burr maple, has a sunburst motif inlaid in sycamore on the lid. Selective edges are finished in ebonized banding to match the fluted, pilaster-edged supports. *1928*

55 in (140 cm) wide

$12,000–18,000   JAZ

Tall cheval mirror made by Beresford & Hicks of London with a burr-walnut-veneered frame on stepped pyramidal feet and supporting an arch-topped, copper-framed mirror glass. *1935*

20¾ in (53 cm) wide

$500–900   JAZ

Mahogany-veneered gentleman's compendium comprising a hanging space and a cupboard above four drawers. The doors have spherical handles with lunette-shaped lock plates. *c. 1920*

43¼ in (110 cm) wide

$1,200–1,800 DN

Rectangular wardrobe by the Rowley Gallery. It has combed decoration to the side panels, a silver finish, and two-over-five mirrored-panel doors enclosing a hanging space. *c. 1930*

47¾ in (121.5 cm) wide

$1,200–2,200 DN

Unusual aluminum cupboard of streamlined, curvilinear form with black Bakelite handles and plinth. It was designed and made by aircraft manufacturer Hawker. *1940s*

50 in (127 cm) high

$2,500–4,000 DOR

Burr-maple-veneered desk with a rectangular top above a frieze drawer and a single pedestal with a drawer over a cupboard. With ebonized handles and plinths. *c. 1930*

38 in (96.5 cm) wide

$2,500–4,000 L&T

Rocket-style china cabinet in walnut veneer. Raised on fin-tail supports, the circular display cupboard has two demi-lune glazed doors with white Bakelite handles. *1930s*

39½ in (100 cm) wide

$1,200–1,800 BW

Small occasional table with a 12-sided top and four tapering legs of square section. Each of its planes is veneered with a panel of mirror glass. *1930s*

20 in (51 cm) wide

$300–500 L&T

Lloyd Loom armchair made by W. Lusty & Sons. Its painted, woven-paper, arched back and square seat are raised on a cantilevered, chrome-plated, tubular-steel frame. *1930s*

31½ in (80 cm) high

$1,200–1,800 DOR

Coromandel-veneered side cabinet made by Whytock & Reid of Edinburgh. The center carcass houses a single drawer above a twin-doored cupboard and is flanked by cupboards raised on stepped plinths. The latter, like the cupboard handles, are painted red. *1930s*

55 in (140 cm) wide

$800–1,200 L&T

Cloud-style couch (from a three-piece parlor suite including two armchairs). Its arch-topped back, scalloped side panels, and serpentine apron are veneered with burr walnut and enclose cream-leather upholstery. *1930s*

30 in (76 cm) wide

$5,000–9,000 (the set) FRE

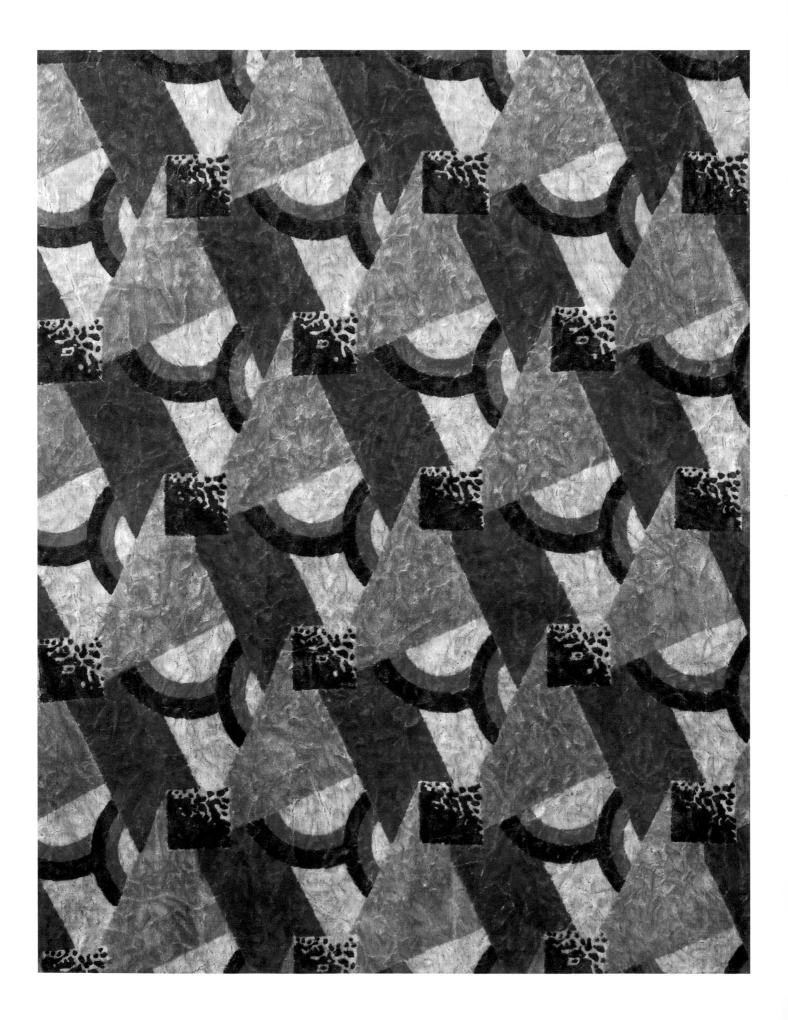

Textiles

Few areas of the Art Deco movement represent the marriage of art and industry as successfully as textiles, a realm that attracted designers from all other artistic fields. Drawing on centuries of experience and skills in the making of clothes, carpets, tapestries, and all manner of fabrics, France soon became established as the world leader in Art Deco textiles.

Both in existence since the 17th century, the two great names in French weaving, Aubusson and Gobelins, operated largely under state patronage. The tradition of excellence they brought to tapestry and carpets enjoyed a successful revival in the interwar years as leading artists designed for them. Luminaries at Aubusson, for example, included Raoul Dufy (1877–1953) and Fernand Léger. In 1911 the Manufacture des Gobelins abandoned the use of natural dyes in favor of synthetics, allowing for an expanded range of colors. Vibrant color is an essential ingredient in most Art Deco fabrics, particularly those designed prior to the mid-1920s.

THE RUSSIAN INFLUENCE
As in most areas of Art Deco, the famous Ballets Russes provided designers with a vast repertoire of motifs and a spectrum of vivid colors that were enthusiastically applied to textiles, mainly by Parisian couture houses. This movement was led by Paul Poiret (1879–1944), who is considered by many to be the father of modern fashion. Poiret opened his own couture house at the age of 25 after brief employment at the House of Worth, and by 1909 he had moved to grand Paris quarters designed by Louis Süe (*see p.29*). Here he would hold decadent soirées on the theme of *Arabian Nights*, with guests adorned in Asian silk costumes, a move that effectively popularized the exotic near-Eastern style of the Ballets and made it Poiret's own.

Between 1900 and 1920, more than 20 new fashion houses were established in Paris, many of them owned and operated by women. However, none of them was as adventurous or extravagant as Poiret's, which ultimately went into liquidation in 1929.

French wall hanging with a raised-pile, velvetlike plush weave in mohair wool. The polychromatic pattern, comprising overlapping triangles, quadrants, stripes, and squares, is classic geometric Art Deco. *1920s–30s* *118 in (300 cm) long* **$2,500–4,000 WROB**

THE FRENCH VANGUARD

Poiret's most remarkable contribution to textile design may be his school Atelier Martine, established in 1911, where fabrics of all types were handmade by girls as young as 12, chosen for their naiveté. The Martine style was strongly influenced by Central European folk weaving and Josef Hoffmann's work at the Wiener Werkstätte, which Poiret greatly admired. Viennese and German textiles are indeed among the finest of the period, many designed with an architectural eye and exquisitely woven by hand. Period and reproduction upholstery by Hoffmann and others often complements Viennese furniture.

The French graphic artist Raoul Dufy was perhaps the most prolific Art Deco textile designer. He shared Paul Poiret's vision and taste and collaborated with him on many projects, including block-printing fabrics using woodcuts carved by Dufy and made at Poiret's studio La Petite Usine. A remarkable series of Dufy wall hangings decorated Poiret's display at the 1925 Paris Exposition. Dufy also designed extensively for the leading French silk- and lace-maker Bianchini-Ferier of Lyons from 1911 until 1930. The preeminent female textile designer

English sleeveless gown made in rose-colored silk velvet, trimmed with machine-stitched gold sequins and with a gold metallic fabric within the deep V-neckline. Its loose-flowing style was a necessity for ease of movement when engaged in Jazz Age pursuits, such as dancing. *c. 1920. 48 in (122 cm) long* **$300–300 AAC**

of the period was Sonia Delaunay (*see p.67*), who united the avant-garde modern paintings of her native Ukraine with modern French taste, mostly in work for the fashion market.

CROSS-MEDIUM APPEAL

After World War I, artists from other fields became increasingly attracted to textiles. Notable Art Deco designers in this category include the architect Eric Bagge (*see p.35*), who designed tapestries for Gobelins; George Barbier (1882–1932), the book illustrator who designed costumes for the stage and movies; and Edouard Bénédictus (1878–1930), a Parisian painter who created upholstery and interior fabrics, including carpets for Brunet, Meunie et Cie. Robert Bonfils (1886–1971) also created fabrics, together with porcelain for Sèvres and bookbindings, though his specialty was graphic design and illustration.

By the mid-1920s, most leading *artistes décorateurs* were applying their talents to fabric design, including upholstery, fabric for room-dividing screens or *paravents*, and wall hangings to complement their interiors. Maurice Dufrène (*see p.33*) was a leading exponent during his management of La Maîtrise interior design studio, as were Paul Follot (*see p.28*), who was responsible for the textiles section of the Grand Palais at the 1925 Paris Exposition, and Jacques-Emile Ruhlmann (*see pp.26–27*), who designed several upholstery fabrics. Another Art Deco furniture designer who created textiles was André Groult (1884–1967), who was not short of sources of inspiration; he was married to Paul Poiret's sister Nicole and related to the theatrical designer Marie Laurencin (1883–1956).

KEY POINTS

With women now free to engage in activities such as dancing and sports, ladies' fashion followed suit and became looser, shorter, or both. Furnishing fabrics drew on diverse sources for inspiration, from romantic motifs such as garlands and rosebuds, to abstract and geometric patterns derived from Cubism, Futurism, and Expressionism, as well as African and South American art and ornament. Similar sources of inspiration also fueled the designs of rugs and carpets, which came to be viewed as works of art in their own right.

Four-panel decorative screen comprising hand-woven tapestry panels with a pattern of stylized tree trunks set against a field of poppies. The plant-form pattern has echoes of William Morris and the Arts and Crafts style but has a more realistic quality that gives it a decidedly more modern twist. *Probably of English origin. 1918–20 94 in (238.75 cm) wide* **$15,000–20,000 DD**

at Eltham Palace, a royal residence up until the 17th century. The interior was remodeled in the 20th century as a luxury Art Deco home. Designed in typically organic colors by Marion Dorn for the palace's entrance hall, the original carpet now resides in the Victoria & Albert Museum.

French low stool with an upholstered cushion set in a rosewood frame with zebra-wood banding. The cushion is covered in a woven fabric with a repeat geometric pattern suggestive of industrial wheels, axles, and other modern machine components and is similar to some of Gerard Sandoz's designs. *1928. 13¾ in (35 cm) high* **$600–900 JAZ**

The finest French upholstery was woven by the Lyons-based firm Prelle, founded in 1752. Prelle still manufactures extraordinary fabrics, including reissues of period Art Deco designs made to original specifications.

THE REST OF THE WORLD

Beyond France and Central Europe, there are relatively few influential Art Deco textile-makers. Americans imported many of their fabrics, and the wealthy still traveled to Paris at least once a year to visit the luxurious haute-couture houses, a tradition that continued until the 1950s.

It is often difficult to identify or attribute designers of fabrics today, since most are unsigned. The best guides are period photographs of room interiors, widely illustrated and reproduced, or period trade catalogs.

Rare woolen rug designed by Eileen Gray with stylized floral motifs framed within linear geometric borders, and worked in a classic Art Deco autumnal color combination of pale rose, burgundy, beige, and gold. *Late 1920s. 114 in (289.5 cm) long* **$12,000–18,000 DD**

Embroidered clutch bag with a geometric pattern in the style of Sonia Delaunay, whose influential geometric patterns employed color to suggest space and movement and were partly inspired by traditional Russian patchwork quilts. *c. 1925. 6¼ in (15.75 cm) high* **$500–900 MOD**

French Textiles

Most French *artistes décorateurs* of the interwar years, including Jacques-Emile Ruhlmann, André Groult, and Maurice Dufrène, designed fabrics, despite being best known in other fields. Searching for their work can be a rewarding enterprise. Most fabrics are unsigned and only attributed through catalogs or other period images, although the work of specialist designers—such as Edouard Bénédictus (1878–1930), a favorite for upholstery among early Art Deco designers—may be signed or well documented. Other designers of note included Raoul Dufy (1877–1953), who worked throughout the period in a distinctive, typically figural style; couturier Paul Poiret (or his studio Atelier Martine); and graphic designers Robert Bonfils and Francis Jourdain. Manufacturers of note include the historic silk-making firm of Bianchini-Ferier and fabric-makers Brunet, Meunie et Cie. It should be noted that several historic fabric houses are still operating and have recently reproduced Art Deco fabrics to authentic standards.

Voided velvet coverlet woven in wool and silk with a stylized fountain pattern. Fountain motifs often appear in early Art Deco designs. *c. 1920*

85 in (216 cm) long

$4,000–5,000 WROB

Voided velvet coverlet woven in black and gray wool with a floral and foliate pattern set within repeat geometric-motif borders. *1920s*

86 in (218.5 cm) long

$4,000–5,000 WROB

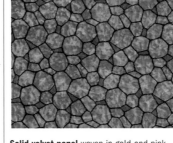

Solid velvet panel woven in gold and pink mohair wool with a dense and stylized stone-and-pebble pathway pattern. *1920s*

53 in (134.5 cm) long

$1,200–1,800 WROB

Solid cotton-velvet coverlet with black stylized spiders and spider webs. Larger webs are in blue against a yellow ground. *c. 1920*

79 in (200.5 cm) long

$1,200–1,800 WROB

Cotton-velvet upholstery fabric with a cylinder-printed leaf pattern in shades of red, brown, and other autumnal colors. *c. 1920*

101 in (256.5 cm) long

$1,200–1,800 WROB

RUSSIAN IMMIGRANTS

Paris became a magnet for Russian artists and intellectuals during the Belle-Epoque, largely due to the enormous impact of Serge Diaghilev's Ballets Russes. From the Paris debut in 1909 throughout the Art Deco years, the music of Igor Stravinsky and performances of Nijinsky injected Russian flavor into Parisian culture. Influential Russian immigrant designers include Romain de Tirtoff (1892-1990), who assumed the name Erté in his early career with Paul Poiret (1879-1944); Leon Bakst (1866-1924); Sonia Delaunay; and graphic artist A. M. Cassandre (c. 1901-68).

Two full plates from a bound portfolio of 20 fabric and wallpaper designs by various artists working in Paris during the 1920s, and including examples from the immigrant Russian artistic community. Collated by the eminent poster artist Adolphe Mouron Cassandre, the designs are permeated with the irregular geometric forms of Cubist decoration so prevalent during this period, and also display the bright colors favored by Cassandre. *1925. 14 in (35.5 cm) long* **$3,000–5,000 SWA**

Length of curtain fabric (one of a pair) woven in black silk and silver metallic thread with a pattern of alternating black stripes and leaf forms, bordered with rows of trees set against ears of wheat and above trelliswork. *1920s*

51½ in (131 cm) long

$1,200–1,800 (each) | **WROB**

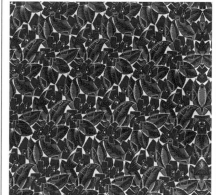

Voided velvet coverlet woven in cotton. It is cylinder-printed with a dense, repeat stylized floral pattern in crimson red and shades of blue. *1920s*

49 in (124.5 cm) long

$1,200–1,800 | **WROB**

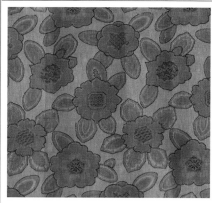

Woven silk panel of upholstery weight with an all-over pattern of flowerheads rendered in shades of pink and blue against a paler pink ground. *c. 1930*

97 in (246.5 cm) long

$1,200–1,800 | **WROB**

Sonia Delaunay

Sonia Delaunay-Terk was born in Odessa, Russia, in 1885 and died in Paris in 1979. Along with her husband, the French Cubist painter and designer Robert Delaunay (1885–1941), she designed graphics and sets for the Ballets Russes. Sonia Delaunay began designing fabrics in the manner of her Cubist paintings before World War I and dresses from about 1914. Her career blossomed after the Great War, when she began selling through her own atelier. Most of her work, including dresses, fabrics, throws, and men's fashions, as well as carpets, were in earth tones and show a Cubist influence. The majority of her Art Deco work was made in the 1920s, reaching a high point at the 1925 Paris Exposition, where she had her own pavilion. After the 1930s, Delaunay devoted much of her time to painting.

Sonia Delaunay silk gauze panel with hand-printed squares, stripes, and rectangles in shades of brown and black against a white ground. The style is informed by Orphism, a strand of Cubism that focused on contrasts of color, especially to suggest a sense of space and movement. *c. 1925*

56 in (142 cm) long

$500–900 | **RSS**

Handbags

Handbags, or—more precisely—evening bags, were a popular fashion accessory in the interwar years, when they were made in a range of styles and materials. Many have survived well and present a good collecting opportunity.

Art Deco handbags, evening bags, and (smaller) clutch bags are plentiful in the modern marketplace. They typically appear wherever Art Deco couture or accessories such as compacts, *minaudières*, cigarette cases, and costume jewelry are traded. The overwhelming majority of handbags were made originally to be inexpensive and eye-catching, and they are not particularly valuable today. Most were made in France or the United States, but some were produced in Germany, Eastern Europe, and Asia.

Handbags—also known as pocketbooks or purses—fall into four main categories: mesh, cloth (or leather), beaded, and bakelite bags. Cloth and leather bags, the most common, typically did not survive well and are rarely of value. Leather bags in good condition may prove

to be exceptional, particularly if they are attributable to designers.

Metallic-mesh bags were made in large quantities in France and are typically of moderate quality. These tend to survive well, and the better examples are signed at the clasp. Less expensive gilt-metal or jeweled clasps are a measure of overall quality.

The clasp is also an important measure of quality in beaded bags, which are typically more elegant and originally more expensive than the mesh variety. Look for luxurious silk linings and compartmentalized interiors (and check every compartment for hidden compacts or other treasures).

Bakelite bags are the most avant-garde in terms of design, and they are growing in value.

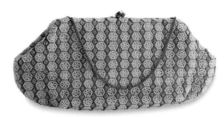

French "Bag by Josef" in white beadwork and woven gilt thread, with an acorn clasp. *1920s. 10 in (25 cm) wide* **$100–180 ROX**

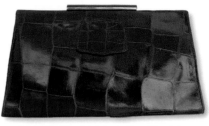

Crocodile-skin clutch bag with a gilt-metal clasp and marked "British Made." *1930s 10¼ in (26 cm) wide* **$120–180 RG**

Leather clutch bag tooled and stained with a floral pattern and lined with beige moiré silk. *c. 1920. 9 in (23 cm) wide* **$40–70 AAC**

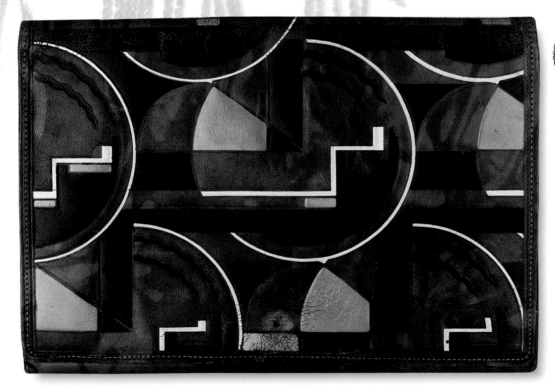

French leather handbag tooled and stained in shades of brown and black with a geometric Art Deco pattern. *c. 1925. 8¾ in (22 cm) wide* **$300–500 QU**

Polychromatic beaded bag with a peacock and floral pattern and a tasseled trim. *1930s. 5½ in (14 cm) wide* **$300–500 AHL**

Metallic beaded bag woven in shades of brown and black with a geometric arrowhead pattern. *1930s. 7 in (18 cm) wide* **$300–400 ATL**

British black leather bag with a silver frame and clasp and a stitched geometric pattern. *c. 1930. 7 in (18 cm) wide* **$500–900 AHL**

Polychrome metallic mesh handbag with a geometric pattern and a gilt-metal clasp. *c. 1920. 7 in (18 cm) long* **$100–180 AAC**

Loop-handled yellow bakelite bag with applied bakelite spiky floral motifs. *1930s 5½ in (14 cm) wide* **$700–900 ROX**

Small suedette handbag with a graduated step pattern in relief and a brass clasp. *1940s. 6¾ in (17 cm) wide* **$300–400 AHL**

Pleated black silk evening bag with an onyx-, carnelian-, and marcasite-studded frame. *1930s. 8¾ in (22.5 cm) wide* **$400–700 TA**

French metallic beadwork bag with diamanté highlights and a foliate fretted gilt-metal clasp. *1930s. 9¼ in (23.5 cm) wide* **$120–200 BY**

Black silk evening bag with a black bakelite frame and clasp, both studded with diamanté. *c. 1930. 8 in (20.5 cm) long* **$300–400 TDG**

European and American Textiles

The best Art Deco fabrics continue the traditions revived during the Arts and Crafts movement. In Britain, the spirit of William Morris and Omega Workshops lives in creations of the Edinburgh Weavers and work by Duncan Grant and others for Allan Walton Fabrics. Most are printed on fabric, since original weaving was not cost-effective for modern designs. Beyond France, exquisite textiles were made at the Wiener Werkstätte for fashion accessories, upholstery, lampshades, and interiors. Many are signed or easily attributed, as are rarer, noncommercial works made at the Bauhaus from 1919 to 1933. Other notable Art Deco fabrics were made in Scandinavia.

In the United States, designers were promoted by fashionable department stores, notably W. & J. Sloane in New York and San Francisco. The tradition continues in New York's ABC Carpet emporium, housed in the original Sloane Building on 19th Street.

Linen and cotton upholstery fabric designed by the St. Edmundsbury Weavers and woven by the Edinburgh Weavers with zigzags and fan shapes in shades of red and yellow. *c. 1930*

27 in (69 cm) long

NPA   V&A

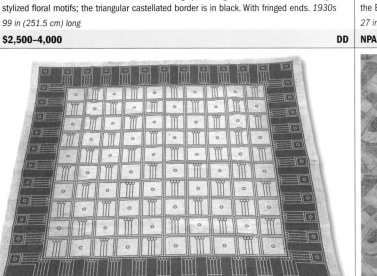

Viennese cotton throw in shades of brown and gray with a geometric pattern containing stylized floral motifs; the triangular castellated border is in black. With fringed ends. *1930s*

99 in (251.5 cm) long

$2,500–4,000   DD

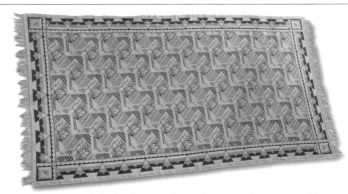

Linen-weave tablecloth with geometric patterns in shades of blue, gray, and white. Designed by Otto Prutscher for Rhomberg of Bavaria and distributed by the Wiener Werkstätte. *c. 1920*

51½ in (131 cm) square

$3,000–5,000   WKA

Upholstery or curtain fabric designed by the Bauhaus School. Machine-woven from cotton and rayon yarns in shades of brown and yellow, it has an abstract pattern of geometric forms. *1920s*

89¼ in (227 cm) long

$700–1,000   RSS

Bahia fabric designed by Julius Zimpel for the Wiener Werkstätte. It is woven with silk threads in shades of red, pink, brown, blue, and black with a geometric pattern. *1925*

29 in (73.5 cm) long

$1,200–1,800   **WROB**

Cotton panel (one of a pair) printed with a Japanese-inspired, repeat plant-form pattern over a geometric trellis ground, in shades of blackish-green, red, mauve, and pink. *c. 1920*

64 in (162.5 cm) long

$1,000–1,800 (the pair)   **WROB**

Ruth Reeves

Ruth Marie Reeves (1892–1966) enjoyed the sophisticated life open to the aesthetic elite a century ago. She was born in California, and between 1911 and 1913 she studied at the San Francisco Art Institute, the epicenter of the unique Californian Arts and Crafts culture, absorbing every influence from east and west. She later traveled to Paris and worked with Fernand Léger, settling in New York by 1930. Reeves is best known for pictorial Art Deco tapestries made to commission for W. & J. Sloane (est. 1881), the New York store that introduced Oriental carpets to North America. Among these tapestries is her Manhattan design of 1932. Reeves was still designing when she died in India in 1966.

Ruth Reeves block-printed cotton tapestry designed for W. & J. Sloane and called The American Scene. Reeves's reputation for representing American culture is perfectly illustrated by this montage of activities from everyday life. *c. 1930*

83 in (211 cm) long

$9,000–12,000   **AMO**

Rugs and Carpets

The best Art Deco rugs and carpets were superbly made, and many survive in good condition. Throughout the period, fashionable interiors favored Western-made floor coverings over traditional Oriental carpets, which had peaked in popularity before 1900. The British carpet-making tradition was revived during the Arts and Crafts period, and several modern designers worked in the Art Deco style, notably Marion Dorn and her husband Edward McKnight Kauffer, whose designs for the Wilton Royal Carpet Factory are scarce but normally signed. French Art Deco carpets are the most desirable. Many are signed, normally with a monogram discreetly woven into one corner. Colors are typically muted, with a tendency toward browns and earth tones, particularly in the 1930s, and pile is deep and unsculpted. Subtle designs, particularly by Ivan de Silva Bruhns, are favored over jazzy themes. Chinese rugs in Art Deco taste were especially popular in the interwar years in the United States and may be found inexpensively.

Detail of a machine-woven woolen carpet with a polychrome Egyptianesque border set against a golden-yellow field. Egyptian patterns and motifs such as these became a fashionable source of imagery following the discovery of Tutankhamun's tomb in 1922. *Mid-1920s*

180 in (457 cm) long

$1,500–2,500   **L&T**

American woolen carpet with a pattern of geometric shapes on a pale beige ground. Although some saturated hues are employed, most of the coloring is in fashionably pastel tones. *1920s*

138 in (350.5 cm) long

$5,000–9,000   **SDR**

French woolen-weave rug with an abstract pattern in the Modernist style. With its combination of bright and muted pastel colors, the design shows the influence of Cubist fine art. *1930s*

76 in (193 cm) long

$3,000–4,000   **DD**

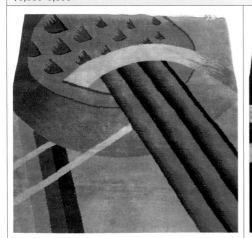

American woolen-weave rug with a highly stylized landscape pattern influenced by Expressionism, an art movement in which distorted shapes are used for emotional impact. *c. 1930*

85 in (216 cm) long

$700–900   **SDR**

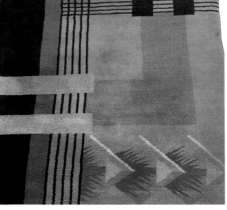

American woolen-weave rug in shades of brown, pink, peach, red, and lilac on a gray ground. The asymmetric geometric design is typical of Art Deco in the late 1920s/early 1930s.

77 in (195.5 cm) long

$700–1,000   **SDR**

Rare Chinese Art Deco–style woolen-weave rug with a nine-dragon pattern and a rainbow-cloud border. Similar rugs were imported from Tientsin in the 1920s and 1930s.

128 in (325 cm) long

$15,000–18,000   **DD**

Pair of machine-woven woolen rugs with fringed ends and designed to be laid on either side of a bed. Asymmetric alone, but symmetrical when employed together, their linear geometric patterns are woven in shades of brown and teal, and set against a tan field. *1930s*

52 in (132 cm) long

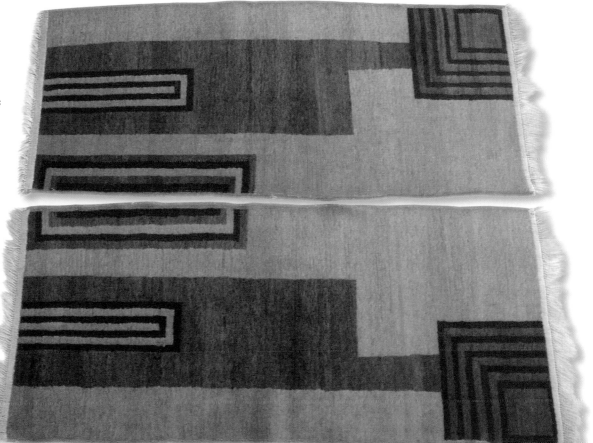

$3,000–4,000   **DD**

Donald Deskey

One of the pivotal figures of the American Modern movement, Donald Deskey (1894–1989) worked throughout the Art Deco period, mainly designing furniture and lighting. However, he is best known for the interior design of Radio City Music Hall, completed in 1932 in collaboration with architect René Chambellan (1893–1955). Designated a New York City landmark in 1978, Radio City was extensively renovated the following year to its original appearance. Most of Deskey's wall and floor coverings, and some furniture, were authentically replaced using preserved drawings and existing pieces. More than 10,000 yards of carpet were rewoven. The restoration was partly funded by selling off original furnishings, including carpeting in various sizes, cut and edged to function as rugs. Radio City carpet is relatively scarce and typically in fair condition. Most bears a distinctive back mark. Deskey strongly influenced American Art Deco carpet design and produced other textiles throughout his career, mainly to commission, including some fabric used on room screens, his furniture specialty.

Original Donald Deskey–designed machine-woven woolen carpet for Radio City Music Hall. The pattern is comprised of a symmetrical patchwork of rectangles, each containing stylized representations of musical instruments, all in shades of purple, rust, and gold. *1932*

82 in (208 cm) long

$1,500–2,000   **SDR**

Fashion

The Art Deco Age of Elegance was firmly centered in Paris, where the fashion industry thrived to satisfy an increasingly affluent and liberated consumer. Haute couture, the most valuable collectible area today, represented the only option for the fashion-conscious wealthy, who would change complete wardrobes by season.

The well-established houses, headed by Paul Poiret, Jeanne Lanvin, and Coco Chanel, saw increasing competition, especially during the Depression years. Smaller labels to look for include Maggy Rouff, Bruyère, Mainbocher, Nina Ricci, and Schiaparelli, all established between 1929 and 1931. A shimmering silk tea gown by Fortuny may be the ultimate Art Deco fashion prize. The value of all fashion depends on condition, and anonymous designs must be finely preserved and high-style. Common items include the ubiquitous cloche, popular throughout the 1920s, and flapper dresses of all types. The best are French beaded creations from the early 1920s. Jazzy men's shoes may be a popular future collectible.

Cloche made of woven straw and decorated with a pale-green velvet ribbon dressed with pinkish-red silk poppies. The small diameter of the band indicates that it was almost certainly intended for a young girl or child. *1920s*

6¼ in (16 cm) high

$800–120   **LH**

Cloche made of woven straw dyed a chocolate-brown color. It is decorated with a satin band dyed a slightly darker shade of chocolate and terminating in a bow. The inside of the hat is fully silk-lined. *1920s*

5¼ in (13.5 cm) high

$300–400   **LH**

V-necked silk costume printed with a floral pattern in shades of pink, peach, gray, and black and descending to an integrated black skirt. With matching scarf. *1920s*

45 in (114.5 cm) long

$500–700   **RR**

Knitwear-style top with integrated pleated skirt. Woven from Macclesfield silk, it has a pattern of graduated horizontal bands in shades of blue. With matching scarf. *1920s*

40 in (101.5 cm) long

$120–300   **JV**

American evening dress with a long-sleeved bodice of green lace with velvet floral appliqué to one shoulder. It has a green silk-chiffon and lace skirt with taffeta underpinnings. *c. 1925*

42 in (107 cm) long

$120–300   **AAC**

American sleeveless evening dress in pink silk with an offset and tied scoop neck, a dropped waist, and flounces stitched around the perimeter of the hem. *c. 1925*

42 in (107 cm) long

$80–120   **AAC**

A CLOSER LOOK

French flapper dress with a sleeveless, V-neck bodice, low waistline, and knee-length skirt. Its beadwork decoration is hand stitched with leaf and other plant-form motifs in autumnal shades of red, brown, black, and gold. c. 1925. 38 in (96.5 cm) long **$3,000–4,000 S&T**

As well as symbolizing the growing emancipation of women, the straight tubular silhouette of this and other flapper dresses was well suited to energetic dancing

Although not by a well-known couturier, this dress's hand-stitched beadwork makes it more valuable than a machine-stitched equivalent

The floral-pattern motifs are formalized in the tapering lines and sweeping curves of this geometric Art Deco composition

Short knee-length skirts, as here, were only fashionable 1926–28. By 1930, hemlines had once again descended to several inches below the knee

Ancient Egyptian–style headdress made in gilt metal with a serpent rising from the headband. The snake is set with amethyst glass cabochons, while the headband is embellished with turquoise-bead-and-gilt tassels. c. 1925

7 in (17.5 cm) wide

$700–900 TDG

English dress belt made of opaque red and white glass beads strung into a pattern of repeat geometric motifs. The wreathlike buckle is formed from white beads. c. 1935

36 in (91.5 cm) long

$180–220 TDG

English silk-chiffon pale-blue dress with horizontal banding at and above the hem and hand-beaded decoration around the neck. 1920s

48 in (122 cm) long

$400–600 RR

American evening dress of black Chantilly lace over peach silk crêpe. It has a silk-chiffon hem and a low waistline with a velvet sash. c. 1925

48 in (122 cm) long

$300–400 AAC

Glass

Demand for new styles of glass grew after World War I, as consumers equated modern taste with optimism and progress. In the early 1920s, technological advances, the building of new factories in Europe and the United States, and improvements in transportation helped forge an exciting era of glass design, with commercial opportunities for both large-scale firms and studio artists.

The interwar years saw several Art Nouveau glassmakers—such as Tiffany, Gallé, and other cameo glassmakers—forced to close their factories. However, a few established companies, notably Daum (*see pp.86–7*) and Steuben (*see pp.100–01*), embraced the new styles and expanded in the 1920s to meet public demand.

New trends in glass design were being set in Europe, just as they had been since the birth of the art-glass movement. The French, especially at Lalique's new factory in Alsace, as well as several of his imitators, pioneered the use of hot metal molds to mass-produce Art Deco glass in every form—from jewelry to architectural elements. The established firm of Daum in Nancy, France, developed new techniques, notably acid-etching, and new forms of vases and lighting rendered in powerful monochromatic glass.

MAIN CENTERS OF PRODUCTION

The explosion in demand for Art Deco glass was most evident in everyday items, especially lighting, perfume bottles, and table glass. The majority of this was met by mass-production in scores of Bohemian glassworks, where traditional skills inherited by modern artisans were applied to a new genre, much of it destined for the vast American market. In contrast to mass-production, several virtuoso glassmakers—notably Maurice Marinot and Marcel Goupy (*see p.84*) in France—thrived in the Art Deco period.

American Art Deco glass is largely inexpensive, often comparable to Bohemian imports and made by European immigrants in the Midwest. The exception is the production of the Steuben Glassworks, the best of which compares to contemporary Scandinavian modern glass.

Clear and cobalt-blue cut-crystal vase by the Saint-Louis Glassworks of Lorraine, France. Its heavy, faceted, ovoid body is cut with stylized floral motifs. *1920s. 6½ in (16.5 cm) high* **$400–600 TC**

COLLECTING GLASS

Decorative glass has been made for about 5,000 years, but it was not until the Art Deco period that sophisticated methods of mold-blowing and carving glass were fully exploited.

Collectors of Art Deco glass have a wide range of choice, including much signed work. All artistic glass of the period may be classified as studio or industrial production, with the overwhelming majority made in the latter category, particularly in the late 1930s. Rarity does not necessarily enhance value, however. Many of the larger makers, led by René Lalique (*see pp.80–83*), have a dedicated following of collectors attracted by availability, variety, and high standards in design, while several small-studio glassmakers remain obscure, despite high-quality work.

It is important to note that glass needs to be in fine condition in order to have value. Minor nicks and scratches are easily removed and may not diminish value, but a crack or flash (internal bruising resembling a shell) can render items worthless. Superficial patinas added to some Lalique can enhance value if authentically restored.

Unlike ceramics, glass is easily polished and ground into new forms, and engraved signatures are easily added. Tall necks can be made short and bases reduced, and a thorough knowledge of original forms is essential.

FRENCH INDUSTRIAL GLASS

French Art Deco glass leads the field in collector interest. Large cameo glassmakers who survived World War I and evolved Art Deco styles are led by the Daum factory, which thrived in the interwar years and is still in operation today. Daum made cameo glass into the 1930s, but the factory's best Art Deco works are acid-etched vases and lighting. Other names to look for include Müller Frères and Charles Schneider (*see pp.88–89*), whose work may be signed Schneider, Le Verre Français, or Charder. The colorful work of André Delatte, made in Nancy from 1921 until World War II, is gaining in value.

French glass struggled for a new identity until the 1930s, when molded glass proved dominant, due largely to economy of manufacture. French industrial makers include Marius Ernst Sabino (1878–1961), who operated two large works throughout the interwar years, making mainly opalescent glass in Lalique style. His Art Deco designs have been widely reproduced since 1960. Other Lalique followers are André Hunebelle, who specialized in larger, geometric vases; Edouard Cazaux, who designed for the firm Degue; the Parisian retailer Etling, which commissioned opalescent and other Art Deco glass from several designers; and the firm of Genet et Michon, which made mostly frosted lighting.

Bottle-shaped vase in cased red over clear glass by the Belgian glasshouse Val Saint-Lambert. Set against a ground of irregular fluting, the primary decoration is in the form of asymmetrical arched and looped cutting highlighted in red. *1930s. 8 in (20.5 cm) high* **$6,000–9,000 MAL**

KEY POINTS

During the Art Deco period, industrial mold-blown glass came into its own. Poly-chromatic cased glass and iridescent and opalescent glass also became fashionable, while the status cameo glass enjoyed during the Art Nouveau era gradually declined. Fashionable patterns and motifs included Egyptian, stylized flora and fauna, human figural (mostly female), and, especially, geometric. New forms included hood ornaments, perfume bottles, and barware.

King Tut–pattern vase made by the Vineland Glass Co. of New Jersey, better known as Durand. Its swirling pattern is inspired by ancient Egyptian decoration that became fashionable following the 1922 discovery of Tutankhamun's tomb. This example has been drilled to serve as a lamp base, hence the low price. *1924–31 6¼ in (16 cm) high* **$300–500 FRE**

Footed cameo-glass vase of slender, waisted form designed by Charles Schneider and signed "Le Verre Français." The layers of glass are in shades of deep blue, pale green, red, yellow, and black, and they are acid-etched with fuchsias set against a distant mountain landscape. *c. 1925 17¾ in (45 cm) high* **$3,000–4,000 FIS**

This 1920s photograph shows René Lalique holding a bowl made of opalescent glass, the medium for which his factory is best known.

Pâte-de-verre was made into the 1930s by Almaric Walter (1859–1942; *see p.91*), whose designs evolved little from Art Nouveau style, and by his rival Gabriel Argy-Rousseau (1885–1953), who developed the art into a unique modern style. Argy-Rousseau's large vases and table lamps are among the most valuable of all Art Deco glass.

BOUTIQUE GLASSMAKERS

French studio glassmaking was led by Maurice Marinot (1882–1960), who worked in glass from 1913 to 1937. He made unique, bubbled-glass globular vessels, most with covers. François-Emile Décorchement (*see p.85*) made translucent Art Deco *pâte-de-cristal*. Other signatures to look for include Henri Navarre and Aristide Colotte, who cast and carved blocks of clear glass, and Marcel Goupy and Auguste Heiligenstein, who both enameled blown glass.

BEYOND FRANCE

Glass production was a key industry in 1930s Bohemia, and the Deco style is reflected in this work. Perfume bottles are particularly popular with collectors today. The scarce British glass in Art Deco taste includes mottled glass from the Scottish Moncrieff works; called Monart, this compares to some Schneider and German glass by W.M.F. and is an emerging collecting area. Glass from the Wiener Werkstätte by designers including Josef Hoffmann is valuable but scarce and often unmarked, as is most of the high-quality work from Ludwig Moser in Karlsbad. Scandinavia developed a neoclassical Art Deco style of figural engraving on clear glass led by Simon Gate (1883–1945) and Edvard Hald (1883–1980) at Orrefors in Sweden. The style was copied in Bohemia and in the US at the Steuben Glassworks. Most Art Deco glass was imported into North America and little was made there, though the late Art Nouveau style of Victor Durand is considered American Art Deco glass.

Footed, tumblerlike vase made by the French glassworks Daum in graduated tints of sea-green glass. Characteristically thick-walled and heavy, it is acid-etched with a geometric pattern in relatively deep relief. *1920s. 11¾ in (30 cm) high* **$3,000–4,000 TDG**

Shallow, circular footed bowl from the Myra-Kristall range made by W.M.F. and named after a site in Asia where archaeologists discovered ancient glass with natural iridescence. This example has a stylized pine cone and leaf pattern etched in red glass with iridescent yellow flashes. *c. 1930 10 in (25.5 cm) wide* **$700–1,500 FIS**

Lalique designed mostly jewelry before World War I.

His career as a glassmaker began with a glass exhibition in 1912.

In 1921 Lalique opened a modern glassworks where all of his Art Deco glass, and all Lalique glass since then, was made.

Lalique exhibited at several American department stores in the late 1930s, attracting an international audience.

Several Lalique Art Deco designs are still in production by Lalique et Cie.

The Lalique company continues to the present day.

René Lalique

Unparalleled in standards of design and technique during the interwar years, René Lalique was remarkably prolific. All pieces bearing his signature were designed by him or directly under his auspices.

Although the name Lalique is well known and respected among glass enthusiasts, René Lalique (1860–1945) did not begin commercial glassmaking until he was almost 50. His first career, as a master jeweler, peaked at the 1900 Paris Exposition. By 1905, he had opened a showroom on the Place Vendôme in the French capital and begun experiments with glass. Within a few years Lalique was designing glass perfume bottles for François Coty.

In 1912 René Lalique held an all-glass exhibition at his showroom. Guests at the opening received a molded-glass invitation medallion. His glassmaking career was well established by the end of World War I, centered in a small factory near Paris. After 1918 Lalique was enticed to the newly French region of Alsace. He built a modern factory, which opened in 1921 in the town of Wingen, near Strasbourg. The factory was set up with all the latest equipment, some designed by Lalique or his son Marc (1900–77), who joined the firm in 1922.

Lalique's approach was thoroughly Modernist: he mass-produced glass using hot metal molds, hot compressed air, and sophisticated decoration techniques. At Wingen he introduced thousands of designs, from tiny jewelry elements to massive architectural panels designed for impressive schemes. Motifs are meticulously modeled or molded into surfaces, and all elements relate closely to each other, including design names, which offer clues to decoration or form.

Above: Mold-blown Piriac vase of trumpet-shape form in blue glass with a center band of fish swimming above water. *c. 1930* *7 in (17.5 cm) high* **$6,000–8,000 RDL**

DOMINATING DESIGNS

René Lalique's new factory in Alsace allowed the manufacture of architectural panels and large cast elements for use in lighting and furniture. By 1930 Lalique offered an ambitious architectural range, specializing in church interiors, wall paneling for commercial and domestic interiors, and outdoor fountains. His contributions to the 1925 Paris Exposition included an enormous figural fountain (dismantled at the end of the fair), taking center stage inside the main entrance, and two pavilions of his own. Several Lalique Art Deco interiors exist today, notably the Asaka Palace in Tokyo and the extraordinary St. Matthew's Church on the island of Jersey.

Press-molded Moissac vase of conical form in amber-red glass with leaf-form decoration in deep relief. *c. 1930. 5 in (13 cm) high* **$3,000–5,000 RDL**

LALIQUE'S FOUNTAIN AT THE 1925 PARIS EXPOSITION

PERFUME BOTTLES

Lalique's career as a glassmaker started with perfume bottles he designed for François Coty about 1907. By 1910, Lalique was manufacturing bottles for both Coty and his own showroom in a small factory near Paris. These met with enormous success, and within a few years his clients included most of the leading perfumeries of Paris. This tradition grew in the interwar years, and many Lalique perfume bottles are exquisitely Art Deco. They can be divided into Maison Lalique, made to be sold, empty, in Lalique retail outlets, and commercial bottles, made for scores of patrons including perfume companies, couturiers, and stores. Many Art Deco bottles were made for Worth in the 1930s, some of which were reproduced in recent years. Original packaging, often designed by Lalique himself, adds considerably to the value. Stoppers and bases have matching engraved numbers.

Left: Maison Lalique Amphitrite perfume flacon press-molded in clear and frosted glass with a blue patina in the form of a fossil, with a kneeling nude woman as a stopper. *c. 1920. 3¾ in (9.5 cm) high* **$3,000–5,000 RDL**

COLLECTING LALIQUE GLASS

Modern collectors find a wealth of Art Deco Lalique, with a wide range of value. Many focus on one category, popularly perfume bottles, vases, or hood ornaments. Recently, more attention has been paid to letter seals, boxes, ashtrays, and drinking glasses, all of which offer the opportunity to "collect the set." Some prefer to concentrate on a motif, such as birds or female nudes, or anything in opalescent glass.

Almost all Lalique glass is signed, the main exception being architectural panels. In general, color adds value, with rare colors such as red topping the list.

Lalique was widely copied, mostly in Bohemia, and it is not uncommon to find inferior glass with spurious Lalique signatures added. Convincing fakes, however, are rare.

INSPIRATIONS

Lalique's golden age as a glassmaker has been called the Age of Speed and the Age of Elegance. Lalique combined these ideas and the wider spirit of the age in Le Style Lalique, as his unique taste became known. His maturity as a designer by the 1920s is evident in his extensive repertoire of influences, but his innovation is shown in a constant attention to modernity, making his late work as fresh as his earliest creations.

HOOD ORNAMENTS

Rare hood ornament by Lalique, called Tête de Paon (number 1140). *c. 1930. 7 in (17.8 cm) high* **$18,000–22,000 WW**

Between 1925 and 1932, Lalique created 28 commercial hood ornaments, most featuring stylized animals or female figures in aerodynamic poses. Most were made only in clear glass. Opalescence and color are rare and normally add value. The base sizes are standard (large or small) and designed to fit chrome radiator-cap mounts, some of which were set up for illumination through colored light filters. Many models were also sold as paperweights or bookends, and a few are still made. Ornaments showing actual use—through provenance, original mountings, or the amethyst tint resulting from exposure to sunlight—are preferred, but value depends largely on rarity.

Left: Ovoid Perruches vase molded with pairs of wooing budgerigars on branches in opalescent glass with an enamel-washed patina in shades of green. *c. 1920. 10 in (25 cm) high* **$3,000–5,000 RDL**

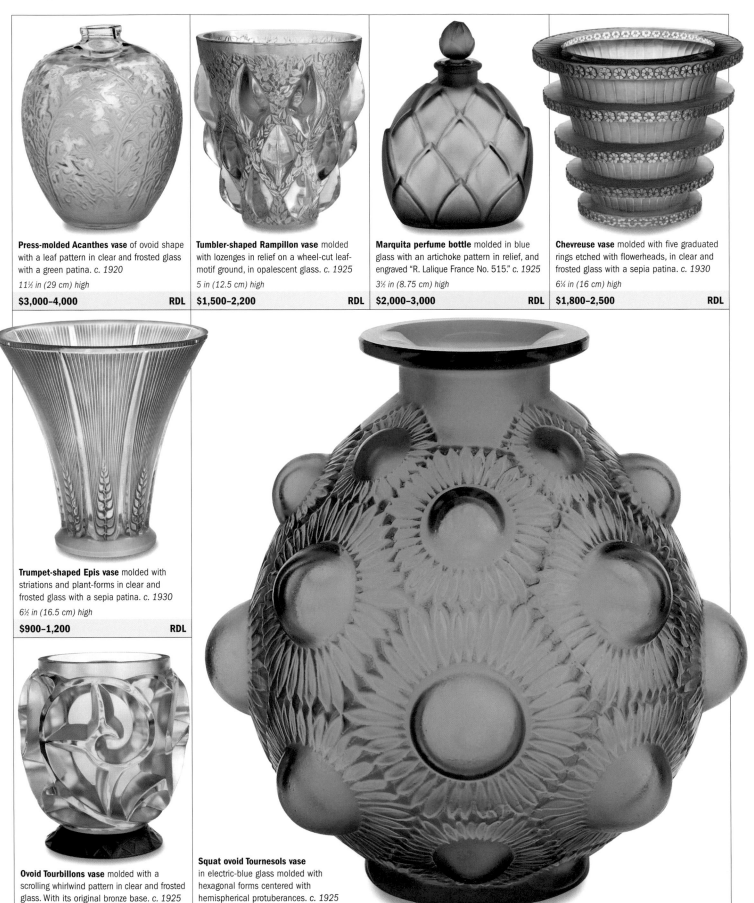

Press-molded Acanthes vase of ovoid shape with a leaf pattern in clear and frosted glass with a green patina. *c. 1920*

11½ in (29 cm) high

$3,000–4,000   **RDL**

Tumbler-shaped Rampillon vase molded with lozenges in relief on a wheel-cut leaf-motif ground, in opalescent glass. *c. 1925*

5 in (12.5 cm) high

$1,500–2,200   **RDL**

Marquita perfume bottle molded in blue glass with an artichoke pattern in relief, and engraved "R. Lalique France No. 515." *c. 1925*

3½ in (8.75 cm) high

$2,000–3,000   **RDL**

Chevreuse vase molded with five graduated rings etched with flowerheads, in clear and frosted glass with a sepia patina. *c. 1930*

6¼ in (16 cm) high

$1,800–2,500   **RDL**

Trumpet-shaped Epis vase molded with striations and plant-forms in clear and frosted glass with a sepia patina. *c. 1930*

6½ in (16.5 cm) high

$900–1,200   **RDL**

Ovoid Tourbillons vase molded with a scrolling whirlwind pattern in clear and frosted glass. With its original bronze base. *c. 1925*

8½ in (21.5 cm) high

$18,000–24,000   **RDL**

Squat ovoid Tournesols vase in electric-blue glass molded with hexagonal forms centered with hemispherical protuberances. *c. 1925*

4¾ in (12 cm) high

$3,000–4,000   **RDL**

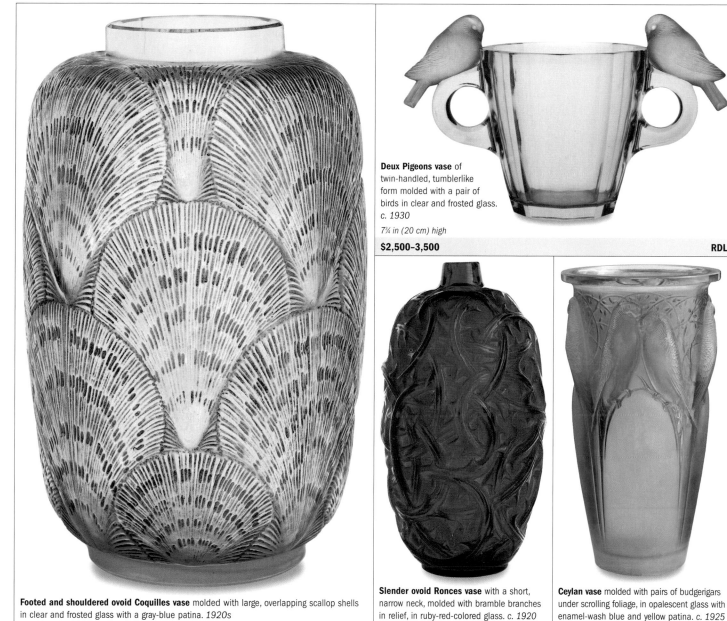

Footed and shouldered ovoid Coquilles vase molded with large, overlapping scallop shells in clear and frosted glass with a gray-blue patina. *1920s*

7½ in (19 cm) high

$1,500–2,200 RDL

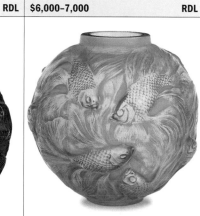

Deux Pigeons vase of twin-handled, tumblerlike form molded with a pair of birds in clear and frosted glass. *c. 1930*

7¾ in (20 cm) high

$2,500–3,500 RDL

Slender ovoid Ronces vase with a short, narrow neck, molded with bramble branches in relief, in ruby-red-colored glass. *c. 1920*

9½ in (24 cm) high

$6,000–7,000 RDL

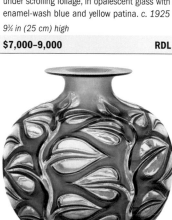

Ceylan vase molded with pairs of budgerigars under scrolling foliage, in opalescent glass with enamel-wash blue and yellow patina. *c. 1925*

9¾ in (25 cm) high

$7,000–9,000 RDL

Shouldered ovoid Esterel vase molded with a plant-form pattern in cased yellow glass with a sepia patina. *c. 1925*

6 in (15 cm) high

$2,500–3,500 RDL

Squat ovoid Ormeaux vase with a narrow neck, molded with an all-over pattern in relief in reddish-amber glass. *c. 1925*

6¾ in (17 cm) high

$2,000–3,000 RDL

Formose opalescent-glass vase molded with a school of fish in relief and with a selective blue patina. *c. 1925*

7 in (18 cm) high

$2,500–3,500 RDL

Ovoid Sophora vase molded with a plant-form pattern in relief, in clear and frosted glass with a green patina. *c. 1925*

11½ in (29 cm) high

$2,500–4,000 RDL

KEY FACTS

Goupy worked in Paris from 1918 until 1936.

Georges Rouard promoted his work from 1919.

Goupy was art director of Geo Rouard from 1929 until 1954.

Clear or pale free-blown vessels are typical of Goupy, as are narrow-necked carafes, small drinking vessels, and small vases.

Pre-1925 pieces tend to be smaller, decorated with flora. Figural decoration appears in later pieces of the 1920s.

Vases dating from the 1930s may be undecorated and geometric in form.

Tableware was made from around 1925 in matching patterns, including simple geometric banding designed to match table ceramics.

Value is added by figural decoration, larger pieces, and vibrant colors.

Marcel Goupy

One of the leading French Art Deco artists, Marcel Goupy supervised all his studio work personally, ensuring that every item created was a distinctive and elegant representation of the style.

Marcel Goupy (1886–1954) studied architecture and interior design at the Ecole Nationale des Arts Décoratifs in Paris. His career took off in 1919, when he met Georges Rouard, who opened a gallery in Paris that year. Rouard promoted leading French glass artists, including Lalique (*see pp.80–83*), Maurice Marinot, and Jean Luce, as well as furnishings and ceramics in modern taste by Jean Mayodon (*see p.111*) and others.

Goupy's free-blown vessels—mostly carafes and vases—are typically decorated by hand with brightly colored enamels. Before 1925 these are often in clear, smoky, or pale-colored glass, sparsely painted on the outer surface with stylized flora in two or three colors.

In the early 1920s, Goupy was assisted by Auguste Heiligenstein, although pieces do not bear his signature. Later in that decade, Goupy developed several new techniques, including the use of colored glazes. These fused to the vessel's surface creating a tangible, marbleized effect, onto which decoration was then added.

In the 1930s, Goupy vases are typically geometric in form and may be decorated only with a superficial layer of enamel sprayed onto the interior. Goupy also decorated ceramics for Haviland in Limoges.

Above: Emerald-colored cut-glass vase with a faceted, funnel-shaped body. With an enameled "M. Goupy" signature. *1930s* 5¾ in (14.5 cm) high **$500–800 QU**

Hand-blown clear-glass vase painted with a rural landscape in shades of blue, green, and gray enamel, and with selective gilt outlining. The rim and base are decorated with thin bands of black enameling. *1920s–30s* 7 in (18 cm) high

$7,000–10,000 **LN**

Ball-shaped clear-glass vase with a gently flared neck with a bulbous collar trailing four root forms. The latter are decorated with red and black enameling. Black geometric motifs are also applied to the body. *c. 1925* 5 in (13 cm) high

$500–800 **QU**

Clear-glass bowl painted around the rim with garlands of trailing red berries in ruby-red enameling. The berries are outlined in gilt and arranged over a black enamel grid. *1920s* 2½ in (6.25 cm) high

$800–1,200 **QU**

François-Emile Décorchement

The ancient art of *pâte-de-verre*, which had been revived in France by Henri Cros and Albert Dammouse before 1900, was successfully evolved by Décorchement into a unique Art Deco style.

Born in Normandy to a family of artists—his father worked with the sculptor Jean-Léon Gérôme—François-Emile Décorchement (1880–1971) mastered the complex *pâte-de-verre* technique after finishing his studies in 1900.

Before World War I, he was making cast, figural pieces and small vessels in Roman form. After 1919, however, he embraced a strong Art Deco style, with early figural detail replaced by geometric forms. All Décorchement vessels are meticulously handmade and typically signed in the mold with a full signature formed as a shell.

From 1903, many bear an engraved consecutive number that may aid in dating.

Typical pieces of the 1920s include vases and footed bowls in deep, mottled colors, including a simulated tortoiseshell. Engraved decoration to the exterior is unusual after about 1925, thereby suggesting an earlier production date.

Décorchement also produced paler, more delicate pieces in translucent *pâte-de-cristal*.

Above: *Pâte-de-cristal* footed bowl in teal, with twin-loop handles and a Classical geometric pattern. *1920s*
10 in (25.5 cm) wide **$3,000–5,000 MACK**

Rare *pâte-de-verre* vase of footed ovoid form with an everted rim. The body's streaks and swirls of beige, orange-brown, and blue-violet inclusions create a *faux-marbre* effect that is complemented by four Classical face masks in relief under the rim. *c. 1925*
5½ in (14 cm) high

$15,000–20,000   **DOR**

Pâte-de-verre footed bowl with octagonal sides and twin handles. Its swirling, smoky reddish-brown and blue-black inclusions have a precious or semiprecious-stone-like quality often evident in Décorchement's postwar pieces. *1920s*
4¾ in (12 cm) high

$15,000–20,000   **MACK**

Pâte-de-verre vase of footed, ovoid form. Although decorated similarly to the vase shown on the left, it is slightly shorter and its in-relief face masks rise partly above a simpler, broader rim. There are also more bubbles prominent in the glaze. *1920s*
4½ in (11.5 cm) high

$7,000–10,000   **MACK**

KEY FACTS

Established in Nancy, France, in 1875 by Jean Daum (1825–85).

Renamed Verrerie de Nancy in 1879, it was operated by Jean Daum and his son Auguste (1853–1909). Brother Antonin (1864–1931) joined in 1887.

Vases and lamps were made with metalwork armatures by Louis Majorelle (1859–1929) from 1900.

Pre–World War I production mostly comprised cameo glass and acid-etched vases, lighting, or decanters.

Most production ceased during World War I.

The production of prewar models was stopped after 1919 to focus on larger, acid-etched vessels and internally decorated pieces with metalwork by Majorelle, Edgar Brandt, and others.

New wares were shown at the 1925 Paris Exposition, under the direction of Paul Daum.

Production ceased during World War II. Henri Daum (1889–1960) reopened the factory in 1946. It is still in operation.

Daum

From its beginning, Daum developed a reputation for outstanding quality, despite being a relatively small enterprise. Art Deco Daum is often monumental and typically displayed alongside contemporary furniture.

The Daum factory's progressive approach was most evident in the dramatic evolution of style after 1919, which makes it easy to separate Daum glass into Art Nouveau and Art Deco. Distinctive pre–World War I pieces rival the work of Emile Gallé, another Nancy native, and include cameo vases and lighting, some with hand-applied ornament or delicately acid-etched with flora or landscapes. Most cameo production ceased after World War I, but the acid technique was refined to produce monumental vases and some lighting in pale or smoky gray, etched with banding or geometric pattern. Some have an outer layer of color, in a variation of the cameo technique, and are thin-walled compared to most monochrome vases. The most desirable acid-etched pieces are those with the deepest color and decoration. The heaviest examples may even be difficult to lift.

By the mid-1920s, Daum also made vases in mottled glass internally decorated with metal foil, usually gold. These tend to be lighter, blown with narrow necks, and less Art Deco in form, as do similar pieces with internal bubble decoration. Daum's mottled and bubbly glass is comparable to similar work by Schneider (*see pp.88–89*), but is less valuable and not widely collected, even when encased in metal mounts.

Daum also produced lighting in the interwar years, including table lamps of mushroom form in clear or pale-yellow acid-etched glass and hanging fixtures in the same taste or with wrought-iron mounts and shades in mottled orange glass.

Paul Daum (1888–1944) managed Daum's Art Deco production. (He was later arrested during the occupation and died in a Nazi camp.) Popular pieces are widely reproduced today, including some convincing Art Deco models reissued by the modern Daum Company.

Above: Twin-handled footed bowl in brown and black frosted overlay glass, cut with simple sweeping lines in shallow relief. *c. 1925. 5¾ in (14.5 cm) high* **$1,200–2,500 DOR**

DECORATIVE MOUNTS

Before World War I, Daum commissioned wrought-iron bases and armatures for lamps and vases from the Nancy firm of Louis Majorelle, best known for making wood furniture. Metal mounts provided a fine complement to Daum's larger Art Deco wares, and many more mounted pieces were produced in the interwar years. Both Daum and Majorelle typically signed such pieces. Less readily identifiable are mounts by wrought-iron master Edgar Brandt or designer André Groult, who also supplied Daum in the 1920s but did not sign their work.

Egyptian cameo-glass vase made from colorless glass with milky powder insertions. It has a vitrified blue outer layer acid-etched with stylized papyrus flowers and olive branches. *1926 11½ in (29.25 cm) high* **$8,000–12,000 QU**

Squat overlay-glass vase with mottled pink, white, and blue powdered-enamel inclusions. It is mounted in an openwork wrought-iron armature designed by Louis Majorelle. *1920s 9¾ in (25 cm) high* **$1,500–2,000 QU**

Pendant ceiling lamp with wrought-iron mountings. The center bowl and shades are in mottled red and yellow overlaid glass with acid-etched floral decoration. *1920s*

41½ in (105 cm) high

$7,000–10,000   HERR

Blown and cased vase with orange, red, and gray-blue streaks and swirls. It is set in a wrought-iron armature with stylized floral motifs designed by Louis Majorelle. *1920–22*

14¾ in (37.5 cm) high

$1,200–3,000   HERR

Ovoid cameo-glass vase with a stubby neck and everted rim. The gray-green frosted body is acid-etched with vertical ribbing alternated with stylized flowers and foliage. *1920s*

13¾ in (35 cm) high

$3,000–4,000   TDG

Blown and cased bulbous vase acid-etched with stylized branches and berries and with speckled peach, tangerine, and black powdered-enamel inclusions. *c. 1930*

6¼ in (16 cm) high

$600–900   VZ

Squat, heavy ovoid vase in pale-green glass, deeply cut with vertical fluting flanked by concave cut panels against a frosted ground. *1930s*

7¾ in (19.5 cm) high

$1,000–1,500   DN

Stocky ovoid vase with an overlay-glass body acid-etched with stylized blossoms, leaves, and branches in orange-yellow and blue-green powder enamels. *1920s*

7 in (17.75 cm) high

$1,800–2,200   QU

Cylindrical clear glass vase acid-etched with vertical ribbing and fluting and mounted in a partly gilded, wrought-iron, footed armature designed by Louis Majorelle. *c. 1925*

16 in (40.5 cm) high

$5,000–8,000   VZ

Large bell-shaped bowl with an inner layer of clear glass overlaid with an outer layer colored with mottled orange and yellow enamels. The outer layer is also acid-etched with a radiating, stylized flower, leaf, and berry pattern. *1920s*

12½ in (32 cm) wide

$3,000–5,000   QU

Schneider

Despite world wars, legal battles, and the Depression, Schneider became a thriving enterprise by the mid-1920s. Most pieces compare to, but lack the refinement in design and execution of, Daum.

Brothers Ernest (1877–1937) and Charles (1881–1953) Schneider moved to Nancy as children. Both began their careers working at the local Daum factory (*see pp.86–87*)—Ernest as a commercial director and Charles, who had studied at the Ecole des Beaux-Arts in Nancy, as a modeler.

Throughout its history, Schneider production resembles the contemporary work of Daum in many aspects, including the use of wrought-iron mounts made at Schneider's own foundry.

In 1913, the brothers started their own venture by reopening a disused factory at Epinay-sur-Seine, near Paris. Within a year, however, they were forced to close the works when both Ernest and Charles were enlisted to fight in World War I. The factory reopened in 1917 to produce medical glass.

Owing to the period of production, virtually all Schneider can be considered Art Deco. Typical pieces include tall vases, made in bubbly or mottled glass, with applied elements of contrasting color, or overlaid Pivoine vases with stylized patterns. Many were made in series and are not totally unique.

Despite the remarkable talent of Charles Schneider, revealed in a Paris museum exhibition in the 1990s, artistic pieces are rare, and Daum is better known for creating unique work to a high standard. However, strong marketing efforts spearheaded by Ernest and sister Ernestine saw the company grow to over 500 employees by the mid-1920s. Schneider's success drew from extensive commercial promotion outside France, largely in the United States, and the pieces' stunning visual impact, which was due to a spectrum of colors developed at the factory, including a deep plum and vivid yellow. A bright orange named Tango became popular in a wide range of French designs, including fashion and fabrics.

Above: Coupe Bijou bell-shaped footed bowl in overlay glass with air bubbles and pale-violet powdered-enamel inclusions on a dark-purple foot. *1918–22. 6 in (15 cm) high* **$1,000–1,500 QU**

LE VERRE FRANÇAIS RANGE

Schneider glass is perhaps best known today through the ware signed Le Verre Français. It was introduced in 1918 and originally designed exclusively for sale in large French department stores. The range was also sold through a Schneider gallery in Paris managed by Ernestine Schneider and became commercially successful as an import to the United States by the early 1920s. Typical examples include tall vases, normally of urn form, some with applied feet or handles. They are etched with stylized flora or figural patterns from deep colors overlaid on pale, mottled ground. The vivid contrast of colors and large scale makes the ware striking and dramatic. Le Verre Français represents Schneider's most modern styles.

Le Verre Français vase of baluster-like form with a ribbed annular knop above the foot. It is made from intercalaire clear and colored glass with mottled and streaked enamel inclusions. *c. 1925 13¾ in (35 cm) high* **$1,800–2,200 FIS**

Le Verre Français Halbrans-pattern vase of baluster-like form made from intercalaire clear and colored glass with mottled enamel inclusions, etched with ducks flying above meadows. *1923–26. 9¾ in (24.75 cm) high* **$2,000–3,000 QU**

Cameo-glass cabinet vase of conical form with bunches of grapes etched in shades of orange over a frosted clear glass ground. Marked "5-66615." *Late 1920s*

3 in (7.5 cm) high

$500–900　　　　**JDJ**

Le Verre Français intercalaire vase with a clear outer layer over a mottled orange layer with applied rosettes, above a clear ground with yellow-powder inclusions. *c. 1930*

13¼ in (33.5 cm) high

$1,200–2,000　　　　**VZ**

Ovoid cameo-glass vase made from a layer of amethyst-colored glass over clear glass. The former is acid-etched with frosted Egyptian-style decoration. *Mid-1920s*

7½ in (19 cm) high

$800–1,200　　　　**JDJ**

A CLOSER LOOK

Le Verre Français Pivoine vase made from cameo glass in a trumpet shape. It has an everted rim and a domed circular foot. The full-height decoration is in the form of stylized peony flowers and leaves, etched in layers of purple, blue, and pink enameled glass over a mottled yellow ground. *c. 1925. 19¾ in (50 cm) high* **$2,500–4,000 FIS**

SCHNEIDER'S "CHARDER" MARK

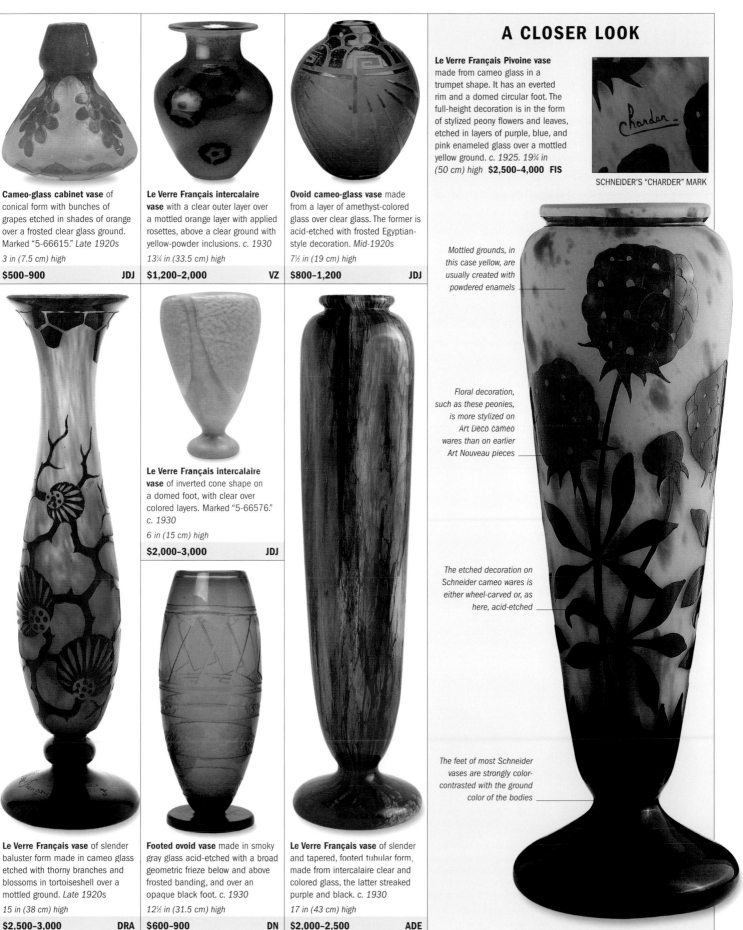

Mottled grounds, in this case yellow, are usually created with powdered enamels

Floral decoration, such as these peonies, is more stylized on Art Deco cameo wares than on earlier Art Nouveau pieces

The etched decoration on Schneider cameo wares is either wheel-carved or, as here, acid-etched

The feet of most Schneider vases are strongly color-contrasted with the ground color of the bodies

Le Verre Français intercalaire vase of inverted cone shape on a domed foot, with clear over colored layers. Marked "5-66576." *c. 1930*

6 in (15 cm) high

$2,000–3,000　　　　**JDJ**

Le Verre Français vase of slender baluster form made in cameo glass etched with thorny branches and blossoms in tortoiseshell over a mottled ground. *Late 1920s*

15 in (38 cm) high

$2,500–3,000　　　　**DRA**

Footed ovoid vase made in smoky gray glass acid-etched with a broad geometric frieze below and above frosted banding, and over an opaque black foot. *c. 1930*

12½ in (31.5 cm) high

$600–900　　　　**DN**

Le Verre Français vase of slender and tapered, footed tubular form, made from intercalaire clear and colored glass, the latter streaked purple and black. *c. 1930*

17 in (43 cm) high

$2,000–2,500　　　　**ADE**

French Glass

France was home to dozens of glassworks during the booming 1920s. Most factories with mechanical production simply made lower-priced interpretations of successful designs by Lalique, Daum, and others. Glass bearing the names of Etling, André Hunebelle, Verlys, D'Avesn, D'Argenthal (made at the Saint-Louis Glassworks in Lorraine), Richard, Degué, André Delatte, and Sabino (a specialist in opalescence) falls into this category.

At the other end of the spectrum in quality and value are several studio glassmakers, headed by Maurice Marinot, who made unique pieces in distinctive styles from about 1912 until 1937. This category includes Jean Sala, Jean Luce, Henri Navarre, and André Thuret. Other noteworthy French Art Deco glass includes the work of Müller Frères of Luneville, founded in 1895 by two brothers who had worked for Emile Gallé and active until 1936. Art Deco Müller includes lighting and vases, most of which compares closely to the work of Schneider in appearance and quality.

Overlay-glass bowl designed by Jean Sala at the Saint-Louis Glassworks. It has a ring of seven acid-etched, ruby-red curlicues set against a rough frosted ground. *c. 1935*

6½ in (16.5 cm) high

$2,000–3,000   VZ

Pale-blue and clear cased-glass vase by André Delatte of Nancy. The sides are etched and enameled in red, gray, and black with stylized jellyfish. *1920s*

4½ in (11.5 cm) high

$800–1,200   JDJ

Clear glass vase by André Delatte of Nancy. It is decorated with birds of paradise among tropical orchids etched in relief and highlighted with graphite-gray enamel. *c. 1925*

17¼ in (44 cm) high

$4,000–7,000   VZ

Cased-glass vase by Legras & Cie. The inner layer has orange-red and brown powdered-enamel inclusions, and the clear outer layer is etched with stylized leaf forms. *c. 1930*

7 in (17.5 cm) high

$800–1,200   VZ

Press-molded glass bowl by Etling et Cie, with eucalyptus leaves and gum nuts in opalescent glass with milky-white, aqua-blue, and greenish-yellow sheens. *1920–30*

9 in (23 cm) wide

$1,000–1,500   OACC

Extremely rare flattened ovoid bottle with stopper by Maurice Marinot. Made from blown and cased glass, it displays swirling, veined, and bubbled marblelike decoration in gray, green, and black, with white enameled geometric motifs around the rim. *1920s*

6¼ in (16 cm) high

$20,000–30,000   LN

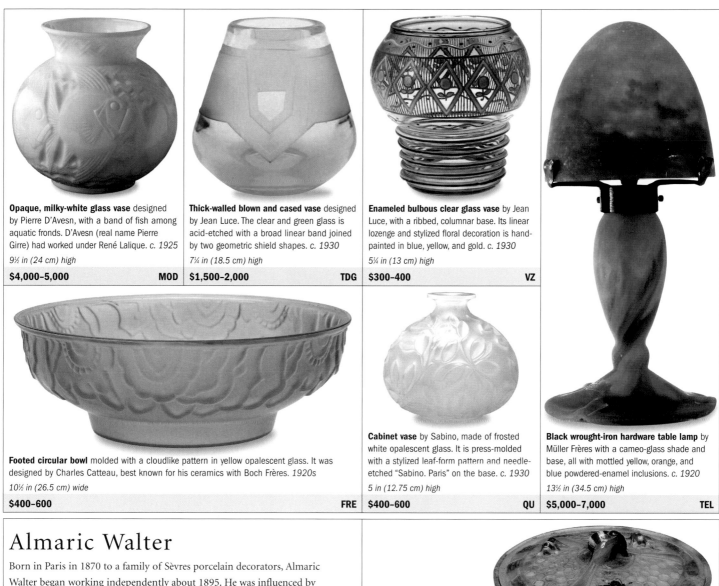

Opaque, milky-white glass vase designed by Pierre D'Avesn, with a band of fish among aquatic fronds. D'Avesn (real name Pierre Girre) had worked under René Lalique. *c. 1925*

9½ in (24 cm) high

$4,000–5,000   **MOD**

Thick-walled blown and cased vase designed by Jean Luce. The clear and green glass is acid-etched with a broad linear band joined by two geometric shield shapes. *c. 1930*

7¼ in (18.5 cm) high

$1,500–2,000   **TDG**

Enameled bulbous clear glass vase by Jean Luce, with a ribbed, columnar base. Its linear lozenge and stylized floral decoration is hand-painted in blue, yellow, and gold. *c. 1930*

5¼ in (13 cm) high

$300–400   **VZ**

Footed circular bowl molded with a cloudlike pattern in yellow opalescent glass. It was designed by Charles Catteau, best known for his ceramics with Boch Frères. *1920s*

10½ in (26.5 cm) wide

$400–600   **FRE**

Cabinet vase by Sabino, made of frosted white opalescent glass. It is press-molded with a stylized leaf-form pattern and needle-etched "Sabino. Paris" on the base. *c. 1930*

5 in (12.75 cm) high

$400–600   **QU**

Black wrought-iron hardware table lamp by Müller Frères with a cameo-glass shade and base, all with mottled yellow, orange, and blue powdered-enamel inclusions. *c. 1920*

13½ in (34.5 cm) high

$5,000–7,000   **TEL**

Almaric Walter

Born in Paris in 1870 to a family of Sèvres porcelain decorators, Almaric Walter began working independently about 1895. He was influenced by Henri Cros and Albert Dammouse, both former employees of Sèvres, who revived the ancient art of *pâte-de-verre* before 1900. Walter's early Art Nouveau style was made at the Daum factory. Following service in World War I, he established his own studio, where he was active until his retirement in the mid-1930s. He later went blind, and he died in 1959.

Art Deco work by Walter includes small, often symmetrical coupes, paperweights, ashtrays, and superb figural panels of translucent *pâte-de-verre* with a muted palette. Pieces are normally signed by Walter and may include a modeler's signature, notably Henri Bergé or Joe Descomps in the 1920s.

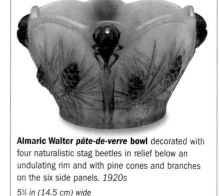

Almaric Walter rare *pâte-de-verre* lidded bowl decorated with honeycombs and with naturalistic busy bees in relief in shades of orange, yellow, green, and black. *1920s*

7 in (18 cm) wide

$12,000–18,000   **QU**

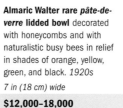

Almaric Walter *pâte-de-verre* bowl in graduated shades of blue glass, with a naturalistic bumblebee detail in orange, blue, and black. It is hand-finished and signed "AWalter Nancy Bergé sc." *1920s*

4½ in (11 cm) high

$1,500–2,000   **QU**

Almaric Walter *pâte-de-verre* bowl decorated with four naturalistic stag beetles in relief below an undulating rim and with pine cones and branches on the six side panels. *1920s*

5¾ in (14.5 cm) wide

$8,000–12,000   **QU**

Perfume Bottles

Few areas of Art Deco collecting are as widespread and heavily contested as perfume bottles. Like fashion, bottle designs allow a glimpse into the interwar culture and represent all tastes and budgets.

The majority of decorative perfume bottles in Art Deco taste were made in France and, more commonly, Bohemia. French bottles, led in quality and value by the work of René Lalique, tend to be of higher standard in design and execution. Prominent manufacturers include Baccarat (which may be signed), Cristalleries de Nancy, Depinoix, and J. Viard (unsigned). French bottles were often made for commercial patrons, including the leading luxury perfumeurs. These are most desirable when found in fully original presentation, including all labels and packaging, and, ideally, unopened. A superbly preserved card box may double or triple the value of a bottle.

Most Bohemian bottles, referred to simply as Czech, or "Czeco Deco," were commonly sold empty as decorative containers and did not have any packaging or labels. Many tend to be elaborate for this reason (the bottle catches the eye, not the packaging or perfume advertising), and may have an Eastern European flavor in coloration or form. Many Czech bottles, especially those with large, Art Deco figural stoppers, are commonly reproduced today, some in the factories where they were made originally, creating confusion for collectors. Czech bottles may be stenciled "Made in Czechoslovakia." The best were made at the Hoffman factory or by the DeVilbiss Company, and are normally unsigned.

Czechoslovakian atomizer bottle with gold-silk sheathing and tassel to the rubber bulb and tube. *1920s. 3¾ in (9.5 cm) wide* **$300–500 TRIO**

Unmarked perfume bottle with a columnar center, fan-shaped stopper, and skyscraper-tiered projections in blue and clear Lucite. *1930s. 6¾ in (17 cm) high* **$400–700 TDG**

Unmarked atomizer bottle of waisted conical form etched with geometric motifs. *1920s. 6¾ in (17 cm) high* **$300–400 TRIO**

Czechoslovakian press-molded clear glass bottle of arched form with a nude-female-under-a-waterfall stopper; the latter is over three times the height of the bottle. *1930s. 10 in (25.5 cm) high* **$300–400 LB**

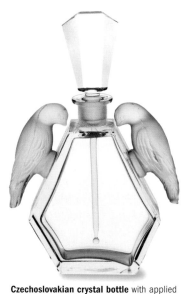

Czechoslovakian crystal bottle with applied bird handles and a bishop's-miter stopper. *1920s. 6¾ in (17 cm) high* **$1,200–1,800 DRA**

Czechoslovakian fan-shaped bottle with a cut and pierced rosette-and-wreath stopper. *1930s. 10½ in (26.5 cm) high* **$300–400 LB**

Nuit de Long Champ bottle by Lubin, with a firework stopper and a ribbed body. *c. 1935 6 in (15 cm) high* **$300–400 LB**

Silver bottle with engraved fluting and a spider-topped stopper wrapped in a serpent. *c. 1925. 3 in (7.5 cm) high* **$200–300 TDG**

Opaque black-crystal bottle by the Hoffman factory with an applied plaque. *1920s 6½ in (16.5 cm) high* **$2,000–3,000 DRA**

Set of three bottles molded in clear glass with sunburst patterns and mushroom stoppers. *c. 1935. Tallest: 5 in (12.5 cm) high* **$120–300 OACC**

Jade-green glass bottle by the Steuben Glassworks. It is molded into an Oriental shape with a teardrop stopper. *c. 1925. 6½ in (16.5 cm) high* **$700–1,000 TDC**

Perfume cube bottle and stand by Bibelot for Lydes, with a bakelite stopper. *c. 1925 4½ in (11.5 cm) high* **$2,000–3,000 DRA**

Ovoid pale-green glass bottle with a jade-green glass stopper and a domed silver cover. *1920s 4¼ in (10.75 cm) high* **$300–400 TRIO**

Val Saint-Lambert

Throughout its celebrated history, Val Saint-Lambert concentrated on traditional cut glass, a decision dating from early ties to Baccarat. The Art Deco period saw some progressive designs, executed with the highest standards of craftsmanship.

By the 1870s, Val Saint-Lambert was established as Belgium's largest glassmaker and one of the largest in Europe. The move from traditional cut glass toward modern taste began in the 1890s, when art director Jules Desprez (and, later, his son Georges Desprez) commissioned designs from leading members of the Belgian Art Nouveau movement, including Philippe Wolfers, Victor Horta, and Henry van de Velde.

The tradition continued upon the reopening of the works in 1919, after several years of closure during the German occupation of Belgium. The new artistic regime was headed by Léon Ledru (1855–1926), whose style evolved from Art Nouveau to Art Deco during his 38-year tenure at Val Saint-Lambert. The vast majority of output in the 1920s remained traditional cut glass, however, and most

Val Saint-Lambert from this period is of high quality in execution but limited collector interest. Art Deco work to look for includes artistic pieces made at the firm's Jemeppe-sur-Meuse glassworks, where glass was free-blown. Signed with an enameled "VSL" monogram, many pieces resemble Müller Frères or Schneider (*see pp.88–89*). Also of interest is the Art Deco work of Charles Graffart (1893–1967), who designed and engraved about 300 vessels in the late 1920s, most with modern figural subjects.

From about 1930 Val Saint-Lambert also made blown vessels resembling the work of Sabino, in frosted and pale smoky or yellow glass. This inexpensive line was introduced in response to the Depression and to the success of similar ware by René Lalique (*see pp.80–83*), but it is not as popular as the cut glass.

Above: Squat vase cased in amethyst over pale-yellow uranium glass and cut with geometric panels, including a ring of lozenges. *1930s. 5 in (12.5 cm) high* **$1,800–2,500 MAL**

GEOMETRIC CUT GLASS

Val Saint-Lambert combined traditional glass cutting in modern taste from about 1925 to World War II in geometrically cut glass vessels. Few companies outside Bohemia made this type of ware, which typically consisted of a deeply colored layer "flashed" on to a clear body and cut in repeating pattern with Art Deco motifs or window facets. Glass in this genre was shown by Val Saint-Lambert at the 1925 Paris Exposition and later sold at the Paris showrooms of Edgar Brandt. Vases cut in this manner were expensive and mostly made prior to the Depression years.

Cased and pedestal-footed vase with an undulating rim, cut with geometric forms on both the inside and outside. The casing is pale blue over red. *1930s. 8 in (20.5 cm) high* **$18,000–22,000 MAL**

Footed ovoid vase cased in amber over straw-green uranium glass, with faceting of the foot, concentric cuts under the rim, and elongated leaf-form cuts to the sides. *1930s 8 in (20.5 cm) high* **$10,000–15,000 MAL**

Tall rectangular vase in clear-over-pink cased glass and with baluster-like cuts to the four vertical edges. *c. 1930*

9¼ in (23.75 cm) high

$1,800–2,500 MAL

Squat vase cased in amethyst over pale-yellow uranium glass and deeply cut to form a repeat geometric pattern of circular, oval, triangular, and pentagonal forms. (Green uranium glass provided an alternative colorway.) *1930s*

6 in (15 cm) high

$2,500–3,500 MAL

Unusual ovoid vase cased in dark amethyst over pale-amber glass, with a castellated band of amethyst around its center. *c. 1930*

5¾ in (14.5 cm) high

$4,000–5,000 MAL

Tapered cylindrical vase on a spreading octagonal foot, cased and cut with a ruby-red glass lozenge pattern over clear glass. *1930s*

12 in (30.5 cm) high

$3,000–4,000 MAL

Very large cylindrical vase cased in clear-over-pale-amethyst glass, cut with vertical striations and a ring of oval lenses. *1930s*

16 in (40.5 cm) high

$4,000–5,000 MAL

Cylindrical vase cased in clear-over-aqua-blue glass, with three annular knops cut with vertical ribs and striations. Conceived by Charles Graffart, this piece is an excellent example of his ability to exploit the high quality and substantial weight of Val Saint-Lambert's crystal. *1938*

13½ in (34.5 cm) high

$10,000–12,000 MAL

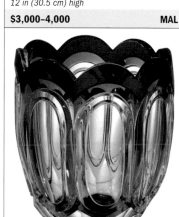

Hexagonal-footed vase in clear glass, cased in blue glass around the scalloped rim and cut with eight ovoid shapes. *c. 1930*

7¾ in (20 cm) high

$4,000–5,000 MAL

European Glass

Although most prominent in France, Art Deco glass was also produced in factories across Europe. The few pieces made under the auspices of the Wiener Werkstätte and attributable to luminaries such as Josef Hoffmann or designed by Otto Prutscher are exceptional in both design and value. Other European glass to look out for includes work made at Leerdam in Holland (notably the Unika range, designed by Andries Dirk Copier from 1923) and Scandinavian modern designs of the 1930s, which often carry signatures.

Mostly, however, European glass is not of the same high quality as French glass. Large factories, including Moser in Karlsbad, deviated little from traditional decoration and cutting techniques. Other Bohemian factories made vast quantities of cheaply molded ware in clear or malachite glass, all widely reproduced today. Loetz in Austria and W.M.F. (Württembergische Metallwarenfabrik) in Germany both produced progressive, geometric designs in iridescent or mottled color.

Savoy vase of undulating, slightly flared, free-form section, designed by the Finnish architect Alvar Aalto for Karhula-Iittala in 1936. This late example was blown in green-tinted bottle glass in a metal mold; pre-1954 versions were blown in wooden molds and have a softer finish. *Late 1950s*

6 in (15.25 cm) high

$700–1,200 L&T

Cylindrical vase designed by Otto Prutscher for Johann Lötz Witwe (Loetz). It is made of opaque white glass with a trellis pattern, overlaid with rose-pink iridescent glass. *c. 1930*

4½ in (11 cm) high

$1,800–2,200 VZ

Internally ribbed vase designed by Elis Bergh while he was art director at Sweden's Kosta Glasbruk. It is mold-blown in blue-tinted glass and signed on the base "B473." *1930s*

10½ in (26.5 cm) high

$200–300 MHT

Purple glass goblet made by Ludwig Moser & Söhne of Karlsbad. It rises from a conical foot via an hexagonal-faceted stem to a spherical bowl decorated with an engraved and gilded frieze of Amazonians among foliage. *1920s*

7½ in (19 cm) high

$200–400 FIS

The Small Grape Harvest vase designed by Frantisek Pazourek and made by Curt Schlevogt. It was press-molded in relief from jade glass and then hand-polished. *1932*

8½ in (21.5 cm) high

$200–300   **BMN**

Cylindrical Bohemian vase from Steinschönau, made from clear and green-tinted flashed glass, cut with vertical and horizontal geometric forms. *c. 1925*

8¾ in (22 cm) high

$400–500   **VZ**

Pale-green crystal jar with a silver-plated lid made by W.M.F. The body and handle are mold-blown with deep ribbing. *1938–39*

8¼ in (21 cm) high

$200–400   **QU**

Bohemian polychromatic flashed-glass vase from the Haida glassworks; probably designed by Adolf Rasche. *c. 1930*

4¾ in (12 cm) high

$200–400   **FIS**

Scallop-rimmed bowl of transparent purple glass on a compressed bun foot. It was designed by the architect Josef Hoffmann for the Wiener Werkstätte. *c. 1920*

9¼ in (25 cm) wide

$8,000–12,000   **LN**

Murano

Glass has been made on the Italian island of Murano since the 13th century, when production moved there to avoid the risk of fire in the neighboring city of Venice. Most Venetian glass made before World War II is in traditional, Renaissance style, characterized by intricate lampwork applied to thinly blown soda glass. Venetian Art Deco appeared about 1925, when Paolo Venini (1895–1959) split from his Muranese partner Giacomo Capellin (1887–1968) to design modern forms. Venini employed progressive designers, including Napoleone Martinuzzi (1892–1977), who worked at Venini until 1932, when he set up with Murano-born Vittorio Zecchin (1878–1947). In the 1930s, Murano introduced innovative glass types and techniques as a prelude to postwar production. Most Murano glass is unsigned and difficult to attribute, so signatures add considerable value.

Baluster-shaped vase designed by Napoleone Martinuzzi for Zecchin-Martinuzzi Vetri Artistici e Mosaici of Murano. Its black-glass body is decorated with spirals of aventurine and has ruby-red glass overlays (*vetro nero e rosso*) on the rim, base, and wavy handles. *c. 1935*

14¼ in (36 cm) high

$8,000–12,000   **QU**

Unmarked Murano vase with a squat body and long, thin neck. It is made from clear over opaque white glass, with applied strings and ovals of black glass. *c. 1925*

11¾ in (30 cm) high

$1,200–1,800   **QU**

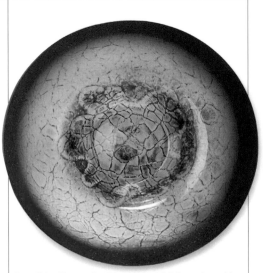

Unmarked Bohemian lidded bowl made from frosted clear glass with blue overlays. The top of the lid and the sides are carved and acid-etched with floral decoration. The lid has a ball-shaped finial and a rim etched with ball motifs. *1920s*

6 in (15 cm) high

$120–300 BMN

Footed ovoid Unika vase designed by Andries Dirk Copier and made by the Leerdam glassworks in the Netherlands. Free-blown in clear and black craquelure glass, it is signed and numbered "Unika C 153." *1930s*

4¾ in (12 cm) high

$5,000–8,000 BMN

Ikora-Kristall–range bowl by W.M.F. of Geislingen. Its mold-blown, shallow, circular form is made from clear and colored cased glass, the latter patterned with green, orange, orange-red, and bright-red oxides. *c. 1930*

15¼ in (38.5 cm) wide

$300–400 VZ

Bohemian iridescent glass vase decorated with a polychromatic abstract pattern comprising streaks and swirls of yellow, orange, red, green, blue, and purple iridescence. Like this example, many Bohemian iridescent pieces are unsigned, and their makers are unknown. *c. 1925*

8¼ in (21 cm) high

$800–1,200 MOD

Trumpet-shaped vase with a five-ribbed collar above the base. Made in clear and colored cased glass by W.M.F. of Geislingen, this piece has a streaked and cloudy marblelike pattern formed by green, gray, and red-oxide inclusions. *c. 1935*

13 in (33 cm) high

$300–500 VZ

Unusual vase from the Leerdam glassworks in the Netherlands. Its clear glass is etched and powder-enameled to depict a nude female leading a stallion. *Late 1930s*

12¾ in (32.5 cm) high

$2,000–3,000   **HERR**

Dexel-Ei (egg) vase designed by Walter Dexel for the Ikora-Kristall range by W.M.F. Its clear, orange, red, yellow, and black body contains numerous fine air bubbles. *c. 1935*

5½ in (14 cm) high

$300–500   **VZ**

Ikora-Kristall–range vase by W.M.F. Its cased-glass body has a strident marblelike pattern in opaque white and shades of green, turquoise, red, and purple. *1930s*

4¾ in (12 cm) high

$120–180   **VZ**

Small Silesian vase by the Josephinenhütte glassworks. Blown from opaque dark-blue glass, the body is hand-painted, in pastel enamels and gilding, with stylized imagery of a bird sitting on a branch surrounded by butterflies. The gilding also lines the rim. *1920s*

4¼ in (10.5 cm) high

$500–800   **VS**

Rare footed cup with a domed lid and ball finial. Made by the Haida glassworks from clear and honey-yellow colored glass, it features a formalized pattern of stylized flower and berry motifs. *c. 1920*

10½ in (26 cm) high

$2,500–4,000   **FIS**

Wilhelm von Eiff

Painter and glass designer Wilhelm von Eiff (1890–1943) specialized in cutting and engraving techniques, and he applied these talents to gemstone and rock-crystal carving. Mostly, von Eiff worked from a studio in Stuttgart, Germany, where he had studied at the School of Arts and Crafts from 1913 and become a professor by 1922. Art Deco works by von Eiff, which are engraved with the initials "WvE," are rare but very distinctive. Most were made during the 1930s and are heavy-walled in clear or smoky glass with a high lead content. Typically, von Eiff's designs included deeply cut geometric patterns in the style of Maurice Marinot.

Wilhelm von Eiff-designed unusual smoky-gray vase made at the School of Arts and Crafts in Stuttgart, Germany. The thick walls of its underlying body are molded and cut with a band of broad, undulating waveforms and are hand-polished to a semimatt finish. *c. 1935*

7¾ in (20 cm) high

$800–1,200   **VZ**

Steuben

From humble beginnings, Steuben grew to become the most respected American artistic glassworks by the 1920s, a status it still holds. Early success was largely due to the talents of British-born Frederick Carder.

Frederick Carder (1863–1963) was a Staffordshire native who studied at the Stourbridge School of Art under John Northwood. Carder later designed for Northwood at Stevens & Williams, where his duties included researching foreign glassmaking techniques. This allowed him to travel extensively; Carder visited Austria and the United States, where he chose to stay after a fact-finding mission, much to the consternation of his former employers.

In 1903 the American glassmaker Thomas Hawkes convinced him to go into partnership to form Steuben, and Carder spent the next 30 years developing dozens of artistic lines, which Steuben produced mostly by free-blowing in colors. The earliest was Aurene, an iridescent glass in gold or blue comparable to Tiffany and mostly made in Art Nouveau forms.

Post–World War I ranges represent Steuben's first Art Deco glass, including distinctive vases and tableware in simulated hard-stone colors, known collectively as Jade Glass. Many of these pieces feature applied feet or handles in ivory color or surface etching in the popular American "Oriental" taste.

Generally, Steuben forms are conventional, many based on Chinese or neoclassical imagery. Although not all ranges can be considered fully Art Deco, Steuben came close to French taste with bubbly vessels made in mottled colors from the mid-1920s. Cluthra vases with simple bubble decoration are also relatively common. Cintra pieces are comparable but have internal striped decoration and are rarer.

Throughout the interwar years, Steuben produced large quantities of tableware, much of it in an elegant Art Deco taste, from silky Verre de Soie glass.

Above: Jade-green fingerbowl with bulbous, tapering sides acid-etched with a stylized plant-form pattern. *c. 1925* *4 in (10 cm) high* **$1,800–2,200 TDC**

WAUGH'S LEGACY

After the Depression, Carder retired and architect John Monteith Gates became Steuben's new art director. He employed designer Sidney Waugh (1904–63) to produce a new range of engraved, clear glass (*see box opposite*). Modern Steuben is the legacy of this work, which compares in style and quality to the best contemporary Scandinavian glass. The crisp, clean-lined, and polished look, a reflection of post-Depression optimism, is evident throughout the modern movement, notably in table glass designed for Steuben by Walter Dorwin Teague from the late 1930s.

Rare plum-colored and clear-cased glass vase with a bulbous base and a long, tapering neck of Oriental inspiration. It is acid-etched with a stylized floral Peking pattern. *c. 1930. 11½ in (29 cm) high* **$8,000–12,000 TDC**

SIDNEY WAUGH

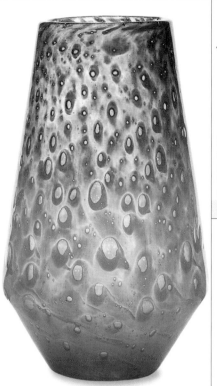

Free-form Grotesque vase with pinching to the sides and in a rare sea-green and clear colorway. It was also produced in light Pomona green, gold ruby, amethyst, dark blue, and amber. *c. 1930*

3½ in (9 cm) high

$1,200–1,800 TDC

Amethyst-colored glass vase of footed, beakerlike form, decorated with a swirling linear pattern created in an optic mold. This amethyst color is relatively common. *c. 1930*

6¾ in (17 cm) high

$300–500 TDC

Shouldered ovoid vase with an everted rim and a conical foot. The semitranslucent body is colored jade green, while the foot is a milky-white alabaster. *c. 1925*

8½ in (21.5 cm) high

$1,200–1,800 TDC

Blown and cased-glass vase from the Cluthra range. Tapering to the rim and base, the body shades from pink into a creamy white; it also displays a mass of internal bubbles, typical of this range. *c. 1930*

8 in (20 cm) high

$1,200–1,800 TDC

A CLOSER LOOK

Cluthra-range vase with a trumpet-shaped bowl and annular- and mushroom-knopped stem, shading from pale green into white with internal bubbles. *c. 1930*

8¼ in (21 cm) high

$2,000–3,000 TDC

Engraved lead-crystal bowl designed by Sidney Waugh. Its near-spherical form is engraved with a frieze of leaping gazelles set within linear borders, with the latter echoed on the four-part stand. *1935. 7 in (18 cm) high* **$25,000–40,000 LN**

Matt-finish copper-wheel engraving of exceptional quality is crisply contrasted against the brilliance of the clear lead-crystal body

Animals, such as gazelles, were sometimes employed on engraved Steuben glass. However, human imagery, ranging from acrobats to Adam and Eve, is more prevalent

Thick walls of heavy lead crystal are typical of Steuben pieces from c. 1932 onward. They instantly convey a sense of high quality

The linear decoration that augments the animal imagery on both the body and the base is quintessential 1930s Art Deco

American Glass

American demand for inexpensive glass grew dramatically after the Depression. Much of this demand was met by the Pennsylvania-based Consolidated and Phoenix glassworks. These two companies, both established in the late 19th century, mass-produced very similar vases, bowls, and table glass in metal molds from the early 1930s until the 1960s. Consolidated introduced the popular Martele range in 1926, and Phoenix produced very similar sculptured-glass vases from 1933 under Kenneth Haley, who designed the ubiquitous Dancing Nymph range of table glass in the mid-1930s. Color and opaque custard glass was used, but most designs are clear with a sprayed color ground, some copied from works by René Lalique. Apart from Ruba Rombic (*see box opposite*), examples are commonly found today and of limited appeal. Of better quality is the work of Baccarat native Victor Durand (1870–1931), made at the Vineland Flint Glassworks in New Jersey and comparable to Steuben or Tiffany.

Pillow-form vase made by the Phoenix Glass Co. of Pennsylvania, with a blue-gray ground and three Lalique-like white flying geese molded in relief; with its original paper label. *c. 1930*

9½ in (24 cm) high

$400–600   JDJ

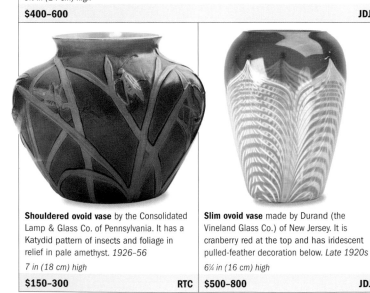

Shouldered ovoid vase by the Consolidated Lamp & Glass Co. of Pennsylvania. It has a Katydid pattern of insects and foliage in relief in pale amethyst. *1926–56*

7 in (18 cm) high

$150–300   RTC

Slim ovoid vase made by Durand (the Vineland Glass Co.) of New Jersey. It is cranberry red at the top and has iridescent pulled-feather decoration below. *Late 1920s*

6¼ in (16 cm) high

$500–800   JDJ

Baluster-shaped King Tut vase made by Durand (the Vineland Glass Co.) of New Jersey. with an iridescent blue ground and iridescent silver-white swirling-vine decoration inspired by decorations found in Tutankhamun's tomb in Egypt. *Late 1920s*

8½ in (21.5 cm) high

$2,500–4,000   JDJ

DEPRESSION GLASS

The first pressed glass was made in the US in the 1820s, and it has been produced in massive quantities ever since. Most Depression Glass was industrially made in West Virginia or the Midwest and either sold through "five and dime" stores or given away as store premiums. Production dates from the early 1920s, with a surge during the Depression years. Intended for daily usage, Depression Glass was rarely ornamental; some pieces were made from molds and in the deep amethyst or gold colors of Victorian carnival glass, but most is pale or clear. Least popular are the historical patterns and copies of expensive formal glass (such as neoclassical Steuben). The most valuable pieces are identifiable by a mark, normally a molded monogram, or a distinctive pattern such as Hocking's Block Optic. Many anonymously represent the best of American economy in design, evoking a neon-lit diner or skyscraper skyline. While most was made for domestic use, some was custom designed for diners, luncheonettes, and soda fountains. Tall glasses for ice-cream sodas are attractive and uniquely American, as are the simple geometric storage containers designed to fit inside kitchen appliances from the mid-1930s until the 1960s.

Machine-molded Depression Glass sugar bowl with a slightly flared rim, solid handles, and vertical fluting and ribbing. Unsigned. *1930s*
4½ in (11.5 cm) wide
$12–18   TAB

Jenny Ware machine-molded mixing bowl by the Jeanette Glass Co. of Pennsylvania. Its split-cut sides imitate cut glass. *1935–38*
6 in (15.5 cm) high
$100–150   DRA

Depression Glass machine-molded jar with cover by the Hocking Glass Co. of Ohio, with a geometric Block Optic pattern. *1929–33*
6¾ in (17.5 cm) high
$80–120   DRA

Machine-molded Depression Glass drinking vessel by the Indiana Glass Co., in the Tearoom pattern for restaurants. *1930s*
6¾ in (17.5 cm) high
$100–180   DRA

Machine-molded Depression Glass candlestick from "iced-tea" tinted glass in a neoclassical form. Maker not known. *1930s*
3¾ in (9.5 cm) high
$40–70   TAB

A CLOSER LOOK

Ruba Rombic whiskey set comprising a decanter, tray, and six glasses. Inspired by Cubist paintings, it was designed by Reuben Haley and made from pressed glass by the Consolidated Lamp & Glass Co. of Coraopolis, Pennsylvania. *1928–32*
Decanter: 9¼ in (23.5 cm) high **$12,000–18,000 CMG**

Art meets science in the derivation of this piece's name: ruba'i is a form of Persian poetry, and the geometric term "rhombic" means an irregular form with no right angles

The multiangular, asymmetrical forms of Ruba Rombic glass transform the two-dimensional principles of Cubist painting into three-dimensional objects

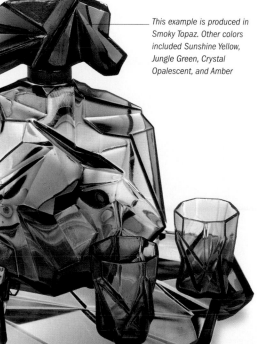

This example is produced in Smoky Topaz. Other colors included Sunshine Yellow, Jungle Green, Crystal Opalescent, and Amber

Machine-molded Depression Glass sugar bowl with a swirling pattern, undulating rim, and C-loop handles. Maker not known. *1930s*
3¼ in (8.5 cm) high
$10–20   TAB

Machine-molded Depression Glass tea plate by the Hocking Glass Co. of Ohio, in the geometric Block Optic pattern. *1929–33*
5½ in (14 cm) wide
$30–50   VGA

British Glass

Great Britain produced some interesting Art Deco glass, even though it was not at the forefront of glass design due to conservatism of consumers and the appeal of imported glass from France, Bohemia, and Scandinavia. Most British Art Deco glass is clear, but exceptions include bubbly Monart glass from Scotland's Moncrieff Glassworks (which compares with the work of Schneider, W.M.F., and Steuben's Cluthra range) and a series of pale-colored geometric vases made at the London Whitefriars Glassworks and designed by William Wilson. The large Midlands firms of Stuart & Sons, Stevens & Williams, Webb Corbett, and John Walsh Walsh also employed freelance designers for artistic ranges in the 1930s. With the exception of Keith Murray, most items are unsigned and not easily identified. Names to look for include Ludwig Kny at Stuart, whose father Frederick decorated the famous Rock Crystal glass at Stevens & Williams, and William Clyne Farquharson, who designed large vases in Scandinavian modern taste for Walsh in the late 1930s.

Cut-glass ship's decanter by Webb Corbett, with a step-cut conical body, two molded annular knops on the neck, and a mushroom-shaped stopper cut with fluting. *1930s*

9 in (23 cm) high

$400–600   AG

Inverted conical-shaped vase cut with graduated horizontal bands of fluting. It was made by Thomas Webb exclusively for the Rembrandt Art Guild England. *c. 1935*

7 in (17.5 cm) high

$400–600   JH

Circular bowl with tapered sides and V-cuts to the rim, made by Royal Brierley and decorated with a geometric pattern of miter, lens, and flute cutting. Pattern number 68449/50. *1937–38*

8¾ in (22.25 cm) high

$600–900   JH

Trumpet-shaped vase made by H.G. Richardson, with an annular knop above a conical foot and deep-cut vertical fluting dividing panels of stylized leaf forms. *c. 1930*

8 in (20.5 cm) high

$500–700   JH

Trumpet-shaped, footed vase designed by Freda M. Coleton for Webb Corbett. Its panels of stylized leaves are divided by vertical flutes. Pattern number 15344. *1938*

10 in (25.5 cm) high

$500–700   JH

Green-tinted cut-glass bowl from the Gay Ware range by the John Walsh Walsh glassworks of Birmingham. Its flared sides are decorated with a shallow-cut floral pattern. *c. 1935*

10 in (25 cm) wide

$300–400   JH

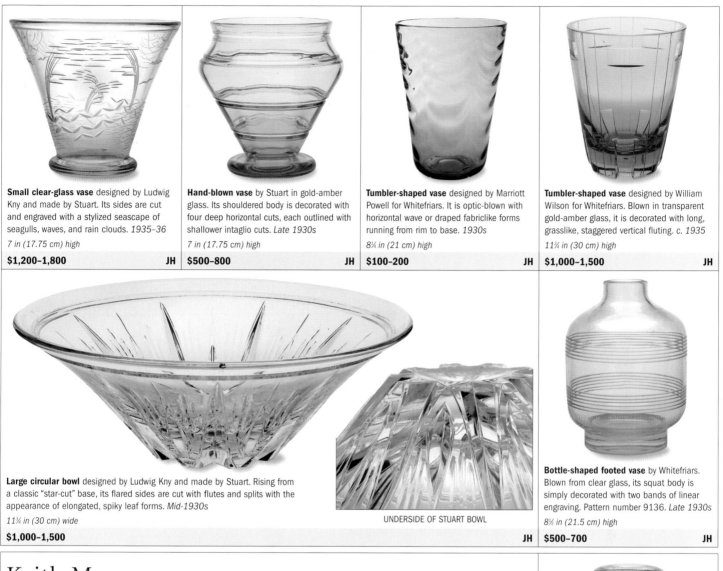

Small clear-glass vase designed by Ludwig Kny and made by Stuart. Its sides are cut and engraved with a stylized seascape of seagulls, waves, and rain clouds. *1935–36*

7 in (17.75 cm) high

$1,200–1,800   **JH**

Hand-blown vase by Stuart in gold-amber glass. Its shouldered body is decorated with four deep horizontal cuts, each outlined with shallower intaglio cuts. *Late 1930s*

7 in (17.75 cm) high

$500–800   **JH**

Tumbler-shaped vase designed by Marriott Powell for Whitefriars. It is optic-blown with horizontal wave or draped fabriclike forms running from rim to base. *1930s*

8¼ in (21 cm) high

$100–200   **JH**

Tumbler-shaped vase designed by William Wilson for Whitefriars. Blown in transparent gold-amber glass, it is decorated with long, grasslike, staggered vertical fluting. *c. 1935*

11¾ in (30 cm) high

$1,000–1,500   **JH**

Large circular bowl designed by Ludwig Kny and made by Stuart. Rising from a classic "star-cut" base, its flared sides are cut with flutes and splits with the appearance of elongated, spiky leaf forms. *Mid-1930s*

11¾ in (30 cm) wide

UNDERSIDE OF STUART BOWL

$1,000–1,500   **JH**

Bottle-shaped footed vase by Whitefriars. Blown from clear glass, its squat body is simply decorated with two bands of linear engraving. Pattern number 9136. *Late 1930s*

8½ in (21.5 cm) high

$500–700   **JH**

Keith Murray

Born in New Zealand, Keith Murray (1892–1981; *see also pp.136–37*) was educated mostly in England. He interrupted his architecture training between 1915 and 1918 to serve in France in the Royal Flying Corps. Murray is best known for the monochrome-glazed, geometric pottery he designed for Wedgwood from 1933 until the 1950s, but he also designed silver for Mappin & Webb from 1934. After unsuccessfully working in illustration, he joined Stevens & Williams of Brierley Hill in 1932. By 1939 he had produced about 1,200 designs, including vase forms and patterns for engraving, the best known of which is Cactus. Most were made in very small numbers and are easily identifiable by style and signature.

Keith Murray-designed shallow clear glass bowl probably made by Royal Brierley (but unmarked). Mold-blown, it is cut around the sides with waterlike diagonal wavy lines. *1930s*

10 in (25.5 cm) wide

$700–1,000   **JH**

Keith Murray-designed Royal Brierley decanter (one of a pair). Mold-blown and with a mushroom stopper, its sides are cut with horizontal waterlike wavy lines. *c. 1935*

8¼ in (21 cm) high

$1,200–1,800 (the pair)   **JH**

Ceramics

By the 1920s, Western art pottery had matured from a Victorian infancy wrapped in Japonisme into a vibrant branch of the decorative arts, with distinctive outgrowths in Great Britain, continental Europe, and the United States. The result is a vast legacy of ceramics, from unique works of art to amusing mass-produced trinkets, providing great opportunities for collecting.

The aspiring collector of Art Deco ceramics has some difficult choices to make. Material is fairly plentiful and classifiable into distinct categories of taste, most of which deserve attention, though they do not necessarily relate to each other. French ceramics, for example, rarely exhibit the geometric zigzag decoration or vibrant colors present on some British and American ware, the starkly architectural composition of some Austrian pottery, or the flamboyant neo-Rococo found in Scandinavia. It is also hard to find artistic parallels to the work of French masters like René Buthaud, whose work ranges from modest, hand-painted vases to gigantic architectural sculpture.

A CHALLENGE FOR COLLECTORS

It would be tempting to consider all Art Deco ceramics as either handmade or mass-produced, but this would be imprecise. The work of Clarice Cliff, for example, is hand-painted on mass-produced blanks, and many studios worked in the manner of a production line.

It is also wrong to assume that mass-production leads to lower value, since many rare, factory-made American and some British pieces are of extraordinary value, while unidentified Art Deco studio ceramics are often inexpensive, regardless of style and quality. In addition, American ceramics are rarely found outside the United States, and many are easily restored or faked, making them difficult to collect. Much the same may be said for British ware in America.

In some respects, these challenges, combined with the still-common lack of documentation, make ceramics one of the most rewarding collecting fields for Art Deco lovers.

Rare Boch Frères vase of octagonal form with stepped sides, finished in a Persian-blue craquelure glaze and decorated with partly red enameled ziggurat metal mounts. *c. 1930. 10 in (25.5 cm) high* **$4,000–6,000 SDR**

Bizarre-range Sunray-pattern vase by Clarice Cliff. To the left of a black staggered, totemlike form above green is a stylized sun radiating orange and mauve beams, while to the right is a stepped orange bridge above an expanse of blue. *1929–30 8 in (20 cm) high* **$3,000–5,000 WW**

FRANCE LEADING THE WAY

As in most Art Deco design fields, France was at the forefront of production, both in variety and standards of manufacture, but few countries were tempted to copy French ceramics as they copied furniture and glass. Some French Art Deco was simply impossible to replicate, such as the extraordinary porcelain made at Sèvres (*see p.110*) from designs by leading French *artistes décorateurs* including Jacques-Emile Ruhlmann (*see pp.26–27*) and Henri Rapin, or the earthenware creations by Henri Simmen, who fitted pots with delicate ivory covers carved by his Japanese wife. Simmen studied under the great ceramicist Raoul Lachenal and matured into an Art Deco studio potter alongside such notable French artists as Robert Lallement, André Metthey, and Jean Mayodon (*see p.111*), all working in singular styles. This area of French ceramics was widely overlooked by collectors until the 1990s but is now highly desirable. Most pieces are signed only with a monogram. French Art Deco ceramics found some following abroad because they were more widely exported, partly due to the promotional role played by Parisian department stores. Galeries Lafayette and Primavera both commissioned and sold large quantities of Art Deco pottery, much made at Longwy in France or by the Belgian firm of Boch Frères (*see pp.118–19*), which was exported throughout Europe and the United States. In this category we must also include porcelain sold by the Parisian firm of Robj, whose whimsical statuettes and figural lamps of the 1920s were widely copied in Eastern Europe and Japan.

THE INFLUENCE OF LOCAL TRADITION

Elsewhere in continental Europe, Art Deco style grew mainly from regional influences. Austrian ceramics are either in the avant-garde styles of the Wiener Werkstätte or, at the other extreme, Goldscheider's (*see pp.112–15*) ceramic versions of popular bronze statuary. Scandinavian, central European, and Italian factories also made statuary, a tradition long practiced in Germany, mostly in delicate porcelain. Hand-painting in elegant fashion was also popular in these established porcelain centers, though few deviated far from tradition, even in the heady 1920s.

THE FEMALE PRESENCE

The British potting industry seized upon Art Deco design with uncharacteristic passion, inspired by a wave of liberation that swept through the country, and much of northern Europe, after World War I. Women had always worked in the potteries as decorators, but the 1920s saw Clarice Cliff (*see pp.124–27*), Susie Cooper (*see p.128–29*), and others rise to international prominence as artists and business leaders. The Poole Pottery (*see p.132*) in Dorset had a comparable impact.

KEY POINTS

While geometric forms are prevalent in Art Deco ceramics, especially those made from the late 1920s, they by no means monopolize the style. For example, numerous vases were produced in classic ovoid, baluster, trumpet, and cylindrical shapes. Similarly, geometric patterns recur, but other motifs also provide inspiration. These range from ancient Egyptian (following the excavation of Tutankhamun's tomb), elegant fauna, notably deer and gazelles, haute couture, and fashionable female pursuits of the Jazz Age, especially dancing.

Porcelain vegetable dish with cover, made by Rosenthal of Bavaria, Germany. Raised on spreading square feet, the body is of gently flared rectangular form beneath an overhanging, slightly domed lid. The bright polychrome decoration consists of diverse geometric motifs set on a white glazed ground. *1923. 4 in (10 cm) wide* **$300–400 QU**

The Sèvres porcelain factory was founded at the Château de Vincennes in 1738, then acquired in 1756 by Louis XV and moved to Sèvres, southwest of Paris. It embraced the Art Deco style from c. 1920 under the direction of Georges Lechevallier-Chevignard.

Earthenware bust of a young woman made under the Katzhütte trademark by Hertwig & Co. of Katzhütte, Germany. Its semi-stylized form, overly large eyes, arched and lined eyebrows, rouged lips and cheeks, and short-cut blond hair all reflect the prevailing fashions of the period. *1930s 8 in (20 cm) high* **$900–1,200 TDG**

The uniquely British form of Art Deco it created was largely uncopied until recently. In addition to these newcomers, established firms like Wedgwood (*see pp.136–37*) led modern British design trends and fashioned a refined Art Deco style suitable for the upper-class home using outside designers and innovative finishes. Smaller companies like Carlton (*see pp.134–35*), Shelley, and James Sadler produced inexpensive and amusing wares for the rapidly spreading middle-class British suburbs.

AMERICAN MASS PRODUCTION

Art Deco somehow lasted longer as a movement in the United States, perhaps due to the Depression, which split the period in two. There was little momentum carried over from the few active Art Deco ceramic designers who survived October 1929 into the 1930s, when a new, economical, and uniquely American Art Deco was born. This style evolved at an accelerated pace into the streamlined style, which finally landed about 1950.

Most American Art Deco ceramic art is mass-produced. The field includes some of the least expensive yet most stylish earthenware ever made, including containers carefully designed to fit inside the modern kitchen appliances with which they were given away.

Earthenware figure of a young lady dancing designed by Joseph Lorenzl and made by the Austrian firm Goldscheider. Fashionable attire in shades of pink and red set against creamy-white skin tones, an elegant and dramatic pose, and a serene expression are recurring features of Lorenzl's designs. *Mid- to late 1920s. 14¼ in (36 cm) high* **$3,000–4,000 WW**

Ovoid Carlton Ware vase with a domed lid and sphinx finial, made by Wiltshaw & Robinson of Stoke. It is polychrome enameled and gilded with an Egyptian-style Tutankhamun pattern on a lustrous cobalt-blue ground. *c. 1925. 10½ in (26.5 cm) high* **$3,000–4,000 WW**

Sèvres was founded in 1738 in Vincennes, but moved to the town of Sèvres in 1756.

It was named a Royal Manufactory in 1753.

Director Théodore Deck (1823–91) introduced Art Nouveau porcelain, which was shown with great success at the 1900 Paris Exposition.

Art Deco porcelain was made in the interwar years and shown at the 1925 Paris Exposition.

Jacques-Emile Ruhlmann designed for Sèvres in the mid-1920s.

Many Art Deco pieces with Sèvres marks were not made at the porcelain factory.

The factory continues to the present day.

Sèvres

Since the 18th century, the name Sèvres has been associated with the highest-quality decorative arts. Some of the finest Art Deco porcelain was made at this prestigious French factory.

Until fairly recently, typical collectors of Sèvres, including museums, focused on porcelain made under royal patronage in the 18th century. This was also true during the Art Deco period, when most porcelain production at this historic factory on the outskirts of Paris was committed to reproducing these wares.

The Modernist tradition, however, thrived at Sèvres, largely thanks to Georges Lechavallier-Chevignard, who became director in 1920. By 1925, several leading designers contributed, notably Jacques-Emile Ruhlmann (*see pp.26–27*), whose Forme Ruhlmann vase and cover were made in several sizes and finishes; Suzanne Lalique, daughter of René (*see pp.80–83*) and best known

as a decorator at Haviland in Limoges; and Henri Rapin, who designed forms and some lighting.

An earthenware studio established at Sèvres in the early 1920s made useful and ornamental ware in Art Deco taste. The best examples are stylized animals by the sculptor François Pompon, notably polar bears with white glaze simulating icy fur. French Art Deco earthenware marked with the Sèvres name is mostly not from the famous works and is of inferior standard. Typical examples are decorative items with azure-blue crystalline glaze or poorly finished statuary.

Above: Large porcelain fish glazed in tones of pink and mustard. It is marked "DN," denoting "pâté dure nouvelle," a custom ceramic mix. *1925. 17 in (43.25 cm) long* **$3,000–5,000 MSM**

Porcelain vase by Jacques-Emile Ruhlmann and pastel-painted with small human figures in a rural landscape. The use of gilding around the rim and foot is typical of Sèvres wares. *1937* *15¾ in (40 cm) high*

$10,000–15,000 **WKA**

Round porcelain box and cover with the latter and the sides decorated in relief with an odeonesque, geometric architectural pattern. This is gilded and strongly contrasted against a mottled vivid-blue and cloudy-green glazed ground. *c. 1925* *6½ in (16.5 cm) wide*

$1,000–1,500 **TDG**

Jean Mayodon

Continuing the French studio-pottery tradition, Jean Mayodon created unique hand-potted art ware. Examples are rare and exquisitely painted with the confidence and precision of a master painter.

In the 1980s, Mayodon ceramics could still be found scattered among the *brocantes* in French flea markets, but you will be extremely lucky to find one today. This artist is now considered notable among a small group of French studio potters, including Henri Simmen (1880–1969) and André Metthey (1871–1920), who developed unique Art Deco styles but continued to experiment throughout their careers.

Jean Mayodon (1893–1967) began his career as a painter; all his work is painterly in execution. Neoclassical and mythological characters figure prominently, typically in muted tones under semimatt glazes on mottled grounds highlighted in gilt. The work has a soft appearance and is lightweight. Small, handthrown vases of Japanese form, plates, and shallow dishes are typical.

In addition to small studio work, Mayodon produced large-scale sculptural pieces and panels, mostly for commercial commissions in the 1930s. His patrons included the ocean-liner owner Compagnie Générale Transatlantique, for which he also designed fountains.

Most examples are signed on the center back with a painted monogram. Mayodon's work is highly distinctive and no forgeries are known.

Above: Round earthenware plate hand-painted with Classical, scantily clad females on a rich brown and gold faux-marbre ground. *c. 1930. 8¾ in (22 cm) wide*
$3,000–5,000 BEA

Hand-painted, footed ovoid earthenware vase featuring a Classical-style nymph on a seahorse. In shades of blue and gray on a craquelure ground and with gilding to the foot and neck. *c. 1935*
9½ in (24 cm) high
$7,000–9,000 VZ

Footed ovoid vase decorated in a painterly style with Classical- or Renaissance-style nude human and animal figures. These are rendered in flesh and hair tones and set against a mottled and slightly crazed ground of brown and gold enamels. *c. 1930*
9¾ in (24.5 cm) high
$10,000–15,000 BEA

Goldscheider

The ceramic figures made by Goldscheider in interwar Vienna are among the boldest in scale and most colorful of all 20th-century sculpture. The vast majority feature elegant female dancers in Art Deco poses.

Ceramic figure of a tall, slender young lady walking a borzoi hound and wearing a long, flowing, floral-pattern blue dress and a broad-rimmed sunhat. Designed by Claire Herozeg, this figure was also produced wearing a red dress. *c. 1930. 17 in (43 cm) high* **$3,000–4,000 WW**

In 1885, Friedrich Goldscheider (1861–1922) arrived in Vienna from his native Bohemia with grand ideas. Over the years, he built his company into a thriving and respected concern, opening retail outlets in Paris, Leipzig, and Florence.

Few firms competed with Goldscheider's unique brand of sculpted ware, mostly made in unglazed red earthenware and cold-painted to simulate Vienna bronze. Statuary, tobacco jars, and jardinières were staple products, together with wall masks, early examples of which often featured male Bedouin faces.

After World War I, as tastes began to change, Goldscheider changed with them, steered by Friedrich's sons Walter (who remained with the company until its closure in 1953) and Marcell, who brought innovative ideas to the company. Marks from this period include the initials "W" and "M." The most successful range was large-scale statuary, designed to serve as centerpieces in stores or homes.

ATTRACTING TALENTED ARTISTS

The best Goldscheider Art Deco figures were modeled by leading sculptors and may bear an impressed artist's signature on the base. Familiar names include Josef Lorenzl (*see pp.204–05*) and Stefan Dakon, whose signature appears on dozens of models, including those with borzoi hounds. Many of the familiar figures of girls dancing in cascading robes were also modeled by Dakon

Above: Caged Bird ceramic figure of a female dancer from a Josef Lorenzl bronze, painted in skin tones and shades of brown, orange, and black. *c. 1925. 18 in (45.5 cm) high* **$3,000–5,000 DOR**

REFLECTING FASHION

Much of Goldscheider's appeal lies in the contemporary costumes, hairstyles, and general appearances of the figures, which superbly represent their period. Fashion was immensely important in the European Age of Elegance, and Goldscheider artists faithfully copied the cut and pattern of modern couture, including accessories such as hats, gloves, makeup, and even jewelry. Some examples are clearly modeled after the elongated mannerism of contemporary fashion illustration, popularized by Paul Poiret and exaggerated in the style of Erté. These fashion "models" are distinct from the more common dancer figures, typically depicted in scanty stage costumes. Complex pieces, including groups or figures with elegant borzoi hounds, are especially sought-after. Many were given pride of place in the home and have survived well, but the popularity of originals has precipitated a wealth of later copies.

This cover of *Vogue* magazine dates from November 1926. At the cutting edge of fashion, *Vogue* was a source of inspiration during the 1920s and 1930s for Goldscheider and other makers of female ceramic figures à la mode.

Pair of dancing girls modeled by Stefan Dakon, with platinum-blond hair and long, flowing dresses split to the waist and painted with a large floral pattern in shades of red and pink. Model number 7868/115/19. *1930s. 13½ in (34 cm) high* **$3,000–4,000 DOR**

ELABORATE MOLDS

Friedrich Goldscheider employed extremely elaborate molds for his early ware, and this tradition continued in the Art Deco period after his death. Several other factories made statuary of comparable scale to Goldscheider, but none was able to match the meticulous attention to molded detail or complex arrangement of elements in Goldscheider's work. Most single pieces were made in several sections using the slip-cast technique to make figures and integral bases in Goldscheider's refined earthenware body. Features including limbs or applied elements, such as animals, were cast separately. Figures were assembled by "luting" elements together when "leather hard" before glaze firing, at which stage seams and other imperfections were carefully removed. Figural groups are rare, partly because of the extra time needed in manufacture and subsequent high retail cost. Most figures are carefully designed to minimize the risk of collapse or wastage during firing. Later Goldscheider figures and copies exhibit shortcuts in the molding process, and unfinished mold seam lines are clearly visible in inferior copies.

about 1930. Other sculptors associated with Goldscheider include Paul Phillipe, Ida Meisinger, Michael Powolny, and Vally Wieseltheir. The latter two artists were associated with the progressive Wiener Werkstätte and may have been attracted to the firm by Marcell Goldscheider, who was impressed by the enterprise and established a small "free-decorating" studio in 1926.

Collectors of Goldscheider look for a vivid but sympathetic use of color, particularly in detailed areas. The more Art Deco, the better. Some models of the Art Deco period were in traditional style, including religious Madonna figures, and these are of less interest to collectors.

In 1938 the family moved to Trenton, New Jersey, where they began a new enterprise. During the 1940s they also collaborated with the Staffordshire firm of Myott, and pieces from this period may be marked "Myott & Goldscheider."

Ceramic figure of a female Asian dancer from a bronze by Josef Lorenzl. Her floor-length headdress covers a harem costume and is painted in shades of blue, green, lilac, and brown with a stylized plant-form pattern. *c. 1920. 18½ in (47 cm) high* **$3,000–4,000 DOR**

NEW WOMEN

Much of the appeal in the popular models by Stefan Dakon or Josef Lorenzl for Goldscheider stems from their use of fashionable women from modern society at a time when most porcelain statuary depicted figures in 18th-century costume. The modern woman of the 1920s was a product of World War I. She was suddenly liberated from a prewar era, when a glimpse of stocking was considered something shocking, and propelled into a society where anything goes.

FLAPPER GIRLS

Goldscheider's figures feature every element of the modern flapper: cloche hats, revealing hemlines, high-heeled shoes, print dresses and shawls, even short-cropped hair and elegant accessories, including long beaded necklaces, clutch bags, and borzoi hounds. Commercial success was aided by the instant recognition of this style throughout much of the affluent world, due to widespread distribution of fashion magazines and Hollywood movies.

Figure of a female dancer cast in ceramic from a Josef Lorenzl bronze. With a "butterfly-wing" dress painted in blue, green, and pale purple. Model number 5715/49/8. *c. 1930*

15¾ in (39.75 cm) high

$3,000–4,000   **DOR**

Ceramic figure of a harem dancer wearing a modern, diaphanous costume and carrying a polychrome shawl decorated with fruit motifs. Model number 5613/70/65. *c. 1925*

18 in (46 cm) high

$3,000–5,000   **DOR**

Restored figure of a dancer by Stefan Dakon. She wears a strapless, floor-length dress and matching hat and gloves, all in shades of green and black. Model number 6551. *1930s*

15¾ in (40 cm) high

$2,000–3,000   **WW**

Ceramic figure of a young woman in a dramatic pose wearing a costume with "butterfly-wing" edges. Cast from a bronze by Josef Lorenzl. *c. 1930*

17¾ in (45 cm) high

$5,000–9,000   **DN**

Figure of a young lady in a dancer's pose by Stefan Dakon. She is wearing a faux animal-print top, a long-trained skirt with a naturalistic floral pattern, and matching shoes, all painted in shades of red and white against flesh tones. *1930s*

15 in (38 cm) high

$5,000–7,000   **BEV**

Figure of a dancing woman by Stefan Dakon. She has blond hair and a long, billowing blue dress with naturalistic floral motifs in shades of red. Model number 8083/220/14. *c. 1940*

13½ in (34 cm) high

$3,000–5,000   **DOR**

Ceramic figure of a female dancer cast from a bronze by Josef Lorenzl, with fashionably short brown hair and a floral-motif strapless dress. Model number 5822/337/15. *c. 1920*

18 in (46 cm) high

$3,000–5,000   **DOR**

Figure of a dancer cast in ceramic from a bronze by Josef Lorenzl, and wearing a halter top and billowing, floral skirt, both trimmed with yellow and black banding. *c. 1930*

19¾ in (50 cm) high

$3,000–5,000   **DN**

Figure of a young lady by Stefan Dakon. She is attired in a romantic theatrical costume painted in shades of brown and gray, and is being licked on the ankle by a small dog. *1930s*

11 in (28 cm) high

$1,200–1,800   **BEV**

Figure of a young lady with a terrier by Stefan Dakon. She wears a modern one-piece, blue-and-white-check swimsuit with matching shoes. Model number 7194/134/31. *c. 1940*

13 in (33 cm) high

$2,000–3,000   **DOR**

Restored figure of a young lady seated on a hatbox by Stefan Dakon. Her check-print dress and shoes are painted in shades of brown and white. *1930s*

10½ in (27 cm) high

$2,000–3,000   **WW**

Rosenthal

One of the best-known and most respected firms in continental ceramics, Rosenthal produced Art Deco designs of the highest quality in both modeling and artistry, with an emphasis on elegance and grace.

Throughout its history, Rosenthal has operated at the cutting edge of modern taste. The interwar years saw the German company attract an international market using mainly commissioned designers and modelers. This tradition continued with Philip Rosenthal, grandson of the founder, who made the factory one of the first in Europe to offer studio ceramics after World War II.

Rosenthal established its retail headquarters in Berlin in 1917, offering delicate figurines and exquisitely painted porcelain. Unlike Meissen (*see opposite*) and older factories, Rosenthal figurines depicted modern subjects or dancers drawn from tales of *The Arabian Nights*. Modelers included Dorothea Charol, who created exotic dancers in

the 1920s, and Claire Weiss, who introduced an Art Deco series of Four Seasons in 1932. Rosenthal also designed a series of Mickey Mouse figurines for Walt Disney in 1931.

Rosenthal's best tableware is hand-painted and signed. Pieces are thinly potted and the porcelain is stark white or ivory in hue, the latter also used on some figurines simulating ivory. All Rosenthal is clearly marked with a distinctive crown and lettering, but many lesser Bavarian makers copied the mark and style. Signatures may also appear molded into the base of the figurine.

Above: Maja porcelain milk jug designed by Friedrich Fleischmann. It features a geometric and stylized plant-form pattern in coral red and gold on a white ground. *c. 1930. 3 in (7.5 cm) high* **$50–100 BMN**

Shouldered vase with a domed lid and a hexagonal body decorated by Kurt Wendler. It has alternating panels of stylized African figures and vertical stripes. *c. 1925* *12½ in (32 cm) high*

$3,000–4,000 **HERR**

Porcelain lidded jar of conical form on a "piecrust" rimmed foot. Designed by Hans Küster, it was decorated by Kurt Wendler with a polychrome Semiramis pattern of stylized palm trees. Model number 850. *c. 1925* *7¼ in (18.5 cm) high*

$300–500 **QU**

Porcelain figure of a dancer, Anita, designed by Dorothea Charol and inspired by Anita Berber, the contemporary "dancer of depravity." Model number 201. *c. 1925* *10¼ in (26 cm) high*

$600–900 **DOR**

Porcelain figure of an Egyptianesque dancer above a coiled snake in a basket. Rosenthal produced numerous figures of snake dancers. *1920s* *10½ in (26.5 cm) high*

$500–800 **GCL**

Meissen

Art Deco represents only a tiny fraction of the output of Meissen, the oldest and largest porcelain-maker of the Western world. However, this style of Meissen is growing in both popularity and value.

Since reconstruction after the Napoleonic Wars (1799–1815), Meissen has consistently drawn on its vast resources of 18th-century design and prestige in both marketing and manufacture. This means that current designs are usually less popular than reproductions wherever Meissen is sold—a fact that is as true today as in the Art Deco years.

Despite the scarcity of Art Deco Meissen, however, quality is exceptionally high in both manufacture and design. Statuary, which ranges from conventional-scale figurines to large groups of ambitious complexity, is most common.

Modelers included Max Esser, who designed an Art Deco stoneware chess set for Meissen in the early 1920s and specialized in animal groups

including mythological figures, and Paul Scheurich, who preferred female subjects. Scheurich also modeled for several Meissen rivals, including Berlin and Nymphenburg.

Colors are rare in Art Deco Meissen statuary, and much is left entirely white, which does not help the value. Most larger figures have an impressed artist's signature along with company marks. The famous Meissen crossed swords, surely the most widely copied ceramic mark, have been used consistently since 1724; however, copies of Art Deco Meissen do not really exist.

Above: Large porcelain charger by Paul Börner with a segmented gilt border and rim encompassing a naked woman feeding grapes to a satyr. *c. 1920. 18 in (45.5 cm) wide* **$7,000–9,000 DA**

Porcelain figure of a badger modeled by Max Esser and from a series of figures entitled Reineke Fuchs (Reynard the Fox), inspired by a German folktale of the same name. *1922*
11 in (28 cm) high
$4,000–7,000 DA

Porcelain figure of a goat modeled, like the badger on the left, by Max Esser for the Reineke Fuchs (Reynard the Fox) series. The perimeter of the base is characteristically defined with gilding. *1923*
7¼ in (18.5 cm) high
$4,000–7,000 DA

Lady with Fan porcelain figure modeled by Paul Scheurich and polychrome painted in delicate shades of pink and blue. Conceived in 1929, this model was produced throughout the 1930s.
18½ in (47 cm) high
$12,000–18,000 DA

The Keramis Pottery was established in 1841 at La Louvière, Belgium, by the Boch family.

The design and decoration of Keramis ware was in the hands of Charles Catteau, who was employed there around 1906–45.

A faience earthenware body or stoneware characterizes all production.

Vibrant hand-decoration is typical on vases, often with symmetrical or frieze patterns.

Most pieces are clearly marked, often with a she-wolf (*louvière* in French, as in the town of origin); many have the impressed signature of Catteau.

The Keramis Pottery remained active until World War II.

Boch Frères

Internationally renowned during the interwar years, the distinctive Art Deco pottery by Boch Frères is still fairly common today. Most of it revolves around ornamental ovoid vases, with larger sizes being more desirable.

During its main period of manufacture, from about 1920 to the late 1930s, Boch Frères' Art Deco pottery bearing the "Keramis" mark was not considered outstanding artistic ware. It was designed to be made in large quantities, using slip-cast bodies with hand-painted decoration to achieve uniqueness and be eye-catching for sale through scores of fashionable galleries and department stores internationally. Commercial popularity made Boch Frères ceramic ware relatively common and inexpensive until recently, when the market developed a new appreciation for its artistically progressive qualities.

Made in Belgium, most Keramis pottery was designed by French-trained artists, notably Charles Catteau (*see box opposite*), to complement French taste. Catteau focused on artistic ware, production of which began at Boch Frères under Alfred William Finch (1854–1930), who designed mostly faience with decoration incised through thick, opaque glazes before World War I. Some Catteau work continues this tradition, but most of it is in vibrant *cloisonné* enamels, typically including azure-blue and yellow, on an off-white, craquelure ground. Large, human figural pieces attain the highest prices, and animals or birds are preferred over the common stylized flora.

Other Boch Frères designers include Marcel Goupy (*see p.84*) and Paul Follot (*see p.28*). The firm's subtlest work, mostly by Catteau, is matt stoneware vases, marked "Grès Keramis," in muted palettes showing Modernist form and decoration. Influences range from Cubism to abstract Expressionism, often with an African or exotic theme in flora or fauna after about 1925.

Above: Stoneware (*grès*) vase of shouldered ovoid form with a stylized cockerel medallion and segmented enameling in brown, green, blue, and black. *1920. 6¾ in (17 cm) high* **$1,200–2,000 MOD**

PRIMITIVISM

Looking for a new repertoire of motifs during the interwar years, many decorative artists explored various exotic cultures, including that of primitive man. In the mid-1920s, a fairly small number of vases with frieze decoration evocative of cave painting was designed by Charles Catteau. They reflect an interest in Cubism, as well as a romantic curiosity of African and other preindustrial cultures that many Belgians and French could now access through their colonies. Some images were directly influenced by Neolithic cave paintings discovered in southern France around that time.

Earthenware vase designed by Charles Catteau. The typical Catteau decoration comprises a linear design with a central frieze of stylized gazelles, painted in green over an ivory craquelure ground. *c. 1925 12½ in (32 cm) high* **$3,000–5,000 MOD**

CAVE PAINTING

Substantially restored earthenware vase with neoclassical Perseus & Gorgons decoration enameled in relief in black on a *cloisonné* craquelure ground. *1920s*

13½ in (34.5 cm) high

$600–900   **FRE**

Rosette-design earthenware vase with bands of incised flowerheads enameled in shades of blue against an ivory-white craquelure ground. *1922*

11¾ in (30 cm) high

$800–1,200   **WW**

Bottle-shaped earthenware vase (one of a pair) by Paul Follot. Vertical stripes alternate with enameled floral medallions against a mottled craquelure ground. *1923–24*

11 in (28 cm) high

$1,000–1,800 (the pair)   **QU**

White-bodied earthenware vase of ovoid shape with a short, flared neck and billowing cloud- or smokelike decoration sponged in shades of blue enameling. *c. 1925*

11¾ in (30 cm) high

$800–1,200   **MOD**

Large, ovoid, white-bodied earthenware vase decorated with stylized pelicans in flight, set above and below stylized white clouds and against blue skies. Typically, the enameling—in yellow and shades of blue—is thickly applied to create the pattern in relief. *1925*

13¾ in (35 cm) high

$3,000–4,000   **PBA**

CHARLES CATTEAU

Charles Catteau (1880–1966) was born into a family of ceramic-industry workers in Sèvres, France. He apprenticed at the famous local porcelain works (*see p.110*) and at Nymphenburg, in Germany, before joining Boch in 1906. Catteau spent the next 42 years at the company, having become an artistic director in 1907. His early work is in Art Nouveau taste, but after World War I he developed a unique style of Art Deco decoration based on exotic cultures, or the avant-garde. Boch Frères was well established as a utilitarian pottery when Catteau joined, but he singlehandedly steered the production of artistic ware. His facsimile signature was used as a promotional device and appears on all his designs.

Stoneware (*grès*) vase designed by Charles Catteau with a stylized leaf-form design in shades of greenish brown against ivory. Its extended, molded foot is typical of Catteau's later work. *1930s*

7½ in (19 cm) high **$1,800–2,200 FRE**

Unusual earthenware vase of cylindrical form designed by Charles Catteau. It features a sketchlike mermaid in a seascape pattern etched in gold. The gold is also applied to two row-of-loops handles. *c. 1925*

11½ in (29 cm) high **$1,200–2,000 MOD**

European Ceramics

Consumer demand in the interwar years led to a wealth of hand decoration on modern ceramics, which fall into two categories: studio pottery and commercial ware. Studio includes work of the Wiener Werkstätte (Viennese Workshops), which appears "hand built" and avant-garde (versions of inferior quality were made by W.M.F. in Germany and Wiener Keramik in Austria), and the work of several French potters, notably Jean Mayodon and Mougin Frères.

After World War I, commercial ware began to appear from K.P.M. in Berlin, as well as firms in Dresden, Limoges, and, at the highest level, Sèvres, France. With the exception of Wiener Werkstätte pieces, which are typically signed with a conjoined "WW" and artist's monogram, most commercial ware was made to be inexpensive and is of inferior design. Many, including "Czeco Deco" and Austrian pieces, which may be unsigned, have the orange and yellow palette of central European origin. The mark "Primavera" appears on pieces sold at the Parisian department store Au Printemps in the 1920s.

Chinese-inspired vase designed by the German painter Ernst Böhm for the Staatliche Porzellan-Manufactur. It is orange-red, with gilt decoration over a white ground. *c. 1930*

12½ in (32 cm) high

$1,000–1,800   QU

Ovoid earthenware vase possibly designed by Charles Catteau for Boch Frères Keramis. It has a flared neck and is hand-enameled with stylized birds and flowers. *c. 1925*

9½ in (24 cm) high

$800–1,200   PBA

Squat ceramic vase designed by Gudrun Baudisch for the Wiener Werkstätte. It has a footed, ovoid body, a long, trumpet-shaped neck, and asymmetric loop handles, with a painted geometric pattern. *c. 1920*

10 in (25 cm) high

$1,000–1,800   WKA

Circular tray in a continental pewter frame with D-loop handles, made by W.M.F. The body of the tray is hand-painted with purplish-blue flowers on a crackled teal ground. *c. 1930*

12 in (30.5 cm) wide

$200–500   FRE

Porcelain vase of multi-tubular profile designed by Ernst Böhm for K.P.M. of Berlin. It has stripes, cross-hatching panels, and other geometric forms hand-painted in blue, orange, yellow, and gold on a white ground. *1928*

7½ in (19 cm) high

$1,200–1,800   QU

Ovoid earthenware vase made at Limoges, France. Framed at the rim and base with black banding, it is decorated with highly stylized figures of mannequins wearing haute couture, in shades of gray-brown against a mottled and streaked red ground. *1920s*

5¾ in (14.5 cm) high

$500–900   QU

Squat ovoid vase by Grès Mougin, of Nancy, France. The body is engraved in shallow relief and highlighted blue, with a stylized landscape containing a Pan-like figure and naked females. *c. 1925*

11½ in (29 cm) high

$4,000–6,000   **MOD**

Ovoid porcelain vase from the Schoenau Porcelain Manufacturers, in Germany. The body is hand-painted with a geometric floral pattern and polychrome banding. *c. 1925*

6¼ in (16 cm) high

$300–500   **QU**

Shallow relief-incised ovoid vase by André Legrand for Mougin Frères. It is painted with a rural landscape of women at toil, under selective matt and shiny glazes. *1920s*

8¾ in (22.5 cm) high

$1,000–1,800   **HERR**

Bulbous ovoid vase by Primavera. It is painted in brown, gunmetal, celadon, and cobalt, with four oval panels depicting nude women surrounded by an abstract pattern. *1920s*

16½ in (42 cm) high

$3,000–4,000   **SDR**

Characteristically colorful vase by Villeroy & Boch of Dresden. Its bulbous body is enameled in orange-yellow; the ribbed foot and neck have glossy black enameling. *1930s*

5½ in (14 cm) high

$300–500   **PBA**

Italian ceramics

Centuries of traditional design stemming from the Renaissance relaxed after World War I, when a few Italian ceramic artists tried something new. Prominent in this movement were the Turin firm of Lenci (*see box p.123*) and the work of Giò Ponti, Angelo Biancini, and other designers for the Società Ceramica Italiana. This company was established by the Ginori family in 1735 in Doccia, near Florence. Ginori porcelain and thinly potted earthenware are painted or transfer-printed in elegant, modern Mannerist style with landscapes or Renaissance figures. Propaganda themes of National Socialism are especially interesting. Most are clearly marked and the extensive range includes tableware.

Footed Temporale vase designed by Gigi Chessa for Lenci of Turin. Of beakerlike form with pinched sides, it is underglaze-painted plain brown on the interior, and with a polychrome idyllic Italian landscape under dark thunderclouds on the exterior. *1933*

10¼ in (26 cm) high

$3,000–4,000   **VZ**

Glazed-ivory earthenware vase designed by Angelo Biancini and made by the Società Ceramica Italiana. It is hand-painted with a polychrome campaign tent at the front and with a young woman in riding gear holding a horse on the reverse. *1938*

12 in (30.5 cm) high

$3,000–4,000   **VZ**

**Circular
wall plaque**
of a female
dancer made
by the Viennese
firm of Goebel und
Hutschenreuther. Set in
a glossy black enameled
frame, she is wearing a long,
billowing, diaphanous dress in shades
of green with floral motifs at the hem. *1930s*

9½ in (24 cm) wide

$300–500 CHS

Czechoslovakian earthenware bust by
Elly Strobach, in the form of a fashionably
dressed young woman smoking a cigarette.
1930s

7 in (17.5 cm) high

$300–500 DN

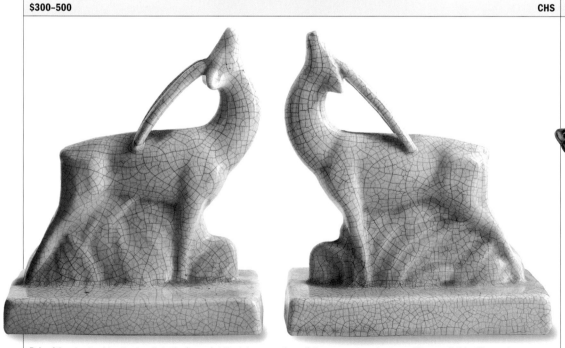

Pair of Czechoslovakian bookends in the form of stylized deer posed over foliage on rectangular bases. They are finished in a pale, creamy-
brown glaze with all-over crazing. *1930s*

6 in (15 cm) high

$800–1,200 DETC

Earthenware bust of a woman's head by
Lotte Calm for the Wiener Werkstätte. It is
painted with white skin, rouge highlights,
black hair, and a floral headdress. *c. 1930*

9¼ in (23.5 cm) high

$5,000–8,000 WKA

Brick-red earthenware cruet set by Susi Singer for the Wiener Werkstätte. It is in the form of a dancing couple, with flanking bowls raised on rocks above the sea. *c. 1925*

4¾ in (12 cm) high

$1,000–1,800 **WKA**

Nude female figure by Lenci of Turin. Seated on a trunk and with a towel draped over her arm, she has the yellow-blond hair characteristic of many Lenci figures. *1930s. 11¾ in (30 cm) high* **$1,200–1,800 SDR**

Continental porcelain half-doll modeled and hand-painted as a 1920s "flapper," with a black bob and wearing a black-trimmed yellow cocktail dress. *1920s*

2¾ in (7 cm) high

$80–150 **F**

Figure of a female dancer by the Wiener Werkstätte. She has a strapless dress hand painted with a polychrome pattern, including geometric motifs and star shapes. *1930*

16¼ in (41.5 cm) high

$1,200–2,000 **QU**

Continental earthenware figure by Sybille May, modeled as a kneeling young woman with a black skirt holding aloft a golden orb. Mounted on a wooden base. *1930s*

8 in (20 cm) high

$800–1,200 **WW**

Pair of porcelain Pierrot & Pierrette figures by Friedrich Heuler for Hutschenreuther. They are sparingly painted in red, yellow, gray, and black against a glossy white ground. *1920s*

9½ in (24 cm) high

$600–900 **QU**

Goldscheider-style bust of a young woman, made in Vienna from brick-red earthenware. She has a serene expression, pale-brown skin, cascading ringlets, and a blue dress. *c. 1940*

12½ in (32 cm) high

$700–1,000 **WKA**

Katzhütte

Large-scale porcelain and thinly cast earthenware figures were made in the German town of Katzhütte from the mid-1920s until the late 1930s. Most depict sleek-bodied animals or young women in elegant poses and fashionable dress. Colors are naturalistic and the overall quality of design and execution compares closely to the better-known figures by Goldscheider (*see pp.112–15*). The best are signed with a maker's mark and impressed modeler's name "Dakon," usually found on the outer base rim. Stefan Dakon (1904–92) also modeled for Keramos and Goldscheider. His work is comparable to that of the Austrian sculptor Josef Lorenzl (*see pp.204–05*), always vibrant and delightful. Dakon's best figures evoke Louis Icart etchings in three dimensions, depicting elegant women and borzoi hounds, for example. Unlike Goldscheider, marked Katzhütte figures all predate World War II.

Katzhütte earthenware figure designed by Stefan Dakon. Modeled as a young girl wearing a flowing dress and a broad-brimmed hat, it is painted in shades of green. Marked "41." *1930s*

16½ in (42 cm) high

$700–1,000 **L&T**

KEY FACTS

Clarice Cliff began work as a lithographer at Wilkinson's Royal Staffordshire Pottery in 1916. She remained with the company until 1963.

She was sent to London's Royal College of Art by her employer for a two-month course in 1927.

She returned to establish her own decorating studio at Wilkinson's adjacent Newport Pottery that year.

Bizarre Ware was introduced in 1928.

Dame Laura Knight designs date from 1932–34.

Art Deco decorating at Clarice Cliff ceased by 1940.

Clarice Cliff

An ordinary girl with extraordinary talent, Clarice Cliff was one of eight children born into a working-class Potteries family. She became nationally respected in the 1930s and is internationally collected today.

Clarice Cliff (1899–1972) was born in Tunstall, in the heart of the Staffordshire Potteries. She showed an aptitude for ceramic art from her early days at Wilkinson's, where the artistic team of John Butler and Fred Ridgway was responsible for her design and decorating training. The most encouragement, however, came from Colley Shorter, the owner's son, whom Cliff eventually married in 1940.

Shorter arranged for Cliff's formal training and helped her set up her studio at the Newport Pottery, which his father had acquired in 1920. It was here in 1928 that Cliff conceived Bizarre, which rapidly grew into a fully modern line, including the familiar patterns Abstract and Banded, all hand-painted in a palette of orange, yellow, green, and black. Most painting was done over a "honey" glaze on Wilkinson's standard, inexpensive earthenware.

PATTERNS GALORE

By the mid-1930s, Clarice Cliff had introduced hundreds of patterns, with evocative names like Sunrise (1929), Gayday (1930), and Tennis (1931). Pattern names may appear on marks, along with the trademark "Bizarre" and a facsimile of Cliff's signature. This mark was used until the 1960s on some ware. Popular patterns were produced over many years, but a few, including Butterfly of 1930, had small production runs and are rare today.

A new branch of Clarice Cliff ware was born in 1932 after the artist's chance meeting on a train with painter Dame Laura Knight (1877–1970), who designed the Circus line for Cliff on commission.

Above: Windbells-pattern wall charger comprising a stylized tree with a black trunk and blue leaves against a red, yellow, and green ground. *1933–34. 10 in (25.5 cm) wide* **$3,000–4,000 SCG**

BIZARRE GIRLS

Clarice Cliff's studio was staffed largely by young, flapper-type female painters with varying talent but a common taste for modernity, all working to the demanding speed and standard of a commercial pottery. After Cliff became artistic director in 1931, the Bizarre girls, many of whom remain anonymous, were encouraged to create their own designs and present them in live demonstrations at store marketing campaigns. One can only imagine the thrill these young women experienced seeing their work exhibited and sold at Harrods or at the International British Art In Industry Exhibition held at Wembley in 1935.

Bonjour-shape vase decorated with a May Avenue pattern in black and shades of blue, green, and red, and with all the elements also outlined in black. *1933. 4 in (10.5 cm) high* **$9,000–12,000 WW**

CLARICE CLIFF

"Delecia"

DECORATION AND FORM

Cliff's Bizarre line was an immediate success. It was introduced in 1928 mainly as a way of decorating old blanks with colorful patterns. This early style and palette remained essentially constant during the Art Deco years. Decoration was entirely hand-applied, mostly by painters working in close quarters with Clarice Cliff, who did limited work herself. From 1929 she began to introduce her own forms, which ranged from starkly geometric in the manner of Jean Luce, to vases of hand-built appearance imitating the work of studio potters such as Bernard Moore. Innovative forms include a honeycomb teapot, conical sugar shakers or cruets, and an inverted conical bowl with cruciform support. Figures are extremely rare and valuable.

An original retail display of Bizarre-range wares with a Delecia pattern. Combined with other motifs, such as flowers or fruit, this pattern consisted of random colored drips known collectively as "runnings." *1931–34*

INSPIRATIONS

By the 1930s, Clarice Cliff had matured from a working-class girl into a sophisticated artistic trendsetter. She drew from a wide range of influences, the main one being, arguably, an innate, almost mischievous, sense of fun entirely consistent with the spirit of the Art Deco age. Beyond this, Cliff was clearly influenced by modern fashion and couture, particularly French fashion illustrations by Georges Barbier and others.

ORIENTAL STYLE

During the interwar years, Chinese and Japanese watercolor scroll paintings were popular in interior design, and a few Clarice Cliff designs show their influence. This free style of semi-abstract painting and lack of perspective or background proved successful in painted pottery, some of which featured patterns of East Asian subject matter.

WARTIME BUSINESS

Cliff conceived or oversaw the design of more than 500 shapes and 2,000 patterns at her studio between 1927 and 1940, when the Newport Pottery was taken over by the government for use as a wartime storage facility.

She did not resume her vibrant, modern decorating after World War II, and spent most of her later years gardening, though she remained at Wilkinson's until 1963 working mainly as an administrator. Sadly, she failed to see the first major retrospective of her work, held at the Brighton Museum in 1972, and she died shortly afterward.

Clarice Cliff ware was sold largely in Great Britain and the Commonwealth countries. It is still relatively uncommon in the United States. Collecting has enjoyed ups and downs since attention began in the 1970s, and most buyers are very discriminating. Some non-Deco traditional forms and patterns were also made but are of little interest today.

Shape 369 vase of stepped and graduated square form, decorated with a Latona Tree pattern with a black trunk and highly stylized blue, orange, green, and red geometric leaves. *1929–30. 7¾ in (19.5 cm)* **$1,800–2,500 WW**

Bizarre-range cylindrical preserve pot with a finialed cover and decorated with a Pine Grove pattern comprising fir trees with red trunks and blue, black, and green foliage, all under rows of fine horizontal blue lines. *1935. 3½ in (9 cm) high* **$400–600 WW**

Cone-shaped sugar sifter from the Bizarre Ware range. It is covered in a honey glaze and features an Oranges & Lemons pattern. *c. 1930*

5½ in (14 cm) high

$2,500–4,000 **WW**

Rodanthe-pattern coffee pot with flared, cylindrical sides and triangular handle and spout. It is hand-painted with stylized flowers in orange, yellow, and gray. *1930s*

7½ in (19 cm) high

$800–1,200 **CHEF**

Bizarre Ware cauldron on a tripod base with a pair of pierced triangular handles. The interior is painted lilac, and the exterior is painted with the Tennis pattern in lilac, green, blue, yellow, and gray. *c. 1930*

3 in (7.5 cm) high

$800–1,200 **WW**

Lynton-shape sugar sifter hand-painted with a Coral Firs landscape pattern with fir trees (and a cottage and cliffs on the reverse). *1933–39*

5 in (12.5 cm) high

$700–1,000 **FRE**

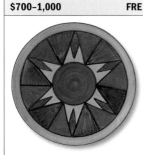

Original Bizarre Ware plate with an early geometric Bizarre design— a radiating pattern of triangle and diamond shapes. *c. 1930*

10 in (25.5 cm) wide

$400–700 **WW**

Stamford-shape teapot with an Orange Roof Cottage pattern. This pattern was also produced in different colorways, as Pink Roof Cottage and Yellow Roof Cottage. *1932–33*

5 in (12.5 cm) high

$2,000–3,000 **WW**

Bizarre Ware jam pot of cylindrical form with a finialed cover. It is hand-painted with a Picasso Flower pattern in orange, red, blue, and green. *c. 1930*

3½ in (9 cm) high

$500–800 WW

Very rare Tolphin jug and bowl set hand-painted with a Sliced Circle pattern comprising radiating lines with circles displaced either side of them. *1929–30*

Jug: 9¾ in (24.5 cm) high

$10,000–15,000 WW

Large Stamford-shape milk jug with a C-shape handle. The body is hand-painted with a Sunburst pattern colored red and orange with yellow and brown. *c. 1930*

4¾ in (12 cm) high

$1,000–1,500 WW

A CLOSER LOOK

Rare miniature vase hand-painted with the Appliqué Lucerne pattern. This Swiss-landscape design is dominated by a five-turret castle with orange-red roofs and black windows set against a blue sky. This item is possibly a tradesman's sample. *1930–31. 3 in (7.5 cm) high*

$3,000–5,000 WW

The sky in this version of Appliqué Lucerne is rendered in blue. However, the alternative colorway to this pattern has an orange sky (and blue turrets)

The configuration of the turrets varies from item to item. There are always five of them, but some are narrower and taller than these

In Appliqué Lucerne, the ground in front of the castle is always yellow and the trees mid-green

The pattern is either framed top and bottom with black and red bands (as here), or black and blue bands when the sky is orange

REVERSE OF APPLIQUÉ LUCERNE

Very rare Bizarre Ware shape 362 vase of ovoid form on a ribbed foot. It is hand-painted with the Football pattern (featuring a net) outlined in black with a green-lined blue net and black, orange, yellow, and purple squares. *1929–30*

8¼ in (21 cm) high

$10,000–15,000 WW

Bizarre Ware shape 362 vase of ovoid form on a ribbed foot. It is hand-painted with a Broth pattern comprising honey-glaze, bubblelike shapes around stylized orange and blue flowerheads. *1929–31*

8 in (20.5 cm) high

$500–900 CHEF

Susie Cooper studied at the Burslem School of Art (1919–22).

Her career as a decorator began in 1922 at the A. E. Gray & Co. pottery, working under her mentor Gordon Forsyth (1879–1952).

The Susie Cooper Pottery was founded in Tunstall in 1929, moving to the Chelsea Works, Burslem, in 1930 and the Crown Works, Burslem, in 1931.

Cooper's pottery met with great success at the 1932 British Industries Fair and the 1935 International British Art in Industry Exhibition.

Transfer-decorated ware was introduced in 1935.

The pottery closed during World War II and Art Deco production ceased before 1950.

Part of the Wedgwood Group from 1966, the Susie Cooper Pottery was finally closed in 1980.

Susie Cooper

An immensely talented ceramic decorator, Susie Cooper brought a sophisticated, modern European taste to the heart of the Staffordshire Potteries. Her work is composed almost entirely of useful tableware.

There are many parallels between Susie Cooper (1902–95) and Clarice Cliff (*see pp.124–27*), but it is unfair to consider them equals and important to identify their differences to appreciate both.

Unlike Cliff, Cooper came from a well-to-do Staffordshire family and was exposed to modern art from an early age. Her sophisticated approach to design used influences from Cubism and progressive European decorative arts, including the Viennese Secession and French Art Deco Modernism. The style she developed is subtler and less provincial than Clarice Cliff, though many modern collectors prefer Cliff's naiveté and uniquely British subject matter.

Cooper's early work was made at the pottery founded by A. E. Gray in Stoke-on-Trent in 1907, which specialized in inexpensive hand-painted modern useful ware. Gray's principal designer during Cooper's tenure (1922–29) was Gordon Forsyth, who introduced the Gloria Lustre ware, some decorated by Cooper, in 1923.

The majority of her Art Deco work was produced at the Susie Cooper Pottery, which she founded in 1929 with a team of six women painters. Here she decorated earthenware blanks in a style that became increasingly sparse and geometric by the mid-1930s. Many of these later works, some transfer-printed after 1935, are very affordable. It is not unusual to find these practical and somewhat timeless sets still in use. Breakfast services were a charming specialty, featuring cups on saucer plates, eggcups, and toast racks.

Susie Cooper's postwar production, including porcelain after 1950, is mostly of limited interest.

Above: Pattern Number 8127 plate hand-painted in shades of red, yellow, orange, green, and black with the geometric Overlapping Triangles design. *c. 1930. 8¾ in (22.5 cm) wide* **$1,200–1,800 SCG**

SUCCESSFUL MARKETING

Beyond her undisputed artistic inspiration, it may be argued that Susie Cooper also had talents that lay in the realm of commercial promotion. She first proved this by successfully maintaining the family retail business following the death of her father in 1919. Cooper was greatly inspired by her employer A. E. Gray, who had begun his career as a china salesman. In the difficult Depression years, Cooper still managed to produce up to 200 of her own designs annually, which she sold through fashionable London showrooms and promoted at British industrial fairs under the bold slogan "No Home is Complete without Susie Cooper."

Paris-shape jug hand-painted with the Moon & Mountains pattern (number 7960) in shades of blue, green, orange, yellow, and black. With the A. E. Gray & Co. galleon back stamp. *1928. 4¾ in (12 cm) high* **$800–1,200 SCG**

SUSIE COOPER

Hand-painted cup and saucer designed for A. E. Gray & Co. Dominated by orange- and lemonlike shapes, it is colored with overglaze orange, yellow, black, and gray enamels. *1929*

5½ in (14 cm) wide

$400–700 SCG

Crayon Lines–pattern plate with a cream-colored earthenware body decorated with a hand-painted underglaze crayon line spiraling from the center to the rim. Marked "No. 912." *c. 1935*

8¾ in (22.5 cm) wide

$80–120 FFM

Dutch milk jug hand-painted with a bright yellow and orange-red Chrysanthemum pattern. With stylized green and black foliage around the base against a white ground. *c. 1930*

4¾ in (12 cm) high

$700–900 SCG

Nursery Ware mug transfer-printed with the Skier pattern (number E/1231). Yellow and orange lines appear on the handle and around the rim. *Mid-1930s*

3¾ in (9.5 cm) high

$500–700 SCG

Demi-tasse and saucer hand-painted with a Graduated Black Bands pattern against a white ground. The interior of the cup and the outside of the handle are hand-painted in green. *1932*

Cup: 2¼ in (5.5 cm) high

$120–180 SCG

Round, lidded box designed for A. E. Gray & Co. with a stylized floral pattern hand-painted in yellow, green, blue, red, gray, and black overglaze enamels. *c. 1930*

2½ in (6.5 cm) high

$500–700 SCG

Lidded butter or cheese dish hand-painted in polychrome overglaze enamels with a pattern comprising semicircular bands offset with rectangles and triangles with sgraffito wave motifs. *c. 1930*

6¾ in (17 cm) wide

$500–700 BAD

Wall Masks

Porcelain wall pockets for flowers were common in Georgian Britain, but mounting purely decorative ornaments is a 20th-century idea, most popular in the 1930s, when wall masks and flying ducks competed for wall space.

Earthenware wall masks in bright colors cheered up thousands of modest homes from the late 1920s until the 1950s, especially in Great Britain, the Commonwealth countries, and the US. They were reasonably priced until recently, when they soared in popularity, and good examples may still be found in situ. Wall masks were typically made in modern taste and most were made to be very inexpensive by British and some Continental firms.

Staffordshire makers include J.H. Cope of the Wellington China Works, Longton (1887–1946), bearing marks "C. & Company" or "C. Ltd"; John Beswick (also of Longton, 1894 to present), makers of well-modeled examples together with

its famous animals and cottage ware; and Clarice Cliff. Wall masks were a small part of Cliff's range. Most were in exotic French style or evoked modern fashion figures, including Marlene Dietrich.

Among the most valuable today are unique pieces made at the Wiener Werkstätte and similarly styled but more common examples made by Goldscheider of Vienna before World War II. Later, British-made Goldscheider masks are less popular. Collectors seek unusual models and generally avoid common motifs such as Spanish ladies or masks with religious appearance. Modern copies in Viennese style are common, as are cheaply made Japanese copies of the period.

Ceramic mask of a young lady in profile with a flower in her hair and a red hat. Made by Cope & Company of Staffordshire. *c. 1935 6½ in (16.5 cm) high* **$300–500 BEV**

Leonardi earthenware wall mask made by the Leonardene Company in London. *Early 1940s. 20 in (51 cm) high* **$500–700 BEV**

Ceramic wall mask of a girl with blue hair wearing a large harlequinesque hat and a black face mask. A monkey sits on her hand and whispers in her ear. Made by Essevi. *1930s. 10½ in (26.5 cm) high* **$800–1,200 CA**

Terra-cotta mask by Goldscheider of a young lady with a serene expression. *1925–28* 4½ in (11.5 cm) high **$700–1,000 SCG**

In-profile ceramic mask of a young lady by Cope & Company of Staffordshire. *c. 1935* 8 in (20 cm) high **$300–700 PC**

Face-on wall mask by Clarice Cliff, depicting Chahar, an Oriental lady with a flamboyant headdress. *1930s.* 11 in (28 cm) high **$1,500–3,000 FRE**

Restored face-on mask of a young lady, Marlene, wearing a yellow and orange Mesoamerican-style headdress. *1930s* 7 in (18 cm) high **$300–500 CA**

In-profile mask of a young lady with fashionably short, wavy blond hair and black earrings, by Cope & Company. *c. 1935* 7 in (18 cm) high **$250–400 BEV**

Terra-cotta mask by Goldscheider of a young lady with white-blond ringlets. *1925–28* 11 in (28 cm) high **$1,200–2,000 SCG**

Terra-cotta mask by Goldscheider of a young lady holding a fan. *1925–28* 10 in (25.5 cm) high **$1,200–2,000 SCG**

Terra-cotta mask by Goldscheider of a young lady with curls holding a tragedy mask. *c. 1925* 13½ in (34.5 cm) high **$1,800–2,200 SCG**

Terra-cotta mask by Goldscheider with wavy orange hair and a green neck bow. *1925–28* 11½ in (29 cm) high **$1,800–2,200 SCG**

Poole Pottery

No other commercial British firm combined traditional potting techniques with modern decoration as successfully as Poole, which created some of the finest British Modernist ceramics in the interwar years.

Prior to World War I, production at Poole was largely limited to slip-cast and molded pottery, including a wide range of monochrome and luster-glazed useful items. Immediately after World War I, however, demand for colorful and artistic ware started to grow.

In 1921, the Carter family went into business with former goldsmith Harold Stabler and the husband-and-wife team of John and Truda Adams to form Carter, Stabler & Adams, later renamed Poole Pottery. Truda Adams would become Truda Carter after her second marriage (to Charles) in the 1940s. Stabler's wife, Phoebe, who used to model for Royal Doulton, also worked at Poole as a designer.

By the mid-1920s, the singular, vibrant, colorful painting of Truda Carter defined the Poole style. Her work, typically of stylized flora in French "1925" taste (but sometimes incorporating deer) is highly sought-after by modern collectors.

Other popular production included John Adams's monochrome or mottled glazed statuary and bookends, and pots with subtle horizontal banding in sprayed muted colors marketed under the name Picotee. In the late 1930s, John Adams also designed a range of Streamline tableware that is eagerly collected today.

Above: Pair of leaping springbok bookends No. 831, made from slip-cast earthenware and finished in a mid-brown glaze. *1930s. 5 in (12.75 cm) high* **$600–900 C**

Trumpet-shaped earthenware vase designed by Truda Carter with a polychrome pattern (333/KN) of stylized flowers, leaves, and zigzag geometric forms. *c. 1935*
9¾ in (24.75 cm) high

$3,000–4,000   **ADE**

Hand-thrown, ovoid stoneware vase with a stylized Leaping Deer pattern (599/TZ) designed by Truda Carter. Its harmonious polychrome palette is applied under a semimatt glaze and dominated by an intense blue repeated in the dentil-pattern rim. *c. 1935*
8¼ in (21 cm) high

$1,800–2,200   **ADE**

Large stoneware platter painted by R. Sommerfelt with an antelope in front of a tree, in black, gray, buff, and selective red highlights, against a white ground. *c. 1930*
16 in (40.5 cm) wide
$600–900   **DRA**

Small earthenware bowl hand-polychrome-painted by Phyllis Ryal with stylized flowers and vegetation, and with a dentil pattern to the top of the rim. *1925–34*
4½ in (11.5 cm) wide
$100–200   **BEV**

Royal Doulton

Among the most respected and prolific firms in the history of British ceramics, Royal Doulton is famous for its extraordinary porcelain figures, some of which represent English Art Deco at its best.

Few artistic wares were produced before Henry Doulton established the Lambeth art studio in 1871. Here, George Tinworth and Mark V. Marshall began modeling rustically realistic pieces. Their legacy is Royal Doulton's figural ware, made initially under the artistic direction of Charles J. Noke at Burslem.

In the early 1920s, Noke convinced Arthur Leslie Harradine to rejoin Royal Doulton, where he had apprenticed in 1887 as a modeler. Harradine had spent the intervening years studying art, living quietly in Canada, and fighting in World War I in France. On rejoining the company, Harradine produced Royal Doulton's most successful figures, notably

The Balloon Seller (introduced in 1929 and still produced today). Several Harradine figures of the interwar years, including Dreamland of 1931, are among the finest examples of English Art Deco, featuring a conservative style of muted palette—hardly avant-garde. Royal Doulton's fully developed Art Deco style can be seen in the vividly geometric Gaylee porcelain tableware, produced in response to successes of similar ware at Shelley and Clarice Cliff (*see pp.124–27*).

Above: Head-and-shoulders earthenware bust entitled "Gladys." Although less common than full-length Royal Doulton figures, she is presented in a characteristically casual pose. Factory number HN 1740 indicates it was made between 1935 and 1949. *5 in (12.5 cm) high*
$600–900 SWO

De Luxe–pattern tea set with a sandwich plate, sugar bowl, milk jug, and six teacups, saucers, and tea plates, each with green and white bands divided by black and silver arcs. *c. 1935*
Cup: 2¾ in (7 cm) high
$600–900 CHEF

Highly desirable Dreamland figure designed by Leslie Harradine and mounted on a table-lamp base. Reclining seductively, the young lady adopts a pose that is rather risqué for its day. Factory number HN1481. *1931–38*
6¼ in (16 cm) wide
$1,500–3,000 DN

Marietta figure designed by Leslie Harradine. The complexion of the young lady is typically "English rose." Like many Royal Doulton figures, she is dressed for a ball—in this case a devilish red and black fancy dress. *c. 1930*
8¼ in (21 cm) high
$600–900 WW

The Carlton Works was founded in Stoke-on-Trent, Staffordshire, by James F. Wiltshaw and Harold T. Robinson in 1890.

The trademark Carlton Ware was first used in the mid-1890s, but today it is mostly associated with Art Deco–period production.

Porcelain was made at the nearby Vine Pottery, under the Carlton Ware trademark, from around 1929.

Novelty ware was introduced in the mid-1920s; most Carlton novelty ware found today is modern.

Luster decoration dates mainly from the interwar years.

Art Deco Carlton Ware has been made in reproductions since the 1970s. The trademark was most recently relaunched in 1998.

The factory remains in operation to this day.

Carlton Ware

Made to be inexpensive and highly ornamental, Carlton Ware typically follows the artistic lead of Wedgwood. It has developed a passionate following in Great Britain, the US, and the Commonwealth.

The Carlton Works and, later, Vine Pottery were overseen principally by Harold Taylor Robinson, who owned and operated several factories, including Parian specialists Robinson & Leadbetter and, from 1920, Cauldon Potteries. Robinson began his career as a maker of porcelain novelties in the 1890s and successfully continued this theme with Carlton Ware.

From its inception, Carlton made inexpensive inferior-quality copies of useful and ornamental ware by established, commercially successful manufacturers. From about 1920 the company copied the distinctive luster-decorated porcelain made at Wedgwood under the direction of Daisy Makeig-Jones and, later, Wedgwood art wares. Other influences include the hand-painted colorful Art Deco of Clarice Cliff (*see pp.124–27*) and Susie Cooper (*see pp.128–29*). Carlton's range was ambitious, featuring ornamental ware and all manner of tableware and other useful items, including large toiletry sets for the washstand.

The majority of Carlton Ware, even in the Art Deco period, was of conventional form and traditional design, much of it in the Chinese taste so popular in 1920s interior design. The Chinese style lent itself well to lustrous backgrounds, made in a range of 12 colors, mostly of speckled or "powder" ground. Interiors are typically in a pale luster finish. Gilded decoration, normally combined with hand-applied overglaze enamels, became a trademark by the mid-1920s but was used less in the 1930s.

Although pure Art Deco by Carlton is relatively scarce, most period pieces show some modern influence. Jazzy motifs in vivid colors are most valuable, especially when featured on geometric forms.

Above: Red Devil–pattern bowl with the devil in a magical landscape. Hand-painted in polychrome enamels over a luster glaze, it is marked "No. 3765." *1920s–30s. 9¼ in (23.5 cm) wide* **$2,000–3,000 WW**

EGYPTIAN INFLUENCE

The 1922 discovery of King Tutankhamun's tomb sparked a modern Egyptian revival that spread through western Art Deco taste. Older companies revived earlier neo-Egyptian models, some designed before 1810. Carlton responded by adapting existing forms to Egyptian manner. Some were among Carlton's most expensive items, including Chinese-form ginger jars fitted with sphinx knops to simulate Canopic jars and finished with hand-painted details. The range was sold under the trademark Tutankhamun throughout the 1920s.

TUTANKHAMUN'S DEATH MASK

Lidded ginger jar printed and hand-painted with hieroglyphs in gilt and polychrome enamels against a deep-blue ground. The Egyptian pattern extends to the large, gilt-and-black pharaoh finial on the lid. *1920s. 12½ in (32 cm) high* **$7,000–10,000 WW**

Circular bowl raised on an X-form foot. It is overglaze hand-painted in shades of blue, yellow, and lilac on a cream ground and features a stylized floral Daydream pattern set within a wave-scroll border. *c. 1930*

9½ in (24 cm) wide

$120–300 PSA

Trumpet-shaped luster-ware vase with a stepped neck and foot. The body is printed and hand-painted with a floral Bell pattern in polychrome enamels and gilt against a mottled red-and-black ground. *1920s–30s*

8 in (20.5 cm) high

$1,000–1,800 L&T

Ovoid luster-ware jug printed and hand-painted with a polychrome Anemone pattern (number 3694) over an orange ground. With a gilded loop handle. *1920s–30s*

7¾ in (19.5 cm) high

$700–1,000 DN

Luster-ware jar and cover printed and hand-painted with a Crested Bird & Waterlily pattern in polychrome enamels against a cobalt-blue ground. *1920s–30s*

6¼ in (16 cm) high

$700–1,000 WW

Flattened ovoid luster-ware vase printed and hand-painted with a Floral Comets pattern (number 3422) in polychrome enamels and gilding against a diagonally segmented ground in mottled shades of blue. *1920s–30s*

6 in (15.5 cm) high

$2,000–3,000 WW

Luster-ware ginger jar and cover of ovoid shape. It is printed and hand-painted with a Floral Comets pattern in polychrome enamels and gilding over a green ground. *1920s–30s*

5½ in (14 cm) high

$1,000–1,500 TDG

Unusual luster-ware bowl with three displaced segments of a circle printed and hand-painted with a Hollyhocks pattern in polychrome enamels over a mottled and streaked green ground. *1920s–30s*

9¾ in (25 cm) wide

$300–500 L&T

KEY FACTS

Keith Murray designed for Wedgwood from 1933 until the mid-1950s.

All Murray designs for Wedgwood are signed with initials or a facsimile signature along with the Wedgwood stamp.

Some of Murray's early designs were produced into the 1960s.

All Murray Art Deco is in matt glaze (green is most common) and normally monochrome.

Norman Wilson glazes appear on some Keith Murray designs after 1937.

Keith Murray

The outstanding Modernist Keith Murray is best remembered for his association with Wedgwood, for which he designed highly distinctive ceramics, achieving considerable commercial success.

Born in Auckland, New Zealand, Keith Murray (1892–1981) was the son of a wealthy Scottish-born father and a New Zealander mother. He moved to London as a boy and was educated at Mill Hill School. In 1915 Murray joined the fledgling Royal Flying Corps and finished World War I with a Military Cross awarded for bravery.

From 1919, Murray studied architecture and spent the 1920s studying and working as a graphic designer and illustrator. His work for Wedgwood began in 1933 under Josiah Wedgwood V, whom he met while in the Midlands designing glass for Stevens & Williams.

Within a year, Murray's first "modern" Wedgwood shapes were exhibited at John Lewis in London, and they met with great commercial success. Building on this, Murray designed scores of shapes for Wedgwood during the 1930s and displayed them in international exhibitions, mostly in Commonwealth countries. Even today, Murray is not well known or collected in continental Europe or the United States.

Murray's work is highly distinctive and easily recognized since it bears his printed signature in facsimile or initials (usually on smaller pieces). These marks were used from 1933 until the postwar years. Most 1930s pieces are in matt green, matt straw, Windsor gray, or moonstone, a semimatt off-white color. After 1937, some shapes used innovative, semimatt glazes developed by Norman Wilson, including Celadon and Champagne. At this time Murray also designed covered boxes, inkwells, bookends, and smoker's accessories. The best pieces are slip-glazed and lathe-turned to create a two-color effect.

Above: Footed ovoid vase with a lathe-turned ribbed body finished in a desirable semimatt, duck-egg-blue glaze. *c. 1935* *11¾ in (30.5 cm) high* **$1,800–2,200 SCG**

ARCHITECTURAL SIMPLICITY

Keith Murray studied architecture at the progressive Architecture Associates in London, completing his degree around 1920. He visited Europe often in the 1920s and was exposed to the International style of the Bauhaus as well as the "Esprit Nouveau" of Le Corbusier and Robert Mallett Stevens. Murray's architectural eye is evident in all his work, which conforms strictly to geometrical proportions, symmetry, and the aesthetic objective of beauty through simplicity. Murray began his own architectural practice in 1936 and was later commissioned by Wedgwood to design a modern extension to the historic Barlaston works.

Trumpet-shaped footed vase with lathe-turned fluting above the foot and below the rim. It is finished in a desirable semimatt black glaze. *c. 1930. 8 in (20.5 cm) high* **$2,500–4,000 SCG**

WEDGWOOD

BARLASTON FACTORY

Shouldered ovoid vase with lathe-turned, shallow annular fluting to the body and finished in a matt pale-yellow glaze commonly referred to as "straw." *c. 1935*

7½ in (19 cm) high

$1,000–1,800   SCG

Large, shouldered, and tapering ovoid vase with lathe-turned, shallow annular fluting to the body and finished in a matt green glaze. *c. 1930*

11¾ in (30.5 cm) high

$1,000–1,800   SCG

Etruscan vase of footed, beakerlike form. It is decorated with annular bands of celadon satin green glaze and with a moonstone ivory-white interior. *c. 1935*

8 in (20.5 cm) high

$1,200–1,800   SCG

Wide-necked ovoid vase with lathe-turned annular bands of ribbing to the barrel-like body. It is finished in a matt green glaze. *c. 1930*

6½ in (16.5 cm) high

$1,200–1,800   SCG

Tapering, ovoid footed bowl with lathe-turned annular ribbing to the body. Its characteristically clean lines are enhanced with a duck-egg-blue glaze. *c. 1935*

6 in (15 cm) wide

$600–1,000   SCG

Large, tapering ovoid bowl with subtle and relatively unusual lathe-turned vertical ribbing to the body. It is finished in a matt green glaze. *c. 1930*

10 in (25.5 cm) wide

$1,000–1,500   SCG

Footed bowl of Classical inspiration, with a singular band of lathe-turned ribbing below the rim. It is finished in a duck-egg-blue glaze. *c. 1935*

6½ in (16.5 cm) wide

$600–1,000   SCG

Lidded tableware jar of cylindrical form with lathe-turned vertical fluting to the body and a vegetal-form finial on the lid. It is finished in a matt green glaze. *c. 1935*

5 in (12.5 cm) high

$600–900   SCG

John Skeaping

Sculptor John Skeaping drew early inspiration from sketches and models he made at London Zoo. After being hired by Wedgwood as a freelance modeler in 1927, Skeaping created 14 animal and bird designs for the firm. His geometrically stylized animal figures and bookends have (except on some later models) an impressed signature on the base. Pieces are typically glazed in matt monochrome. Common models, such as the Sea Lion, are less valuable, as are those in paler glazes, especially cream or ivory. The animal range, including Fallow Deer, Kangaroo, Duiker Tiger, and Monkeys, appealed to the Commonwealth market. Rare models in black basalt and Norman Wilson glazes are the best.

John Skeaping Fallow Deer sculpture with a stylized preening form above stylized vegetation and a chamfered rectangular base. It is finished in a glossy ocher glaze. *c. 1935*

7 in (18 cm) high

$400–600   WW

British Ceramics

Art Deco ceramics were made in large quantities at scores of British factories, mostly in Staffordshire. The majority of this ware is unmarked and kitschy, leaving room for little more than decorative value. Among the highest-quality and most desirable items are designs by Shelley of Longton, mostly dating from 1925 until the late 1930s. Shelley specialized in modern, Art Deco porcelain tableware in shapes and patterns designed by artistic director Eric Slater with names like Vogue and Mode. No other company rivaled Shelley in this market.

Most British Art Deco ceramics are inexpensive earthenware, painted or transfer-printed in an eye-catching palette and form and loosely in the style of Clarice Cliff. Marked pieces in this genre include Royal Winton (famous as a maker of Chintz ware), made by Grimwade Ltd., pieces by A.E. Gray & Co., and S. Fielding & Co., which made Crown Devon ware in the 1930s.

Shelley Potteries 40-piece tea set from the Vogue range. Its inverted, conical-shaped vessels have solid, triangular handles. This set is decorated with the interlocking-rectangle pattern 11792. *1930-33*

$4,000–6,000   **CHEF**

Bretby Art Pottery vase of tapering square section with an indented base forming bracket feet and ribbed diagonal panels. *c. 1920*

6¼ in (16 cm) high

$300–500   **DN**

Fielding's Crown Devon Ware vase in the form of a stylized lily, hand-painted with polychrome flower and leaf forms. *1930s*

6 in (15 cm) high

$150–200   **BAD**

The Corn Girl by Allan G. Wyon of Ashtead Pottery. Holding a sheaf of corn, she is seated on a blue-glazed pillow on a black base. *1927*

7¾ in (20 cm) high

$500–900   **J&H**

Unattributed porcelain half-doll with short hair, a serene expression, and a brightly colored, geometric-pattern coat. *1930s*

3¼ in (8.5 cm) high

$60–120   **F**

Royal Winton Fan vase with hand-painted, stylized sunflower motifs in shades of yellow, green, and red against a yellow and white ground. *Early 1930s*

9 in (23 cm) high

$500–800   **BEV**

Grimwades (Royal Winton) Byzanta Ware lidded urn decorated with floral imagery in the colors, luster, and gilt trim typical of these wares. With an acornlike finial. *Early 1930s*

8¾ in (22.5 cm) high

$300–600 BAD

Unmarked water jug with a curved spout, cylindrical neck, and conical base painted with dots and rings. The solid handle is modeled as a stylized saxophone player. *1930s*

9½ in (24 cm) high

$250–400 WW

Burleigh Ware Pied Piper jug probably designed by Harold Bennett. It is molded on the body in shallow relief and typically brightly hand-painted and enameled. *1930s*

7 in (18 cm) high

$500–800 BEV

Crown Ducal earthenware vase of high-waisted and footed ovoid form. It is hand-painted with a rural landscape with overhanging trees in the foreground. *1930s*

8½ in (21.5 cm) high

$250–400 OACC

Crown Devon octagonal-sided pot with a chamfered overhanging rim. The latter is hand-painted in black, while the body is similarly decorated with a geometric pattern in black, burnt orange, tan, and yellow ocher, all under a transparent glossy glaze. *c. 1930*

3¾ in (9.5 cm) high

$250–400 BAD

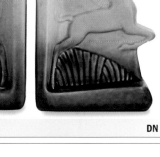

Pair of Royal Lancastrian bookends modeled as antelopes leaping over stylized foliage with their horns sweeping majestically behind them. They are finished in a semimatt, shaded green glaze. *1930s*

6¼ in (16 cm) high

$300–500 DN

Myott

The Staffordshire Potteries firm of Myott, Son & Co. was established in 1897 and merged with Alfred Meakin in 1976. In the interwar years, Myott made traditional useful ware (which has little value today) and large quantities of inexpensive modern lines. The best have a jazzy, Art Deco look in the style of Clarice Cliff. Myott also made pleasingly simple blue-banded ware and a range of luster-decorated semiporcelain for the dressing table inspired by Wedgwood's Fairyland and Butterfly luster. Most pieces bear a maker's mark but cannot be attributed to individual designers. Today Myott it is mostly collected in Great Britain and Canada.

Myott Pottery Fan vase hand-painted with a geometric pattern in shades from Myott's autumnal color palette. This classic shape was also produced with other geometric/abstract patterns and in a pastel-blue, green, pink, and mauve palette. *1930s*

9 in (23 cm) high

$500–700 BEV

Myott Pottery Pyramid vase with an Orange Flowers pattern (number 8668). Other patterns and colorways for this shape included Bluebells, Pastel Trellis, Yellow Flowers, and Pencil Trees. *1930s*

8½ in (21.5 cm) high

$250–400 RH

The Cowan Pottery Studio was founded as a small enterprise by Reginald Guy Cowan in 1913.

A new, larger pottery opened in Rocky River, near Cleveland, Ohio, in 1920.

Cowan headed the Ceramic Department at the Cleveland Institute of Art 1928-33.

Cowan Pottery closed in 1931 following financial troubles brought on by the Depression from 1929 onward.

Cowan Pottery

A successful enterprise that made large quantities of mostly inexpensive useful ware, Cowan Pottery is best known for a few remarkable artistic designs, among the most valuable of all American Art Deco ceramics.

Reginald Guy Cowan (1884–1957) was the Midwestern visionary and talented ceramic artist who modeled many of Cowan Pottery's figural designs. By the height of production in 1929, his firm employed more than 40 people using nine kilns. The range of ware was impressive: figures, figural vases, and useful ware of all description, including a full architectural line that encompassed tiles, doorknobs, and outdoor ornaments.

His greatest contribution to American Art Deco is not the figural "flower frog" for which Cowan is best known, but the gathering of a group of about 20 talented artists. Found mostly through Cowan's ties with the Cleveland Institute of Art, these artists were commissioned to design artistic ware from about 1927 to closure in 1931. The list included sculptor Alexander Blazys (1894–1963), Waylande De Santis Gregory

(1905–71), Margaret Postgate (1880–1953), A. Drexler Jacobson (1895–1973), and Victor Schreckengost (*see below*). Waylande Gregory was the most prolific, designing almost as many models as Cowan himself. He specialized in mythological subjects and modern allegory in a unique and distinctive style. Following the closure of Cowan, Gregory worked from studios at the Cranbrook Academy near Detroit.

Cowan pottery is not especially rare and most is relatively low in value. Flower frogs are ubiquitous and normally in monochrome matt glaze. Figural sculpture is more popular, particularly if attributable to a commissioned artist. Many examples are marked with a stamp or (on early redware pieces) incised mark and may have the artist's initials. The trademark "Lakeware" was impressed from 1927 to 1931.

Above: Pair of unicorn bookends designed by Waylande Gregory, and finished in a glassy, mottled ocher and mahogany glaze. *c. 1930 7¼ in (18.5 cm) high* **$400–600 SDR**

VIKTOR SCHRECKENGOST

A highly influential potter, Viktor Schreckengost (1906–2003) had a long and varied career devoted to the practice and teaching of ceramic artistry. His brief time at Cowan (1930–31) resulted in several designs now considered among the best, and most valuable, of all American Art Deco ceramics. These include a Danse Moderne figural plaque, a Sports design wall vase, and, most notably, the Jazz punch bowl of 1931 (*see opposite*). Made in a limited edition of 50, it is incised with scenes of New York on New Year's Eve under an Egyptian Blue glaze.

VIKTOR SCHRECKENGOST

Earthenware figure entitled Burlesque Dancer by Waylande Gregory. Its stylized female form was modeled on the dancer Gilda Gray, who posed for Gregory after he saw her perform in Cleveland, Ohio. *1930. 17½ in (44.5 cm) high* **$6,000–10,000 CWN**

Chinese Bird vase designed by R. Guy Cowan and finished in a bright, lustrous Egyptian blue-green glaze. c. 1925

11¼ in (28.5 cm) high

$1,200–1,800   **SDR**

Porcelain wall plaque from a series entitled The Hunt, designed by Viktor Schreckengost with polychrome underglaze decoration on a cream ground. 1931

11¼ in (28.5 cm) wide

$1,500–2,200   **SDR**

Rare and highly stylized pelican bookend (one of a pair) designed by A. Drexler Jacobson and finished in black, silver, and bronze glazes. c. 1930

5½ in (14 cm) high

$3,000–5,000 (the pair)   **SDR**

Flamingo flower frog modelled by Waylande Gregory. Designed to stand in water and hold flowers, it is finished in an Oriental pinkish-red glaze. c. 1930

11 in (28 cm) high

$400–600   **CWN**

Female flower frog entitled Debutante designed to stand in water and display flowers, finished in a custom ivory glaze. Modeled by R. Guy Cowan. 1928

10 in (25.5 cm) high

$500–700   **CWN**

Nautch Dancer sculpture by Waylande Gregory, modeled on the dancer Gilda Gray wearing a traditional East Indian form-fitting dress known as a nautch. 1930

18½ in (47 cm) high

$6,000–10,000   **CWN**

A CLOSER LOOK

Exceptionally rare punch bowl from a limited edition of 50, designed by Viktor Schreckengost. Officially entitled New Year's Eve in New York City, it is best known as, simply, The Jazz Bowl. *1931. 14 in (35.5 cm) wide* **$60,000–80,000 DRA**

New Year's Eve motifs, such as stars, streamers, and champagne bubbles, are also applied to the interior of the bowl, two of which were purchased by Eleanor Roosevelt

The festive New Year's Eve and jazz-club imagery is in the form of sgraffito decoration carved into the colored slip

The punch bowl is highly desirable because its dynamic imagery perfectly captures the essence of New York during the Jazz Age

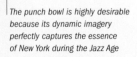

Coloration of the underlying porcelain body is achieved by applying a black slip and then a contrasting Egyptian blue-green overglaze

Rookwood

The largest manufacturer of art pottery in the United States, Rookwood made its name with Arts and Crafts ware. Its Art Deco production, however, also presents interesting opportunities for the modern collector.

Maria Longworth Nichols, who grew up in a wealthy Cincinnati family, founded Rookwood in 1880. She was devoted to ceramics, Japonisme, and the Arts and Crafts ethic from an early age and employed the finest artists from Europe, the United States, and Japan. By the start of World War I, Rookwood was thriving, with an extensive range of useful and ornamental ware, most made in the shiny Standard Glaze introduced in 1883.

Rookwood began to decline in both prosperity and output in the 1920s—the firm suffered considerably during the Depression years, eventually going into receivership in 1941. As a result, Rookwood's Art Deco was made during the company's leanest years. Much of it is of simple, economical design and manufacture. Typical examples include small slip-cast vases in pleasing shapes glazed in monochrome matt green, blue or pink, or cast bookends, paperweights, and other desk accessories in similar glazes, which may be mottled by the late 1940s. Architectural ceramics, including tiles, plaques, and garden fountains, were made from about 1905 until 1935, but most are in Arts and Crafts style. They may not be signed.

Few pieces made after the late 1920s are in the Rookwood tradition of artist potting. Exceptions include the work of the Danish Jens Jensen (1895–1978) and Louise Abel, who came to Rookwood at age 26 in 1920 and decorated until 1932. Art Deco artistic Rookwood may be in Jewel Porcelain glaze, introduced in 1915 for use on the soft porcelain body.

Art Deco Rookwood is certainly underpriced compared to earlier pieces and may present good buying opportunities for collectors.

Above: Floral-form Production vase with an exterior emerald-green matt glaze and an interior canary-yellow glaze. *c. 1925* *5½ in (14 cm) high* **$180–220 DRA**

ADOPTING MODERN DESIGNS

Throughout its history, Rookwood employed artist-designers, mostly to decorate ware. This tradition continued into the 1930s, though many of the early artists had retired by then and were not replaced. Danish immigrant Jens Jensen brought a breath of fresh European air when he arrived at Rookwood in 1928. A sophisticated oil painter, Jensen was familiar with modern French and Scandinavian taste. His work for Rookwood, made until about 1948, is signed with a stylized monogram. Jensen's wife, Elizabeth Barrett, also designed in modern taste for Rookwood.

Jewel Porcelain vase of slender shouldered ovoid shape, painted by Jens Jensen with an all-over stylized floral and foliate pattern in shades of brown, pink, and indigo "butterfat" glaze on an ivory ground. *1932* *7½ in (19 cm) high* **$4,000–6,000 DRA**

Large and unusual vase slip-painted by Elizabeth Barrett with a group of dancing women silhouetted in black against a brilliant sky-blue ground. *1935. 11¾ in (30 cm) high* **$4,000–5,000 SDR**

Trivet tile molded in relief with a large rook in a jet-black glaze set against an Oriental-style trellis, which, like the border, is in a glossy indigo glaze, contrasted with a glossy white ground. *1927*

5½ in (14 cm) square

$900–1,200 DRA

Footed ovoid Production vase molded with a ring of whimsical seahorses in relief under a frothy green matt glaze. *1921*

8 in (20 cm) high

$800–1,200 DRA

Barrel-shaped Production vase with a wide rim, molded with a stylized wave-scroll pattern in relief under a light-blue matt glaze. *1932*

4½ in (11.5 cm) high

$300–500 DRA

Shouldered ovoid vase with sprigs of flowers in relief and squeezebag-painted flowerheads by William Hentschel. *1929*

5¼ in (13 cm) high

$1,200–1,800 DRA

Rare Production paperweight designed by Louise Abel in the form of an eagle. It is finished in a brown-tinted, glossy gunmetal glaze. *1934*

8 in (20 cm) high

$1,000–1,500 DRA

Production bookend (one of a pair), modeled as a frog on a bed of mushrooms and finished in a Celadon glaze described as "a soft misty gray-green." *c. 1925*

4½ in (11.5 cm) high

$400–700 (the pair) SWO

Aventurine glazed vase of Oriental bottlelike form, painted by Linda Epply around its bulbous body and foot with large, stylized blossoms in shades of deep, muted green and blue. *1920*

15½ in (39.5 cm) high

$5,000–7,000 SDR

Trumpet-shaped porcelain vase painted by Janet Harris with blossoms, fruit, and leaves between two layers of semitranslucent, matt Velum glaze. *1930*

8½ in (21.5 cm) high

$1,500–2,000 BEL

Jewel Porcelain vase incised and painted by Jens Jensen with birds and leaves on a white-and-amber ground, under a glossy, crackled overglaze. *1944*

15¼ in (39 cm) high

$2,500–3,500 DRA

The trademark Rozane was used by Roseville from 1905.

Floral decoration was introduced by Roseville art director Frank Ferrell after 1918.

The Futura line was introduced in 1924. Pinecone and Moderne both date from the mid-1930s.

Art Deco elements can be found in most Roseville from the mid-1930s until the 1950s.

Art Deco Roseville has been convincingly copied, with fake marks, in Southeast Asia since the 1990s.

Roseville

Abundant in the United States, Roseville pottery was mostly made as an inexpensive alternative to Rookwood and Weller. Modern collectors pay special attention to the Art Deco lines and have fastidious taste in color variation.

In 1892 a consortium of local businessmen took over the J. B. Owens Pottery in Zanesville, Ohio, creating the Roseville Pottery. Established in 1885, Owens principally copied Rookwood Standard Glaze ware. Roseville continued this tradition with Rozane, a range made under Frederick Hurten Rhead (1880–1942), who was art director from 1904 until 1908; Rhead also designed Art Deco ceramics elsewhere in America in the 1930s.

By the Depression, Roseville was one of the largest potteries in the United States, with a range extending from artistic ware to garden ornaments. Art Deco Roseville dates mostly from the mid-1930s, though two notable exceptions exist: the Tourist and Futura ranges.

The Tourist line, featuring automobiles and figures in recreational pursuits, dates from the World War I years (1914–18). Decorated mainly in browns and greens on a cream ground, the rare and valuable Tourist items have a peculiarly

British early Art Deco flavor of a type found in railroad posters. The other exception is the less subtle, and more common, Futura line. The best examples are among the most progressive Art Deco American ceramics of their age.

The common Pinecone line, made in numerous forms, all featuring pine cones, is less desirable. Like most Roseville, the line was made in several color variations, which determine value today (though tastes change periodically), with most pre–World War II items featuring brown or orange blended into russet. Blue and pink are more typical of postwar production, which continued with the popular Pinecone until Roseville's closure in 1954. Other Art Deco lines include Moderne of 1936, made mostly in monochrome glaze.

Above: Futura-range vase with a brown telescopic neck rising from a blue-black angular-shouldered body and flanked by angular C-shape handles. *1920s–30s. 8½ in (21.5 cm) high* **$200–300 DRA**

FUTURA LINE

Roseville's most Art Deco line was introduced in 1924 and made until about 1928. Unlike earlier Roseville, and most made since, Futura used exclusively modern forms, undecorated except for a geometric pattern. Futura also saw the introduction of blended glaze colors, typically combining pink with gray or blue in vivid contrast. Modern collectors focus sharply on Futura, and prices have risen dramatically in recent years. Little of this line is found outside the United States. Futura is unmarked except for a paper label, which rarely survives.

Rare Futura-range Arches vase with a pair of arched handles spanning a slender, square cornet-shaped neck rising from a layered, bell-shaped body and a squat ovoid base. In shades of brown and gray. *1920s–30s. 14¼ in (36 cm) high* **$3,000–4,000 DRA**

Futura-range vase of footed form with a broad, square cornet-shaped body. It is decorated with a chevron pattern in mottled gray and two-tone mottled shades of pink. *1930s. 7 in (17.75 cm) high* **$700–900 DRA**

Pinecone-range cornucopia-shape vase in shades of reddish brown and yellow shading into dark brown at the foot. *1931*

8¾ in (22 cm) high

$300–400   **PAC**

Pinecone-range footed and waisted bulbous vase with twig handles and a Pinecone pattern molded in relief. *1931*

7 in (17.75 cm) high

$2,000–3,000   **DRA**

Futura-range footed vase of tapering, square-section trumpet form with buttressing to the corners, in a blue-gray glaze. *1920s–30s*

6 in (15.25 cm) high

$500–700   **DRA**

Futura-range footed vase of squat, bulbous form with a telescopic neck. With its original paper label. *1920s–30s*

8½ in (21.5 cm) high

$180–300   **DRA**

Futura-range Tank vase finished in a matt and mottled burnt-orange glaze graduating into blue. Roseville's very rare Tank vase is highly sought-after and thus invariably commands a substantial price. *1920s–30s*

9¼ in (23.5 cm) high

$10,000–15,000   **DRA**

Futura-range footed vase of flat rectangular form with gray-blue diagonal stripes in relief against a paler gray-blue ground. *1920s–30s*

8 in (20.25 cm) high

$400–700   **DRA**

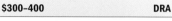

Twin-handled jardinière with a stepped neck and foot and a shouldered ovoid body with leaf decoration in relief. *1920s–30s*

7 in (17.75 cm) high

$300–400   **DRA**

Futura-range tapering vase of star-shaped section on a stepped circular base. Decorated in matt pink and green glazes. *1920s–30s*

9½ in (24 cm) high

$180–300   **DRA**

Futura-range Aztec bowl on a plinthlike base, molded with a geometric pattern in relief and finished in matt glazes. *1920s–30s*

8 in (20.25 cm) wide

$400–700   **DRA**

Futura-range hanging basket with a tapering and shouldered conical body, sectioned and molded with leaf motifs. *1920s–30s*

9½ in (24.25 cm) wide

$180–400   **DRA**

American Ceramics

The majority of American Art Deco ceramics was made in large quantities during the post-Depression years. Typical finds include matt-glazed Tutone vases and jardinières made by Weller in Zanesville, Ohio, in the 1930s and 1940s. The most successful and best-known tableware is Fiestaware, introduced by the Homer Laughlin China Co. in 1936 as an inexpensive Depression-era line. Early Fiestaware came in a range of five colors: red, cobalt blue, pale green, ivory, and yellow; turquoise was added in 1937. By 1940, consumers could choose from over 50 designs, most with simple, concentric patterns and monochrome glaze. Fiestaware is widely collected: rare forms or colors are especially sought-after, and unusual items fetch extraordinary prices, though most is affordable enough to use. It has been widely reproduced since the 1990s.

At the upper level of value and popularity are studio works by virtuoso ceramic artists, including Waylande Gregory and Victor Schreckengost, who also designed for Cowan.

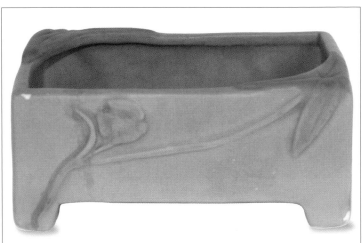

Tutone-range planter by the Weller Pottery. It is of rectangular form and molded in relief with two flowerheads, stems, and leaves. These, like the four block feet and the perimeter of the base, are in gray and set against a pink ground. *Late 1920s*

7 in (18 cm) long

$90–180　　　　　　　　　　　　　　　　　　　　　　　　　**BEL**

Tutone-range vase by the Weller Pottery. It is of triangular section on a stepped base and molded in relief with a stylized plant form on each side. The plant, like the base, is selectively highlighted in green against a purplish-pink ground. *Late 1920s*

11¾ in (30 cm) high

$150–200　　　　　　　　　　　　　　　　　　　　　　　　　**BEL**

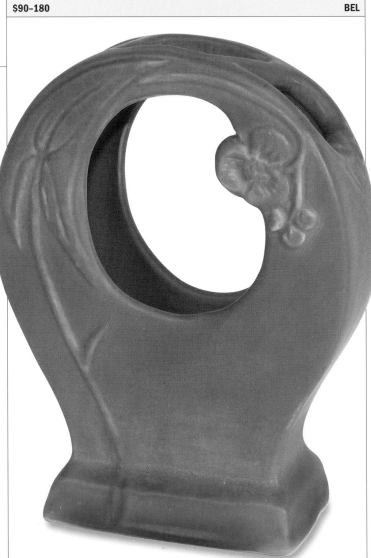

Tutone-range vase by the Weller Pottery. Of basketlike form with an integral cutout handle and a stepped base, it is molded in relief with a curving plant form. This, like the base, is selectively highlighted in green against a pink ground. *Late 1920s*

7½ in (19 cm) high

$180–220　　　　　　　　　　　　　　　　　　　　　　　　　**BEL**

Rare Fiestaware pitcher designed by Frederick Rhead for the Homer Laughlin China Co. This example, probably a one-time trial, is extremely unusual because the body is finished in a brilliant-red glaze from the Hall China Co. *Late 1930s*

7 in (18 cm) high

$3,000–5,000   **K&R**

Fiestaware pitcher by Frederick Rhead for the Homer Laughlin China Co. Although designed in 1935, this later piece is finished in the chartreuse-green color introduced to the range in the 1950s.

7 in (18 cm) high

$400–600   **K&R**

Figure of a circus bareback rider and horse by Viktor Schreckengost, entitled Madam Kitty. It is painted in matt yellow, blue, and orange on an ivory ground. Schreckengost studied under Michael Powolny in Vienna in the 1920s. *1930s*

8¼ in (21 cm) high

$4,000–6,000   **SDR**

Large terra-cotta wall plaque originally designed by Paul Bogatay for the Ohio State University. The stylized polo players in its center are decorated in cuerda seca, in reddish-brown, teal, umber, and black against a white ground. *1934*

16 in (40.5 cm) wide

$3,000–5,000   **SDR**

Rare owl figurine by the Weller Pottery. It is of stylized form and finished in a semi-matt pale-blue glaze. This is an example of the animal figurines introduced by Weller during the Depression, which were molded, glazed, and fired in one cost-effective process. *Early 1930s*

9¾ in (24.75 cm) high

$700–900   **BEL**

Russel Wright

Few 20th-century designers were as prolific as Russel Wright (1904–76), who applied his talents to most fields of industrial design in the Art Deco period and after World War II. In 1937 Wright was commissioned by the Steubenville Pottery of Steubenville, Ohio, to design a line of inexpensive tableware. The firm specialized in commercial table ceramics made in heavy earthenware with monochrome glazes. He produced the American Modern line, which was made until the 1960s, in the popular streamlined style he had pioneered. Examples are inexpensive today and some bear Russel Wright's signature in the mark.

Russel Wright American Modern-line teapot manufactured by Steubenville. This example is finished in the Bean Brown color. *Late 1930s*

5 in (12.75 cm) high

$500–700   **MI**

Russel Wright American Modern-line water pitcher manufactured by Steubenville. It is finished in Coral, one of the company's early colors. *Late 1930s*

11¾ in (30 cm) high

$120–200   **MI**

Jewelry

Art Deco jewelry ranges from some of the most luxurious and elegant fine jewels ever made to inexpensive mass-produced plastic "cocktail" items. As with most categories of Art Deco, design and production were centered in France, but indigenous modern styles also evolved in Scandinavia, the United States, and elsewhere, including Mexico.

The interwar years saw a leap in the popularity of jewelry and a wealth of new forms, including clips for dresses, strands for hats, shoulders, and arms, and elongated necklaces in flapper mode. Inexpensive jewelry, such as glass creations by René Lalique (*see pp.80–83*), neo-Baroque semiprecious fantasies by Coco Chanel (*see p.153*), and molded plastics, introduced "costume" to a world familiar only with paste, or imitation gemstones. Known as "cocktail" in the period, this category represents the largest source for modern collectors. Costume jewelry collecting trends are still unfolding as new research uncovers forgotten firms and designers, many of whom signed their work.

ACCESSORIZING IN THE AGE OF ELEGANCE

Fine Art Deco jewelry falls into two principal categories: gemstone and Modernist. Gemstone jewelry was made by all leading firms using the abundance of diamonds and colored stones that flooded into the West by the 1920s, often set in platinum, which usurped gold as a fashionable setting. Value is gauged by carat weight and maker's mark, above style.

Modernist French jewelry was made by smaller firms, headed by Georges Fouquet, and individualists such as Jean Dunand and Gerard Sandoz. It features innovative materials, such as glass and enamels, sometimes set with precious metal or gems. Demand is limited to Art Deco or jewelry collectors, and value depends on attribution and current fashions.

Outside France, Georg Jensen (*see pp.162–63*) and the Danish School made distinctive modern silver jewelry. Their style was copied in the United States and Mexico, where native culture and turquoise were added to create a unique blend of Art Deco jewelry.

English openwork platinum brooch of stepped, triangular form, set with 59 diamonds of graduated size and two large, faceted, prong-set aquamarines. With original box (not shown). *c. 1920. 2¼ in (6.5 cm) long* **$12,000–15,000 KAU**

Silver-plated lapel clip comprising openwork of rectangular form set with four rows of circular-cut rhinestones divided by three horizontal rows of square-cut ruby-colored rhinestones. Beneath these is a slightly elongated slab of black bakelite with chamfered edges. *c. 1930 3 in (7.5 cm) high* **$180–220 PAC**

FRENCH GEMSTONE STYLE

Most French Art Deco gemstone jewelers were well established by the 1920s, and many still thrive today. The main ones include: Boucheron (founded 1858); Cartier (1847); Chaumet (1780); Mauboussin (1827), which favored exotic, colored stones; and Van Cleef & Arpels, founded in Paris in 1906 and active in New York from 1929. They made heavy use of diamonds, contrasted with sapphires or rubies and set geometrically in platinum. Diamond bracelets were especially in demand, as were parures, or matching sets with necklace, earrings, brooch, and ring. Jewelry of this type was (and still is) popular in the United States, where it was retailed by French jewelers in their own boutiques, or by Americans, notably Tiffany & Co. and its Fifth Avenue neighbor Harry Winston, which opened in 1932.

Most examples of gemstone jewelry are discreetly marked and may have original leather boxes. Smaller jewelers copied this taste using lower standards of manufacture and stones. Jewelry of this quality is typically unsigned and affordable, and it has been reproduced in recent years.

The Art Deco gemstone style continued into the 1950s, when geometric arrangement gave way to organic patterns and larger, colored stones.

Gabrielle "Coco" Chanel (here in a 1930s Cecil Beaton photograph) is one of the legendary stars of French couture. Credited by Christian Dior with revolutionizing fashion "with a black pullover and ten rows of pearls," Chanel also promoted costume jewelry as chic.

INDIVIDUAL CREATIONS

Outstanding French artists who designed and made their own jewels include Georges Fouquet (1862–1957), who began under Art Nouveau influence, and his son Jean Fouquet (1899–1964), who started his career in 1919 and favored pure geometry. The best Modernist Fouquet combines bold, African-inspired images with Cubism, using glass, onyx, coral, and enamels after designs by Jean Fouquet, Eric Bagge (*see p.35*), and André

KEY POINTS

In the 1920s and 1930s, new forms of jewelry emerged to complement changes in fashion: more prominent earrings for shorter hair; brooches for lapeled jackets; and ladies' watches. Precious metals and stones were still used in high-end pieces, but jewelry made from base metals, plastics, and rhinestones also became fashionable. Form and decoration were inspired by the Machine Age, Cubist and Minimalist art, and Egyptian and Mesoamerican vocabularies of ornament.

Gold-washed silver scarab pin filled with alternated sections of turquoise, purple, green, red, and white enamel, and a single, carved, ruby-red glass cabochon. Other popular Egyptian-revival motifs included snakes, palm trees, and sphinxes—the latter with the body of a lion and the head of a pharaoh, ram, hawk, or falcon. *1920s 1½ in (4 cm) wide* **$300–400 MARA**

Leveille. The Japanese-inspired jewelry by metalworker Jean Dunand (1877–1942) from 1924 until the mid-1930s is rare and notable. He worked mostly in contrasting red and black lacquer, often decorated with eggshell fragments in the *coquille d'oeuf* technique. Other makers of note include Jean Desprez (1889–1980), Raymond Templier (1891–1968), who specialized in starkly modern platinum and diamond or enamel creations, and Gerard Sandoz (b. 1902), who designed from about 1920 to 1934. Sandoz grew up in a Parisian jewelry family and developed an evolved Arts and Crafts style combining geometric patterns with mostly semiprecious materials.

Celebrated as the world's leading Art Nouveau jeweler by 1900, René Lalique turned to glassmaking as a second career in 1912. His glass jewelry, offered in hundreds of designs until the late 1930s, was inexpensive and fashionable with the flapper generation. Several original designs are reproduced today by the modern Lalique Company.

WORLDWIDE STYLES

A conservative British Art Deco style emerged briefly in the 1930s, including men's accessories shaped largely by Alfred Dunhill (est. 1893) and the London retailer Aspreys (active from 1848). Led by the Danish silversmith Georg Jensen, a thriving jewelry movement that brought a Modernist slant to the earlier style produced throughout the period in Copenhagen.

Most jewelers in the United States copied the French gemstone style, and it was still common for fashionable and wealthy Americans to purchase their jewelry in France. An interesting Art Deco style also grew in Mexico, where artist-craftsmen, some native and some from the United States, made silver, enamel, and turquoise jewelry by hand in traditional centers, notably Taxco. The best of this was made by William Spratling (1900–67).

English platinum brooch of half-moon clasp and scrolling fabriclike form. It is filled with pavé-set diamonds of circular cut and graduated size, contrasted with two adjacent curved rows of sapphire cabochons and two rows of baguette-cut sapphires. *Late 1920s. 2 in (5 cm) high* **$3,000–5,000 WW**

Silver bracelet by the French designer Gerard Sandoz. The geometric design is achieved by the application of black, gray, and red enamels, contrasted with white eggshell lacquer. Sandoz's geometric designs often have a machinelike quality, while many others are inspired by Cubist fine art. *c. 1925. 2¼ in (5.5 cm) wide* **$40,000–60,000 JES**

American watch brooch with a rectangular silvered face in a silver setting of winged and stepped geometric form. The latter is set with circular-cut diamonds of graduated size, square-cut emeralds and sapphires, and baguettes of black onyx. *c. 1925 2¼ in (5.75 cm) wide* **$25,000–40,000 JP**

Louis François Cartier (1819–1904), who took over the workshops of his mentor Adolphe Picard, founded Cartier in Paris in 1847.

Cartier moved to its current headquarters on Rue de la Paix in 1898, expanding to London in 1902 and New York in 1909.

Art Deco jewelry was made under the leadership of Alfred Cartier (1841–1925) and his three sons: Louis, Pierre, and Jacques.

Cartier jewelry was made in Paris and New York during the Art Deco period.

Cartier

Called "the king of jewelers" by Edward VII, a favorite patron and collector, Alfred Cartier created a firm that drew on generations of excellence and prestige to establish itself as the ultimate Art Deco luxury retailer.

By the death of patriarch Alfred Cartier in 1925, Cartier boutiques operated throughout the affluent world, including the countries around the Persian Gulf. The Paris headquarters were run by Louis Cartier, the New York store by Pierre (1878–1965), and the London branch by the youngest brother, Jacques (1884–1942).

Family and corporate unity resulted in consistent styles and standards, designed to attract the wealthiest clientele with a taste for Modernism. Cartier used a variety of innovative materials, including black onyx, Chinese jade, and enamels. Designers were mostly anonymous, in the old tradition of French jewelry houses. Cartier Art Deco has few rivals in quality of execution and boldness in design, however, and is easily distinguished. All pieces are stamped with firm and French *poincons*, and fakes are rare. Original boxes are a valuable addition to any Cartier jewel.

In addition to jewelry, the firm also made vanity and cigarette cases, objets d'art in the manner of Fabergé, watches, and clocks for home and travel, notably the famous Art Deco Mystery clocks, with invisible movements.

Above: 1920 pendant bar pin in black and white enameled pot metal, flanked by a pair of diamonds. With its original case (not shown). *1920. 2 in (5 cm) wide* **$1,500–2,200 JHB**

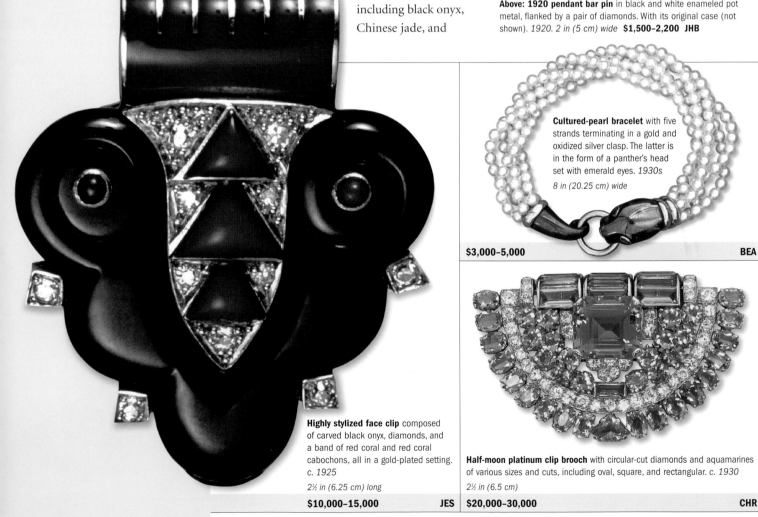

Cultured-pearl bracelet with five strands terminating in a gold and oxidized silver clasp. The latter is in the form of a panther's head set with emerald eyes. *1930s*
8 in (20.25 cm) wide

$3,000–5,000 **BEA**

Highly stylized face clip composed of carved black onyx, diamonds, and a band of red coral and red coral cabochons, all in a gold-plated setting. *c. 1925*
2½ in (6.25 cm) long

$10,000–15,000 **JES**

Half-moon platinum clip brooch with circular-cut diamonds and aquamarines of various sizes and cuts, including oval, square, and rectangular. *c. 1930*
2½ in (6.5 cm)

$20,000–30,000 **CHR**

Chanel

Few individuals have injected as much fantasy and flair into modern culture as Coco Chanel, whose legacy still dictates policy within the company she founded in 1912.

Gabrielle "Coco" Chanel (1883–1971) began her remarkable career as a milliner before World War I, and by the early 1920s she had established her signature style of simple and comfortable but elegant fashion. She claimed to design only clothes she would want to wear herself, a statement equally applicable to her jewelry.

Although her fashions, and the perennially popular No. 5 fragrance she introduced in 1922, are considered the ultimate in luxury, Chanel jewelry was always intentionally in the realm of costume, a concept she is credited with inventing and popularizing. "When you make imitation jewelry, you always make it bigger," she once said.

Chanel was attracted to jewelry design as early as 1911, under the influence of Paul Iribe, who designed for Jean Lanvin, among others. She did not launch her Variations line until the early 1930s, however, when post-Depression culture allowed new acceptance of inexpensive materials in jewelry and fashion. By then, Chanel moved in the artistic circles of Pablo Picasso, Salvador Dalí, and Jean Cocteau (for whom she designed movie costumes). Her jewelry captures their surrealistic world, inspired by a Baroque and Byzantine past.

Above: Rare frog pin with green, black, and red enamel on a lead casting and pavé-set rhinestones on the eyes and webbed feet. *1927*
2¼ in (6 cm) long **$2,500–4,000 CRIS**

Rare palm-tree pin with a sombreroed figure. It is decorated in red and pink enameling and rhinestone baguettes on a gold-plated pot-metal casting. *1930s*
3 in (7.5 cm) high

$4,000–5,000   **DD**

Rare gold-plated pin manufactured in France. It is in the shape of a leaf made up of a burst of six-pointed stars of graduated size—smaller at the tip, larger at the stalk. *1930s*
4¼ in (11 cm) long

$3,000–4,000   **WAIN**

Highly stylized floral pin with a gold-plated metal casting set with green, blue, and red *pâte-de-verre* stones and beads. These are interspersed with rhinestones of graduated size and terminate with faux pearls and two larger red *pâte-de-verre* cabochons. *1920s*
4¼ in (10.5 cm) high

$2,000–3,000   **BY**

French Jewelry

During the Belle-Epoque (1890–1914), Paris became established as the center of modern jewelry design, with luminaries such as René Lalique, Henri Vever, and the Fouquet family. French Art Deco jewelry, made almost exclusively in Paris, is considered the world's finest in design and manufacture, particularly if attributable to a prominent maker. Lavish platinum and diamond jewelry was popular during the period, often pavé set and geometrically arranged with colored gemstones, onyx, or carved Chinese jade. Despite the sheer brilliance of these jewels, a simple enamel design in Modernist taste by a leading designer may outstrip them in value. Signed pieces are most highly sought-after, but unsigned, wearable fine jewels, particularly bracelets, also compete well.

Art Deco jewelry was produced into the 1950s. Modern reproductions also exist, but they tend to be of inferior standard in manufacture and gemstone, and spuriously signed. Original boxes are a big asset, often indicating the retailer or manufacturer.

Very high-quality clip (one of two halves) with diamonds of graduated size and various cuts set in sterling-silver castings. *1920s*

2½ in (6.25 cm) wide

$90,000–120,000 (the set)　　　JP

Vase-of-flowers pin with carved Fruit Salad pastes and clear-crystal rhinestones set in a sterling-silver casting. *Early 1920s*

2 in (5 cm) high

$300–400　　　CRIS

Pair of ear clips with an oviform jade stone and a semicircle of small diamonds set in a gold and platinum casting. *c. 1930*

¾ in (2 cm) wide

$3,000–4,000　　　BEA

Sterling-silver bracelet set with crossed and interlaced bands of clear-crystal rhinestones. Along its center, these are contrasted with four ruby-colored paste cabochons. The bracelet is secured with a V-spring clasp. *Late 1920s*

7½ in (19 cm) long

$900–1,200　　　RG

Platinum-setting bracelet with a central medallion flanked by a pair of loops. In addition to the rows of natural pearls, the bracelet is set with chaton-cut diamonds. Both are contrasted in the medallion and loops with onyx highlights. *Early 1920s*

7½ in (19 cm) long

$1,200–1,800　　　JP

Silver shield-shape pendant with a geometric pattern of dark- and light-blue enamel and arrowheads of clear-crystal rhinestones. *1930s*

2¼ in (6 cm) long

$1,200–1,800　　　TR

Sterling-silver bracelet with foliate and floral motifs in deep relief, and with a large, faceted, emerald-green paste at its center. *c. 1930*

1¾ in (4.5 cm) high

$1,200–1,800　　　TR

Rectangular gold brooch with geometrical-design openwork. It is set with more than 80 diamonds in various sizes and has a large brilliant-cut diamond at its center. The diamonds are contrasted with pear-cut and baguette-cut blue-sapphire highlights. *1930s*

2¼ in (5.5 cm) wide

$1,800–3,000　　　KAU

Rare platinum ovoid brooch by Marchak of Paris. Edged with black enamel, it is set with a five-carat, sugarloaf-cut emerald and onyx flowerheads on a bed of pavé-set diamonds. *1925*

2¼ in (6 cm) wide

$30,000–40,000 **MACK**

Platinum-link bracelet secured with a V-spring clasp and set along its center with blue-sapphire baguettes flanked by trios of diamonds. *1920*

7½ in (19 cm) long

$60,000–90,000 **JP**

Unsigned bib necklace composed of staple-linked, matt-finish, gold-plated sections of various geometric forms. The three largest sections are decorated with triangles of black enameling. *1930s*

17 in (43 cm) internal circumference

$700–900 **CRIS**

Boucheron

This historic French firm was founded in 1858 by Frederic Boucheron (1830–1902) and still operates from Place Vendôme, home to the luxury trade in Paris. From its inception, Boucheron set the standard for generations of fine jewelers in style and quality. The firm has always specialized in gemstones, and most examples are clearly marked with a stamp. Post–World War I fashions saw a demand for bracelets and brooches that Boucheron met with glittering success. Platinum became the metal of choice by the early 1920s, usurping gold, and diamonds were typically cut baguette or *en baton* (as rectangular rods), often contrasted with sapphires. In the 1920s Boucheron introduced "white jewelry," setting just diamonds into platinum. Many French and American Art Deco jewelers copied the Boucheron style.

Scrolling floral-spray fur clip (one of a pair). The platinum setting is encrusted with diamonds of graduated size, many of which are pavé set and three of which are large and emerald-cut. It has some damage. *c. 1935*

2½ in (6.25 cm) wide

$30,000–40,000 (the pair) **FRE**

Boucheron hinged bangle-bracelet cast in gold and platinum. It features two bucklelike terminals encrusted with brilliant-cut diamonds framing four rows of invisibly set baguette- and square-cut blue sapphires. Boucheron also designed a clip in this style. *1930s*

7½ in (19 cm) internal circumference

$40,000–50,000 **JES**

Interlocking ring-and-bar pin made by Bonnet of Paris for Van Cleef & Arpels. The platinum bar is set with 14 four-carat, caliber-cut Burmese blue sapphires, while the platinum rings are set with 84 six-carat, round-cut diamonds. A large round-cut diamond centers the bar. *c. 1930*

2 in (5 cm) wide

$15,000–20,000   FRE

Hanging-basket-of-flowers pin with ruby-, sapphire-, and emerald-colored Fruit Salad paste flowerheads. Each flower has a tiny faux-pearl center. The basket itself, a sterling-silver casting, is set with good-quality round- and baguette-cut clear-crystal rhinestones. *Early 1920s*

1½ in (4 cm) wide

$300–400   CRIS

High-quality articulated platinum bracelet set with diamonds in various cuts, including square and round, and with five large carved emerald stones along its center. *Late 1920s*

7 in (17.5 cm) long

$90,000–120,000   NBLM

Bow-shaped platinum clip of excellent quality, set with swirls, arcs, rows, and clusters of diamonds. These are in various cuts, including baguette, rectangular, chaton, and rose, and they are contrasted with a perimeter arc of nine prong-set ruby stones. *1930s*

2¼ in (5.5 cm) wide

$10,000–15,000   MACK

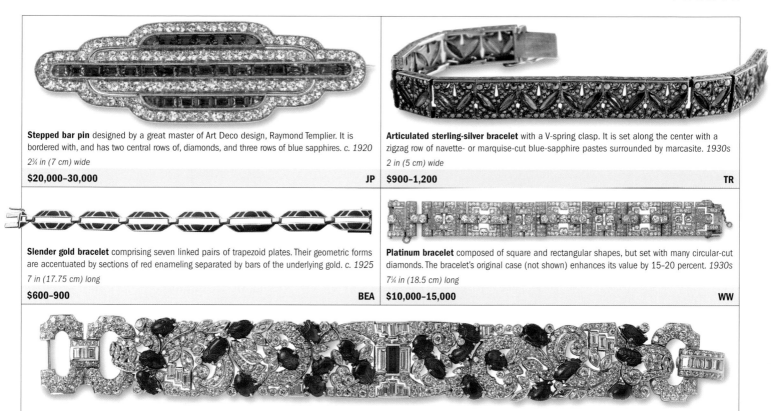

Stepped bar pin designed by a great master of Art Deco design, Raymond Templier. It is bordered with, and has two central rows of, diamonds, and three rows of blue sapphires. *c. 1920*
2¾ in (7 cm) wide

$20,000–30,000   **JP**

Articulated sterling-silver bracelet with a V-spring clasp. It is set along the center with a zigzag row of navette- or marquise-cut blue-sapphire pastes surrounded by marcasite. *1930s*
2 in (5 cm) wide

$900–1,200   **TR**

Slender gold bracelet comprising seven linked pairs of trapezoid plates. Their geometric forms are accentuated by sections of red enameling separated by bars of the underlying gold. *c. 1925*
7 in (17.75 cm) long

$600–900   **BEA**

Platinum bracelet composed of square and rectangular shapes, but set with many circular-cut diamonds. The bracelet's original case (not shown) enhances its value by 15–20 percent. *1930s*
7¼ in (18.5 cm) long

$10,000–15,000   **WW**

Articulated platinum bracelet with diamonds of various cuts set to simulate foliate motifs. These are interspersed throughout with prong-set rubies hand-cut to simulate fruits. *c. 1935*
7 in (17.75 cm) long

$90,000–120,000   **MACK**

Exceptionally elegant articulated platinum bracelet with a pierced, bucklelike centerpiece and a V-spring clasp. It is set all over with small diamonds of various cuts (including chaton), contrasted with twin, full-length bands of hand-cut green emeralds. *1920*
7 in (17.75 cm) long

$100,000–130,000   **JP**

Van Cleef & Arpels

Founded in 1906 by Alfred Van Cleef and his brother-in-law Charles Arpels, this luxury firm still operates alongside its biggest rival, Boucheron, on Paris's Place Vendôme. Van Cleef has always been simpler and more modern than Boucheron and produced some of the finest designs in Art Deco jewelry. In the 1920s Van Cleef introduced the "invisible setting," using stones precisely cut to slot into a parallel setting, giving the appearance of having no support. Colored Southeast Asian stones—in particular rubies, sapphires, and emeralds—were popular, together with Chinese jade elements and black onyx. Since 1939 Van Cleef has also operated in New York.

Bucklelike brooch of silver casting and set with round-cut clear-crystal rhinestones of graduated size. These are configured in straight and diagonal rows and as four stylized flowerheads. The centers of the latter are set with four jade-green paste cabochons. *1930s*
3¼ in (8.5 cm) long

$300–500   **RG**

Van Cleef & Arpels platinum ring of overtly Machine-Age, chamfered spherical form, with an equatorial channel set with caliber-cut rubies. *1940s*
1 in (2.5 cm) wide

$9,000–12,000   **MACK**

Theodor Fahrner

Pforzheim, a German jewelry center since the late Middle Ages, was never more active than during the long career of Theodor Fahrner, who successfully marketed affordable Art Deco jewelry to a demanding world.

Theodor Fahrner (1868–1928) was well placed to compete in the growing market for fashionable, nonprecious jewelry. This field had gained popularity during the Art Nouveau and Craftsman years under the influence of René Lalique (*see pp.80–83*) in Paris and Georg Jensen (*see pp.162–63*) in Copenhagen. Fahrner's manufactory in Pforzheim had long produced high-quality decorative jewelry, but it began employing talented outside designers in the 1890s, a tradition continued in the 20th century. Before World War I, designers included Patriz Huber (1878–1902) and Ludwig Knupper (active 1902–05), a leader in the Jugendstijl movement. The most prominent, however, was architect Josef Maria Olbrich (1867–1908), who trained in Austria under Otto Wagner and helped found the Vienna Secession. Olbrich was an important pioneer of the Modern movement; he planted the seeds of Art Deco at Fahrner with his abstract, clean-lined forms and use of geometry. As well as jewelry, Olbrich designed in many other fields, from buildings and furnishings to automobiles.

A PERIOD OF CHANGE

After World War I, Germany began a process of economic and political reconstruction that allowed the birth of movements as extreme as the Bauhaus and National Socialism. Fahrner steered a cultural middle course through the interwar years, gaining an international clientele for the Art Deco jewelry he made with high standards of design, manufacture, and efficiency in Pforzheim.

Above: Silver-gilt brooch with soldered corded wire, blue cut-glass triangles, and a central amazonite bar. *1927. 2¼ in (5.5 cm) wide*
$1,800–2,200 TR

GEOMETRIC DESIGNS

The use of pure geometry in design is a uniquely Art Deco concept, born in reaction to the florid Art Nouveau taste and nurtured by the compelling desire to control ornament that encompassed and unified the Modern movement. Fahrner's Art Deco jewelry was made to suit international tastes. The geometric variety responded equally to a contemporary German pursuit of order, Europe's exploration of Aztec and Inca cultures, and American Skyscraper style, which imposed architectural lines on everyday objects and made geometry chic and modern. Most geometric designs date from the 1930s and are made in silver set with starkly contrasting colored stones or marcasite. These are most favored by modern Fahrner collectors.

Silver and marcasite pendant set with a band of coral squares above six rectangular and three elongated baguette-faceted stones of black onyx. *c. 1930. 2½ in (6 cm) long*
$5,000–7,000 TR

Print advertisement for Fahrner-Schmucks jewels originally placed in *Die Dame* magazine. It promotes the spring 1933 collection of high-quality yet affordable Art Deco-style jewelry.

QUALITÄT UND STIL
NEBEN PREISWÜRDIGKEIT
SIND DIE MERKMALE DES
FAHRNER-SCHMUCKS
FRÜHJAHR 1933

SIGNATURE MARKS

Chased silver-gilt pendant embellished with marcasite fruit and berry forms, around a large, prong-set blue-glass stone. Its hexagonal shape was combined in other pieces with turquoise enameling, smoky quartz, and coral. *1930s* *2¼ in (5.5 cm) wide* **$300–500 BMN**

MARKS

Unlike most Art Deco jewelry of this quality, the majority of Fahrner's work is clearly marked, normally with a series of stamps indicating the maker and standard of precious metal. Fahrner began adding marks in the late 19th century, and much of his Art Nouveau or Jugendstijl jewelry is also readily identifiable. The mark may be limited to an impressed "F" accompanying the mark of a retailer or distributor, normally "MB & Co." for Murrle Bennett, whose name may also appear on original boxes for Fahrner jewels. Small items such as earrings may bear only a stamped "TF" in block capitals within a circle. Larger items of the Art Deco period are usually fully marked, with Fahrner's name, "TF" in a circle, and a number indicating the standard of the silver. This varies from 935 to 925 (sterling standard) and occasionally 835. Gold is normally of a low standard. The French trademark-protective "Deposé" was commonly stamped on Jugendstijl and Art Deco Fahrner jewelry sold in Europe.

FAVORED MATERIALS

Most Fahrner jewelry was made in silver, but low-grade gold, steel, and gilt-metal wire were also used as ground. Throughout the period, Fahrner relied heavily on cut marcasite, a white iron pyrite used since the 18th century as a substitute for diamonds. Marcasite was generally preferred to the similar cut steel, since it did not oxidize. Translucent stones such as amethyst and aquamarine were less popular after World War I, replaced by opaque glass, onyx, enamel or quartz, and more exotic minerals mostly from South America, Russia, and Africa. Colors, normally supplied in semiprecious stone, seed pearl, or enamel, were chosen to meet modern fashions. As a consequence, lapis lazuli or blue glass adorned Egyptian-style jewels after the discovery

of King Tutankhamun's tomb in 1922, while the fascination with Aztec and Inca cultures in the late 1920s saw a proliferation of black and red combinations. By the mid-1930s, one popular line was of thinly gauged silver contrasted with simple black onyx or enamel, in keeping with the post-Depression taste for simplicity.

By the advent of the Art Deco period, Fahrner jewelry was available internationally, due in part to the marketing and distribution efforts of wholesale jewelers Murrle Bennett & Co., based in London.

Fahrner pieces can be found throughout Europe and the United States today and are not uncommon, but there is no more supply and high quality and comprehensive marks are key ingredients of increasing demand.

USE OF MATERIALS

Theodor Fahrner developed the use of semiprecious and hard stones by the 1880s and can be credited with popularizing their use internationally during the interwar years. The setting of these materials in jewelry and silver objects dates from ancient times but first returned to fashion during the European Arts and Crafts movement, notably in the various Norse and Celtic revival movements in Great Britain, Scandinavia, and Northern Europe. Fahrner typically set semiprecious stones in contrast with marcasite.

SEMIPRECIOUS STONES

Fahrner employed an extraordinary variety of semiprecious stones, all widely available in Europe by the 1920s thanks to the efforts of large wholesale distributors and increased trade with Asia and South America. Popular stones included opal, chalcedony, turquoise, lapis lazuli, amazonite, amethyst, black and colored onyx, and all manner of quartz, typically set in silver. Fahrner's semiprecious stone jewels were less commercially successful in the United States, where they competed with the more popular silver and turquoise native jewelry from Mexico and the American southwest.

Silver-gilt bar pin with openwork fruiting foliage around an aventurine quartz cabochon and flanked by two triangles of black enamel. *c. 1925. 2¾ in (7 cm) long* **$1,000–1,500 RBRG**

Pair of pendant earrings in the form of three graduated silver-and-marcasite shields, linked by graduated coral baguettes and terminating in faceted black onyx lozenges. *Late 1920s*

2 in (5 cm) long

$2,000–3,000   **TR**

Shield-shape brooch of pierced silver casting decorated with dark-blue enameling and gilt borders and enlivened with lapis stone and faux-amethyst cabochons. *1930s*

2 in (5 cm) long

$1,200–2,000   **TR**

Silver-and-marcasite teardrop pendant with applied curlicues set against green enameling and encircling a ring of seed pearls set around a green-glass cabochon. *1920s*

2 in (5 cm) long

$700–1,000   **TR**

Silver-framed pin set with two large and eight small pearls around a gold-framed, oval ivory centerpiece pierced with a stylized geometric floral pattern around an emerald-colored glass cabochon. *Late 1920s*

2¼ in (5.75 cm) long

$800–1,200   **TR**

Silver-framed bar pin pierced at the ends and chased at the sides with stylized floral motifs with marcasite highlights, all around a large aquamarine glass baguette. *1930s*

2 in (5 cm) wide

$800–1,200   **TR**

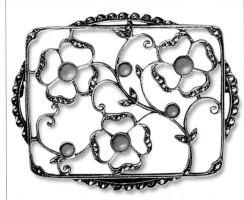

Silver-and-marcasite framed pin with stylized stems, leaves, and flowerheads enlivened with matt rock crystals and six turquoise cabochons of graduated size. *Late 1920s*

1½ in (3.75 cm) wide

$2,000–3,000   **TR**

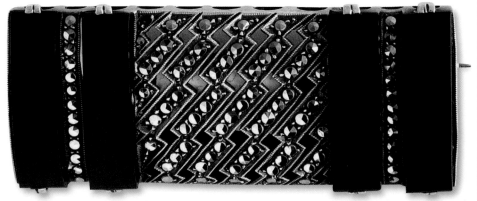

Silver-framed bar pin of rectangular form. It has a zigzag silver, marcasite, black enamel, and matt rock-crystal center panel flanked by pairs of black onyx rectangular bars in turn divided by rows of marcasite balls. *1930s*

2¼ in (6 cm) wide

$4,000–6,000   **TR**

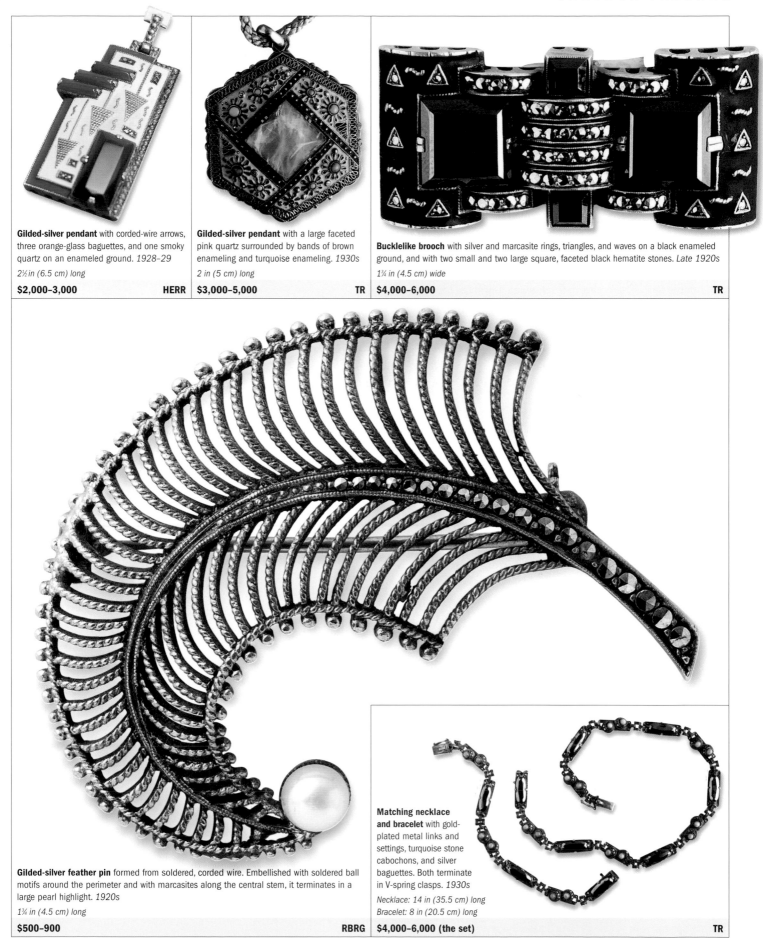

Gilded-silver pendant with corded-wire arrows, three orange-glass baguettes, and one smoky quartz on an enameled ground. *1928–29*

2½ in (6.5 cm) long

$2,000–3,000   HERR

Gilded-silver pendant with a large faceted pink quartz surrounded by bands of brown enameling and turquoise enameling. *1930s*

2 in (5 cm) long

$3,000–5,000   TR

Bucklelike brooch with silver and marcasite rings, triangles, and waves on a black enameled ground, and with two small and two large square, faceted black hematite stones. *Late 1920s*

1¾ in (4.5 cm) wide

$4,000–6,000   TR

Gilded-silver feather pin formed from soldered, corded wire. Embellished with soldered ball motifs around the perimeter and with marcasites along the central stem, it terminates in a large pearl highlight. *1920s*

1¾ in (4.5 cm) long

$500–900   RBRG

Matching necklace and bracelet with gold-plated metal links and settings, turquoise stone cabochons, and silver baguettes. Both terminate in V-spring clasps. *1930s*

Necklace: 14 in (35.5 cm) long
Bracelet: 8 in (20.5 cm) long

$4,000–6,000 (the set)   TR

Georg Jensen

The unique style fashioned at Georg Jensen's factory on Copenhagen's Ragnagade from 1918 is found mostly on flatware and holloware. However, jewelry has only recently become popular and may still be found at a reasonable price.

Jensen jewelry is of high quality and was never inexpensive, but it was mass-produced and is not especially rare. By the time of his death in 1935, Jensen had showrooms in Brussels, Barcelona, Berlin, Copenhagen, Geneva, London, New York, and Paris. The style was widely copied by silversmiths in Scandinavia, the United States, and Mexico, and some models were made into the post–World War II years, so close attention to Jensen's meticulous marking system is important. Brooches are most common, and attributable to designers through reference numbers. Examples by Arno Malinowski show the evolution in design from Nordic imagery into fresh Modernism. Bracelets are scarcer and more popular today, as are pieces mixing silver and stones or amber.

Openwork silver brooch by Arno Malinowski (design number 256), with an oval frame encompassing a deer kneeling among stylized flowers and foliage. *c. 1930s*
1¾ in (4.5 cm) wide

$500–900   SF

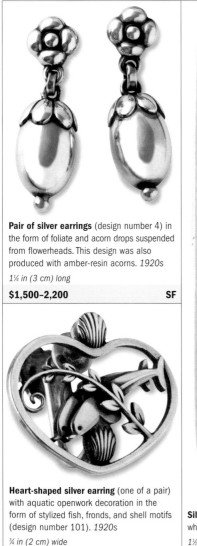

Pair of silver earrings (design number 4) in the form of foliate and acorn drops suspended from flowerheads. This design was also produced with amber-resin acorns. *1920s*
1¼ in (3 cm) long

$1,500–2,200   SF

Heart-shaped silver earring (one of a pair) with aquatic openwork decoration in the form of stylized fish, fronds, and shell motifs (design number 101). *1920s*
¾ in (2 cm) wide

$900–1,500 (the pair)   SF

Silver openwork brooch by Arno Malinowski (design number 250), of square form. It is filled in the center with a large, diagonal ear of wheat, which is flanked by a pair of fat little birds—also stylized—one in flight and the other perched. *c. 1930s*
1½ in (4 cm) wide

$500–1,000   SF

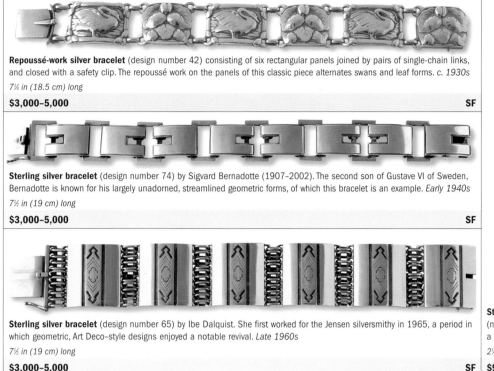

Repoussé-work silver bracelet (design number 42) consisting of six rectangular panels joined by pairs of single-chain links, and closed with a safety clip. The repoussé work on the panels of this classic piece alternates swans and leaf forms. *c. 1930s*

7¼ in (18.5 cm) long

$3,000–5,000 SF

Sterling silver bracelet (design number 74) by Sigvard Bernadotte (1907–2002). The second son of Gustave VI of Sweden, Bernadotte is known for his largely unadorned, streamlined geometric forms, of which this bracelet is an example. *Early 1940s*

7½ in (19 cm) long

$3,000–5,000 SF

Sterling silver bracelet (design number 65) by Ibe Dalquist. She first worked for the Jensen silversmithy in 1965, a period in which geometric, Art Deco–style designs enjoyed a notable revival. *Late 1960s*

7½ in (19 cm) long

$3,000–5,000 SF

Sterling silver pendant brooch by Harald Nielsen. This design (number 217b) is modeled as a bunch of grapes hanging from a pair of leaves partially obscuring other grapes. *Mid-1940s*

2½ in (6.5 cm) long

$900–1,500 PC

Sterling silver bracelet (design number 86) by Harald Nielsen. It is comprised, along its articulated length, of alternating pairs and trios of navettes—or marquise-shaped forms—and each is flanked on either side by quartets of tiny, berrylike balls. *1940s*

7½ in (19 cm) long

$2,000–3,000 SF

Skonvirke

The Danish Skonvirke (literally "beautiful work") movement is mostly associated with jewelry-making in the Arts and Crafts tradition, beginning in the 1890s. It later evolved into a unique Art Deco style and flourished until World War II. The best known Skonvirke jewelry-maker was Jensen himself, but dozens of other names appear in marks, from individual craftsmen and women to larger companies, notably Mogens Ballin (1871–1914), an early employer and mentor of Jensen, and Bernard Hertz. Individuals include Kay Bojeson (1886–1958), S. Jacobsen, and Evald Nielsen (1879–1958), who was prolific during the 1930s in a style comparable to Jensen's.

Skonvirke openwork silver brooch designed by Evald Nielsen with a dove perched among foliage, and set with three ruby glass cabochons of graduated size. Nielsen's designs embraced both Arts and Crafts traditions and Art Deco style. *c. 1930*

2 in (5 cm) wide

$500–700 VDB

European Jewelry

By the interwar years, much jewelry in Europe was mass-produced to satisfy huge new demand—both locally and from the United States, where many European firms had established footholds by 1920. The majority, and usually best quality, was made in France, but most countries made fashionable jewels. The largest producers were in Germany, at the traditional goldsmithing centers of Augsburg or Pforzheim, near the Black Forest, which made mainly silver, semiprecious stone, and marcasite work. Similar work was also done in Austria. Most continental Art Deco jewelry interprets fashionable Parisian designs, especially the work of Cartier, whose "tutti-frutti" bracelets were widely copied with lower-grade diamonds and sumptuous colored stones. Much of the work popular today is starkly geometric. Interesting silver jewelry was also made in Scandinavia as an extension of Georg Jensen's style, and well-made glass-beaded "flapper" necklaces were mass-produced in Czechoslovakia, using Bohemian and Venetian beads.

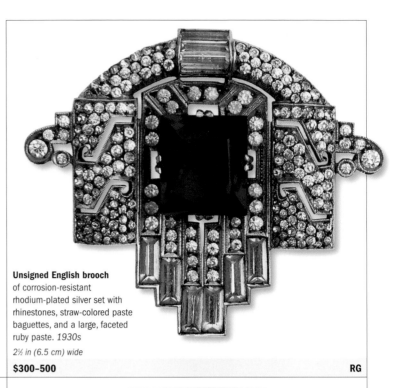

Unsigned English brooch of corrosion-resistant rhodium-plated silver set with rhinestones, straw-colored paste baguettes, and a large, faceted ruby paste. *1930s*

2½ in (6.5 cm) wide

$300–500 RG

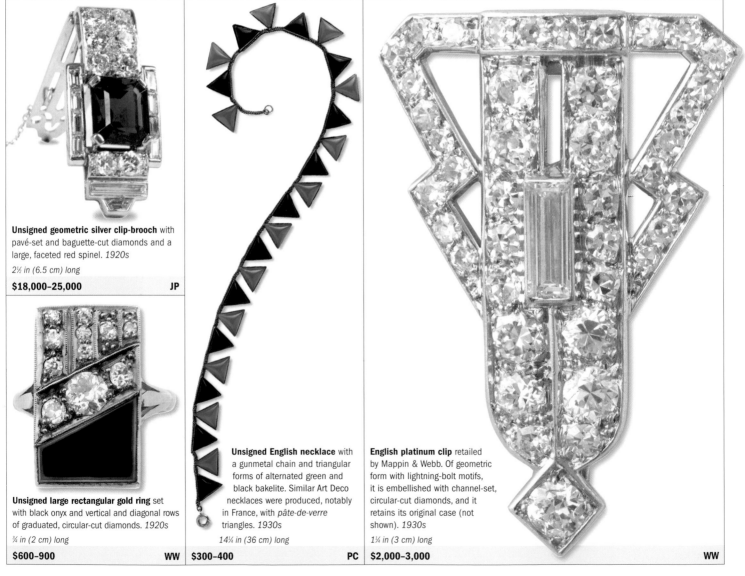

Unsigned geometric silver clip-brooch with pavé-set and baguette-cut diamonds and a large, faceted red spinel. *1920s*

2½ in (6.5 cm) long

$18,000–25,000 JP

Unsigned large rectangular gold ring set with black onyx and vertical and diagonal rows of graduated, circular-cut diamonds. *1920s*

¾ in (2 cm) long

$600–900 WW

Unsigned English necklace with a gunmetal chain and triangular forms of alternated green and black bakelite. Similar Art Deco necklaces were produced, notably in France, with *pâte-de-verre* triangles. *1930s*

14¼ in (36 cm) long

$300–400 PC

English platinum clip retailed by Mappin & Webb. Of geometric form with lightning-bolt motifs, it is embellished with channel-set, circular-cut diamonds, and it retains its original case (not shown). *1930s*

1¼ in (3 cm) long

$2,000–3,000 WW

164

Unsigned English silver bracelet with openwork decoration in the form of stylized floral and foliate motifs, set at intervals along their length with oval, jade-green glass cabochons. *1920s*

7 in (18 cm) long

$400-600   **RG**

Unsigned platinum bracelet, possibly of Dutch origin, with seven articulated, openwork panels of chamfered rectangular form set with diamonds of graduated size and various cuts. *1920s*

7¾ in (20 cm) long

$12,000-18,000   **NBLM**

Unsigned platinum "duette," or double-clip, in the form of a pair of stylized plant forms set with circular-cut diamonds of graduated size and eight ruby beads. They can be worn together, as here, or separately. *1920s*

1¾ in (4.5 cm) long

$12,000-18,000   **MACK**

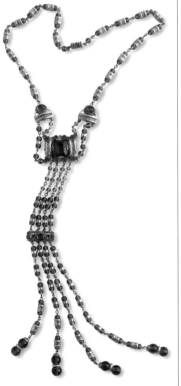

Czechoslovakian flapper necklace strung with round-, oval-, and square-cut glass beads, and with gilt-metal links and spacers. *1920s*

Pendants: 8½ in (22 cm) long

$300-400   **ECLEC**

A CLOSER LOOK

Sterling silver bracelet designed by Wiwen Nilsson for Anders Nilsson of Lund, Sweden, and set with a large faceted rock crystal flanked by two slabs of black onyx. *1930s. 2½ in (6.25 cm) wide*
$6,000-7,000 JES

Elegant, understated contrasts of color—between clear rock crystal, silver, and black onyx—enhance the precision and simplicity of form characteristic of Nilsson's work

Sharp angles and clean lines, uninterrupted by elaborate or unnecessary ornament, are a recurring feature of Nilsson's 1930s Modernist Swedish designs

Nilsson designed for his father's firm, Anders Nilsson (AN), from 1923. Prior to that, he worked at Georg Jensen's Paris workshop while studying at the Académie de la Grande Chamuière

Watches

Few fields of collecting have enjoyed the rapid surge in activity experienced by wristwatches in the last decade. Although Art Deco watches are fairly common, mostly in the form of inferior versions of the Cartier Tank model or other famous period designs, the modern collector is highly discriminating. Value is greatest in the Swiss firm Patek Philippe, which concentrated on craftsmanship and complexity above style. Art Deco elegance is best seen in French watches made to complement jewels by Cartier, Patek's closest rival in value and collectibility. Lesser Art Deco watches have elegant appeal, but few have more than decorative value. Most men's watches are still inexpensive, particularly those of American manufacture. Swiss origin normally helps, but brand names are more important. Many ladies' evening or "cocktail" watches were made for limited use and have survived well. Most are valued principally by their gemstone content. Poor condition drastically reduces value in most instances, since repairs are expensive and difficult to achieve.

Ladies' platinum cocktail wristwatch set with small diamonds. Its circular dial is silvered and has black Arabic numerals. With its original black leather strap. *1920s*

Face: ¾ in (2 cm) wide

$500–900 GHOU

Gold-plated gentleman's wristwatch with a black leather strap, made by the American Elgin National Watch Co. Its elongated "tank" case is a desirable feature. *1930s*

Face: 1½ in (3.75 cm) long

$300–400 ML

Platinum-cased ladies' wristwatch by Cartier of Paris. Enclosing a square white face with Roman numerals, its case and deployment buckle for the leather strap are set with diamonds. Its Parisian manufacture commands a premium over New York-made equivalents. *1920s*

Face: 1 in (2.5 cm) wide

$40,000–60,000 SOM

Ladies' purse watch made by Movado of Switzerland with a silver-gilt case enclosing a square ivory baton dial that can be concealed within a sliding outer case of silver gilt. The latter is flanked and inset with bands of black enamel. Its case is hallmarked "London Import." *1928*

Face: 2 in (5 cm) wide

$300–500   **F**

Ladies' fob-pin watch with a 17-jewel Swiss movement behind a circular face set in a round, *cloisonné*-enameled case. *1920s*

Face: 2 in (5 cm) wide

$200–300   **TAB**

Ladies' platinum-cased wristwatch set with diamonds and enclosing a silvered dial with black Arabic numerals, above a 15-jewel Swiss movement. With its original mesh strap. *1930s*

Face: ¾ in (2 cm) wide

$400–500   **DN**

Ladies' cocktail watch with a polished steel case enclosing an ivory dial with gilt numerals. Signed "Rolex," it has a non-Rolex crown and bracelet. Its minute hand is missing. *1930s*

Face: ¾ in (2 cm) wide

$200–300   **F**

Ladies' cocktail watch with a square face enclosed by six rows of caliber-cut sapphires divided and bordered by diamonds. Its winder is tipped with a sapphire cabochon. *1920s*

Face: 2 in (5.25 cm) long

$5,000–7,000   **DUK**

Calibre 101 cocktail watch by Cartier, with a white face above an EWC (European Watch & Clock) movement. The stepped platinum case is set with diamonds and rubies. *1920s*

Face: ¾ in (2 cm) wide

$40,000–60,000   **SOM**

Plastic Jewelry

Jewelry can be categorized as "fine" or "costume," and plastic has always been placed in the latter group. Some Art Deco plastics, however, now rival their glittering cousins in value, a trend that appears likely to continue.

Plastic jewelry—mostly inexpensive, "fancy"-style items—became common in the 1920s. By 1930, the wide variety available had breathed new life into affordable jewelry, offering modern collectors an inviting and appealing legacy.

Bakelite was originally patented in 1907, but the word is now used generically to describe a large number of different vintage plastics. Varieties such as the American Catalin and the clear Lucite may be identified within that term. Some period plastics imitated luxurious and expensive natural materials, such as certain types of celluloid for tortoiseshell and Ivorine for ivory.

Collectors favor bright colors such as cherry red, oranges, yellows, and greens. Bangles are among the most common items found. Look for color and deep or bold designs that are intricately hand-carved. Higher prices are attained by reverse-carved and painted transparent pieces, or those in which colors have been combined and laminated together. Brooches often display high levels of design and artistry and can be inset with rhinestones or metal ornament. Novelty and figural shapes are among the most popular and desirable pieces today.

The soaring value of Art Deco–style bakelite jewelry has led to some forgeries. Modern copies are produced in different plastics, which have a different feel and are often lighter in weight. Mold seams and colors that vary slightly from the originals are also indications. If in doubt, always compare to an authentic original. Many vintage plastics give off an unforgettable chemical odor when rubbed.

Black bakelite torch-and-buckle pin with floral motifs and gold incisions and edging. *c. 1930. 4¼ in (11 cm) long* **$70–100 ABAA**

Red-and-black bakelite buckle with stylized plant-form motifs. *Late 1920s. 3¼ in (8 cm) high* **$60–90 JBC**

Cast phenolic bangle with three bands of color shading from green into yellow. *1930s 3¼ in (8 cm) wide* **$300–400 BY**

Cast phenolic bangle with two black bands flanking a yellow and a red band. *1930s 3 in (7.5 cm) wide* **$300–400 BY**

Bakelite belt buckle comprising stylized, mirror-image leaf forms in black and amber-red. *1930s. 3½ in (9 cm) wide* **$70–120 ABAA**

African mask pin in black and red bakelite with chromed-steel eyebrows and mouth. *1920s. 2½ in (6.5 cm) long* **$300–500 RITZ**

Chromed-steel pin of geometric form with a faceted red bakelite insert. *1930s 2½ in (6.5 cm) long* **$70–150 ABAA**

Cast phenolic necklace with black and cream lozenge-shaped segments and pendant. *1930s. 2¼ in (6 cm) drop* **$200–300 BB**

Apple Juice bakelite necklace with a carved geometric pendant set with rhinestones. *1930s. 2¼ in (5.5 cm) drop* **$200–300 PAC**

Bakelite snake bangle in black and ivory, set with rhinestones and tiny brass cabochons. *1930s. 9 in (23 cm) circ* **$50–100 ABAA**

Unsigned English necklace with alternating geometric forms of silver and green and black bakelite. *Late 1920s. 15 in (38 cm) circ* **$250–300 RITZ**

Shield-shaped brooch with a zigzag pattern in cream and red bakelite. *1930s. 2 in (5 cm) wide* **$300–500 PAC**

English geometric-form bracelet with arcs of red bakelite and chromed steel. *Early 1930s. 7½ in (19 cm) circ* **$250–300 RITZ**

Apple Juice bakelite brooch reverse-carved and painted with petal motifs. *1930s 2 in (5 cm) wide* **$300–400 BB**

Oriental landscape brooch framed and rendered in black, green, and white bakelite. *c. 1930. 2¼ in (5.5 cm) wide* **$70–150 GKA**

169

American Jewelry

The vast majority of Art Deco jewelry made in the United States was an interpretation of fashionable French taste. By the 1930s the luxury French jewelers, including Cartier and Van Cleef & Arpels, were established in New York, competing with American firms such as Harry Winston, Black, Starr & Frost, Marcus & Co., and Tiffany & Co. Regional jewelers of note included Shreve, Crump & Low (Boston), Galt & Bros. of Washington, DC, Brock & Co. of Los Angeles, and Shreve & Co. of San Francisco.

More than half the fine jewelry for these and other retailers was already being made by the late 1920s in New York by William Scheer & Co. Examples are typically platinum or sterling silver, conservative in style but of uniformly high quality. Retailer marks were not common, except on boxes. In general, flashy Hollywood-style Art Deco is less popular than simple design, unless it has celebrity provenance. Egyptian-style jewels, designed following the discovery of King Tutankhamun's tomb in 1922, were also popular.

Ear-shaped brooch with bands and loops of diamonds, some pavé set, in platinum settings. It features various styles of gemstone cuts, including baguette, trapezium, chaton, and rose. *1930*
1¾ in (4.5 cm) wide

$20,000–30,000　　　　　　　　　**MACK**

Filigree-worked platinum ring set at its center with an old, large, European cut diamond, which is contrasted with caliber-cut, blue-sapphire accents, also of European origin. *1920s*
Top: ½ in (1.5 cm) wide

$20,000–35,000　　　　　　　　　**MACK**

Filigree-worked platinum ring with diamonds of various cuts and sizes set to a geometric pattern. The hexagonal ruby at its center is augmented with caliber-cut ruby accents. *1920s*
1 in (2.5 cm) wide

$10,000–15,000　　　　　　　　　**MACK**

Platinum ring of buckle design, pierced with scroll and star motifs, set with two bands of diamonds flanking a band of rubies and with a sapphire cabochon on each side. *1930*
1 in (2.5 cm) high

$7,000–9,000　　　　　　　　　**MACK**

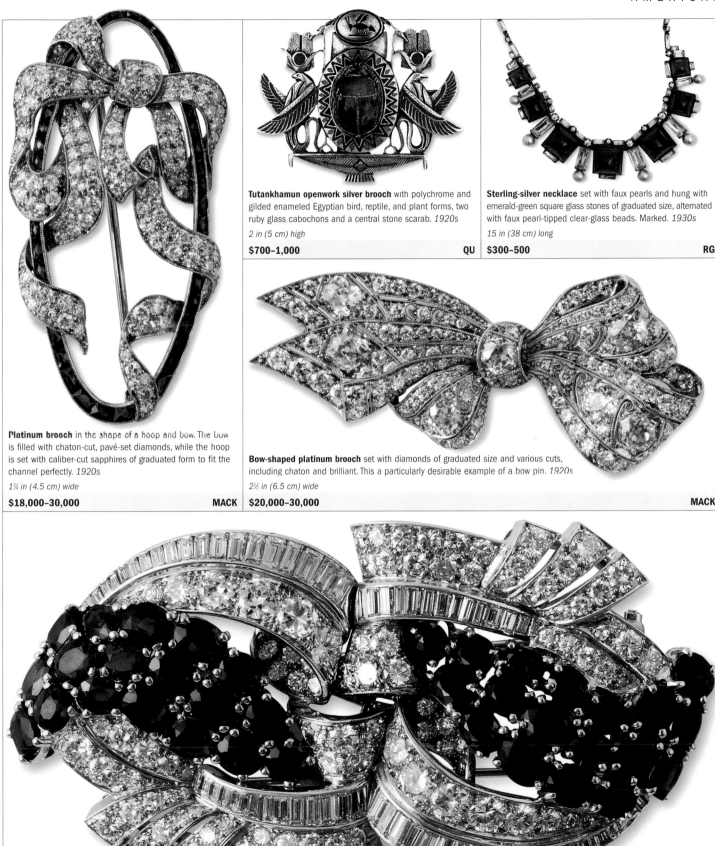

Tutankhamun openwork silver brooch with polychrome and gilded enameled Egyptian bird, reptile, and plant forms, two ruby glass cabochons and a central stone scarab. *1920s*

2 in (5 cm) high

$700–1,000   **QU**

Sterling-silver necklace set with faux pearls and hung with emerald-green square glass stones of graduated size, alternated with faux pearl-tipped clear-glass beads. Marked. *1930s*

15 in (38 cm) long

$300–500   **RG**

Platinum brooch in the shape of a hoop and bow. The bow is filled with chaton-cut, pavé-set diamonds, while the hoop is set with caliber-cut sapphires of graduated form to fit the channel perfectly. *1920s*

1¾ in (4.5 cm) wide

$18,000–30,000   **MACK**

Bow-shaped platinum brooch set with diamonds of graduated size and various cuts, including chaton and brilliant. This a particularly desirable example of a bow pin. *1920s*

2½ in (6.5 cm) wide

$20,000–30,000   **MACK**

Platinum "duette" pin set with diamonds of various sizes and cuts and chaton-cut sapphires. Also known as a "double-clip," the pin can be worn in one piece or split between two lapels. *1930*

1½ in (4 cm) wide

$30,000–40,000   **MACK**

Silver and Metalware

Art Deco style can be found in all its varieties and standards on metalwork—from the meticulous handwork of master craftsmen to inexpensive stamped aluminum or chrome housewares. It is also found on every scale—from massive architectural grillework to tiny silver powder compacts. Collectors tend to focus on one area or one maker, and there are plenty to choose from.

Working metal or silver is an ancient art. Several of the best Art Deco makers carried on the tradition of handcraftsmanship, using techniques well established by the European Middle Ages.

The Machine Age, however, saw a dramatic acceleration in technology, much of it originating in heavy industry, including the making of cars and aircraft. These developments led to innovative techniques, new materials, and mass-production being applied to decorative metalworking in Europe and, especially, the United States, where the gleaming metal cap of New York's Chrysler Building symbolized the importance of steel and chrome in the interwar economy.

HANDCRAFTSMANSHIP IN METAL

Art Deco metalwork can be categorized into two main types: handmade (including work made with innovative mechanical techniques and hand-finishing) and machine-made.

Most Art Deco wrought-iron pieces are meticulously handmade. Cast-iron production with industrial viability began in England during the first quarter of the 18th century, and by 1900, metalworkers (centered in Germany) offered statuary, garden ornaments, lighting fixtures, and even jewelry in cast and wrought iron. Furnishings were typically ecclesiastical or for the garden. It was the French Art Deco masters who made wrought-iron furniture chic and respectable, particularly for dining or console tables and floor lamps.

Other handmade metalware includes the work of Georg Jensen (*see pp.178–81*) in Copenhagen and Jean Puiforcat (1897–1945) in Paris, and the technically and artistically demanding French dinanderie. This technique of inlaying brass by hammering in other metals has been around since the Middle Ages and is a specialty of the French town of Dinant, near Liege.

American silver powder compact with copper highlights, made by The Evans Case Company and depicting a pair of leaping gazelles set against a floral and foliate ground. *1930s. 3 in (7.5 cm) wide* **$600–900 DD**

LEADERS IN THE FIELD

Wrought iron burst into fashionable interiors after World War I, and because of its virtually indestructible nature, it remains as a legacy throughout the western world. The French School was led by Edgar Brandt (1880–1960), who opened his own workshop in 1919. Brandt made massive contributions to the 1925 Paris Exposition and later opened a studio in New York, where his work can be seen in the Cheney Building (1926). Brandt made everything from architectural installations to paperweights and radiator covers, and he also developed autogenous welding, allowing the welding together of different metals. Other notable French makers include Raymond Subes (1893–1970) and Paul Kiss (*see p.177*), both furniture specialists.

In the United States, remarkable metalware was made by Wilhelm (William) Hunt Diederich (1884–1953), a Hungarian immigrant active in New York making elegant firescreens, weather vanes, and lighting from wrought and sheet metal, and Oscar B. Bach, a neo-medievalist, who also supplied interior metalwork for the Chrysler and Empire State buildings.

Handwork was imperative in the metalwork of the Wiener Werkstätte and other contemporary factories in Germany. Artists of note include Josef Hoffmann (1870–1956) and Dagobert Peche (1887–1923), whose thinly wrought creations in silver and gilt metal border on the fantastical. The finest examples are stamped with maker and designer monograms.

The rarest and most valuable Art Deco metalwork is by Jean Dunand (1877–1942), a Swiss immigrant who began his career as a coppersmith in Paris in 1903. Best known for lacquer panels of the 1920s, he also worked in hammered metals throughout his career and excelled in dinanderie. His main follower was Claudius Linossier (1893–1955), who trained with Dunand before launching an independent career in Paris in the 1920s.

MASS-PRODUCED SILVERWARE

Most Art Deco silver was made using mass-production techniques common to the trade since the 18th century. Handmade silver typically evolved from the Arts and Crafts movement, as

Brass French vase (one of a pair) of stepped shape—a form often found in Mesoamerican architecture and ornament, which became fashionable during the Art Deco period. Additional decoration is in the form of a panel of embossed, stylized floral motifs. *c. 1925.* 6¼ in (16 cm) high
$1,500–2,500 (the pair) MOD

KEY POINTS

During the Art Deco era, traditional metals and alloys such as silver, bronze, brass, copper, tin, and pewter were still employed extensively, but relative newcomers such as stainless steel, chrome, and aluminum came to the fore. In contrast to the Art Nouveau style, metalware became less convoluted in terms of shape and decoration. Simple, angular, or streamlined geometric forms proved particularly popular, but stylized figural imagery, notably of animals, also became the height of fashion.

Square wall mirror with a carved and gilded metal frame, designed with by Dagobert Peche for the Wiener Werkstätte and made by Max Welz. *1922.* 18¼ in (46 cm) square
$25,000–40,000 WKA

American wrought-iron gate (one of a pair) fashioned in the style of Wilhelm Hunt Diederich, with leaping hounds and stags in a stylized landscape. *1930s.* 62¾ in (159.5 cm) high
$18,000–22,000 (the pair) SDR

THE RISE OF INDUSTRIAL DESIGN

Generally speaking, only signed or attributed Art Deco metalwork is of significant value. Most is mass-produced sheet metal with stamped decoration, made to satisfy the booming domestic demand for ornamental houseware in the interwar years. The 1925 Paris Exposition helped popularize certain styles and motifs, widely reproduced in the United States. Standards tended to diminish during the Depression years, though innovative companies successfully combined mass-production with talented designers. Although this "industrial design" movement found most momentum in the United States, it is firmly rooted in central Europe, particularly in developments at the Bauhaus and the studio of Peter Behrens (1868–1940), who designed some valuable and early Art Deco metal appliances.

The front entrance hall of Claridge's Hotel in London, which was remodeled with fine Art Deco ironwork by Oswald Milne in 1929-31.

French silver-plated tea and coffee set by Jean Iétard. It comprises tea and coffee pots, a creamer, and a covered sugar bowl. Rising from ribbed bases, all are of unembellished cylindrical form and have angular handles and circular finials made of hardwood. *c. 1930. Creamer: 4 in (10 cm) high* **$10,000–18,000 (the set) OE**

with Georg Jensen, who combined new machinery with the finest artisanship.

Most of Jensen's imitators made little by hand. In France, Jean Puiforcat set extraordinarily high standards for design and craftsmanship. A World War I hero, Puiforcat began his independent career in Paris in 1921. He relied entirely on geometric design, combining hard stones, exotic wood, and ivory into his ware. Some original designs for flatware and holloware are still made by the Puiforcat Company. Most Art Deco silver made in continental Europe and the United States can be considered interpretations of Puiforcat's style.

Silver candelabrum (one of a pair) by Georg Jensen. Raised on a domed and spreading circular foot, two scrolling foliate-like stems rise to support its three trumpet-shaped candle sockets. *c. 1935. 6½ in (16.5 cm) high* **$25,000–35,000 (the pair) SF**

Unsigned American aquarium with a glass liner set in a footed, wrought-iron frame fashioned on one side with stylized and scrolling aquatic plant forms and a pair of bronzed carp. *c. 1925 15½ in (39 cm) wide* **$1,200–1,800 MOD**

Christofle

The impressed mark "Christofle" has been a symbol of quality in design and manufacture for over 150 years. Art Deco Christofle ranges from superbly made silver objects to mass-produced metal of "hotel" standard, but few disappoint.

With more than 1,500 employees, by the 1920s Christofle was the largest metalworks of its kind in France. Paris rivals included Maison Cardeilhac (est. 1802), makers of high-quality work comparable to Aspreys, and Gustave Keller Frères (est. 1857). Products in the Art Deco period were highly varied, ranging from furniture mounts to extensive flatware services, mostly in historic styles.

Only period Christofle in modern taste attracts Art Deco collectors, particularly the items made for the Compagnie Générale Transatlantique, operators of the *Normandie* and other luxury liners. Most bear the company's distinctive "CGT" monogram. This mark has

been fraudulently stamped on all manner of inexpensive Art Deco metalware in recent years, and it is wise to cross-reference.

Christofle enjoyed a boom in the Art Deco period and followed the lead of other French companies by commissioning designers, mostly after 1930, when luxury trade was less reliable and artists sought commercial work. French Art Deco designers who worked for Christofle include Maurice Dufrène (*see p.33*), André Groult, Paul Follot (*see p.28*), Louis Süe and André Mare (*see p.29*), and the Italian Giò Ponti.

Above: Silver-plated champagne bucket designed by Luc Lanel for the luxury French cruise liner *Normandie*. *c. 1935*
8 in (20 cm) high **$1,500–2,200 DOR**

Silver-plated twin-socket candlestick (one of a pair) designed by Giò Ponti in the form of crossed cornucopias tied to a center arrow. Model number 6055. *1920s*
8 in (20.5 cm) high

$5,000–7,000 (the pair) QU

Octagonal copper tray with selective silver plating, the latter etched in the center with a rectangular pattern made up of various abutted and interlocking geometric forms. It is signed "Christofle B 199 G" on the underside. *1930s*
18¼ in (46.5 cm) long

$900–1,500 QU

Paul Kiss

Wrought iron enjoyed a renaissance in the interwar years. Paul Kiss can largely be considered a follower of iron master Edgar Brandt, but his work is of the highest quality in execution, design, and ambition.

Wrought-ironmaking is arguably the most labor-intensive of all Art Deco crafts, requiring considerable skill, strength, patience, and artistry. This results in few convincing fakes, although it is common to find inferior work stamped with a spurious mark, normally "E.Brandt." Most work by Paul Kiss (1886–1962) is impressed "P. Kiss Paris" and identifiable by heavy use of ornament and surface annealing, in the manner of Brandt.

Although Kiss's range included furniture, such as a console table and mirror made for Paul Poiret, architectural gates, and facade details, the majority of his production consisted of lighting and small objects, including vase mounts and desk items. Floor lamps were a specialty much admired at the 1925 Paris Exposition, where Kiss set up a boutique on the Pont Alexander III, next to Sonia Delaunay (*see p.67*).

Along with Brandt, Kiss's Paris rivals were Nics Frères, a firm operated by a Hungarian immigrant family; Gilbert Poillerat, who worked mostly in the 1930s and after World War II; and Raymond Subes (1893–1970), who apprenticed with the legendary Paris ironworker Emile Robert. Like Kiss, Subes worked to commission with architects and designers and made an extensive range of furniture.

Above: Wrought-iron inkwell with floral tracery, fluting, beading, and a bud finial, on an onyx and iron base with a rope-twist side and scrolled ends. *c. 1920. 13¾ in (35 cm) wide* **$9,000–15,000 CALD**

Wrought-iron wall hook with an oval backplate in the form of a scrolled floral medallion. The protruding hook is in the shape of a partially open seedpod with a pealike finial. *c. 1925*
9½ in (24 cm) high

$6,000–8,000   **MOD**

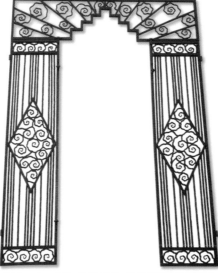

Wrought-iron door frame in the form of two sidelights below a transom forming a stepped arch with a sun-ray pattern. Like the sides, the transom is embellished with scrolling floral motifs. *1920s*
96 in (244 cm) high x 62 in (157.5 cm) wide

$30,000–40,000   **DD**

Large Palm Tree floor lamp with an integral matt-finish glass shade supported in a wrought-iron stand. The latter is patinated black and has a tapering stem of overlapping trapezoid-like sections rising from a square base forged with geometric motifs. *1928*
74¾ in (190 cm) high

$9,000–15,000   **CSB**

Georg Jensen

Jensen silver has been admired for its quality since World War I. His unique Danish style blossomed in the Art Deco years under careful management and with contributions from a small group of talented designers.

After graduating from the Royal Danish Academy in 1892, and a short-lived stint as a ceramic modeler, Georg Jensen (1866–1935) began his remarkable career in silver as a jewelry designer for Mogens Ballin (1871–1914), who also worked in copper and pewter. Here Jensen first used his signature flower-bud and grape-cluster motifs.

There are many silver designs that are attributed to Jensen, including the classic budding five-light table candelabrum of 1918. However, he also had a talent for finding young, gifted designers to work for him. From 1905 Jensen employed up to 60 workers at his workshop; in 1918, he opened a modern factory in Copenhagen, where the workforce expanded to 250 by the mid-1930s.

One of the preeminent artists employed by Jensen was Johan Rohde (*see opposite*), whose Konge or Acorn flatware is one of the most successful patterns in history.

At the height of production in the 1930s, Acorn was available in 272 pieces.

JENSEN'S POOL OF TALENT

Comparable to Rohde's organic style is the work of Henning Koppel (1918–81), best known for the design of an extraordinary covered fish server and for his unique Modernist approach, in contrast to the familiar Jensen style. Other artists of note include Arno Malinowski (1899–1976) and the sculptor Gundorph Albertus (1887–1970), who joined Jensen in 1911 and was responsible for the Cactus and the starkly Art Deco Relief (also known as Parallel) flatware patterns. Both are among the 11 Art Deco period flatware patterns still in production, from an original line of 33.

Above: Pyramid-pattern silver teapot designed by Harald Nielsen, with a stepped lid, ball finial, and ebony handle. Design number 600. *c. 1920s. 5½ in (14 cm) high* **$6,000–7,000 SF**

COMMERCIAL SUCCESS

Georg Jensen relied heavily on investors in his early career, which saw several failed business ventures. Even his early attempts at silversmithing were largely unsuccessful. By the mid-1920s, however, Jensen had achieved international popularity and commercial success, fueled by a bold campaign of expansion leading to stores in Brussels, Barcelona, Berlin, Geneva, Paris, Stockholm, New York, Buenos Aires, and London before 1935. By the 1950s the company even operated a floating boutique on the SS *Queen Mary*. Jensen's signature style proved compatible with virtually all interior design, from Rococo to neoclassical. The biggest draw was flatware services, which greatly outshone any competitor in variety and comprehensiveness.

Silver cocktail shaker designed by Harald Nielsen, with a plain, tapering body, stepped foot and neck, and a seedpod finial. Design number 462. *c. 1925* *10 in (25.5 cm) high* **$6,000–8,000 SF**

JENSEN'S NEW YORK SHOP

JOHAN ROHDE

After studying medicine, Johan Rohde (1856–1935) trained in painting and graphic arts at the Royal Danish Academy, also attended by Georg Jensen, in the early 1880s. Rohde began designing for Jensen in 1906, at which time he taught anatomical drawing at the Art Studio School he had founded in Copenhagen. Rohde became a permanent designer in 1913, but maintained an active career as an artist, putting on several one-man shows in Europe and the United States until the 1930s. He is best known for two Jensen designs: the Acorn flatware pattern of 1916 and a jug of sleek, naturalistic outline designed in 1920. In departure from the characteristic Jensen style, Rohde's vessel has little or no applied ornament and relies on subtly hammered surface texture and careful design. The jug features a handle that, though made separately, appears to grow organically from the lip. In addition to painting and work for Jensen, Rohde also designed furniture and textiles.

Johan Rohde-designed silver water jug with an ebony-insert handle. This classic streamlined form (design number 432) was conceived by Rohde c. 1920, but not put into production until c. 1925. 8¾ in (22.5 cm) high
$7,000–9,000 SF

CRAFTSMANSHIP

Georg Jensen was born in Raadvad, an idyllic rural community north of Copenhagen, and drew much inspiration from the place he called "Paradise on Earth." He grew up immersed in the Skolwerk movement, which looked romantically at Danish medieval history in an attempt to revive preindustrial techniques and standards. Jensen, who spent most of his career working in this ethic, can be largely considered an Arts and Crafts silversmith, despite ultimately opening a large factory in 1918 where much of the work was done mechanically.

FINISH AND SIGNATURE

The subtly elegant, satiny surface of most Art Deco Jensen was achieved by hand-annealing the surface, then immersing the piece in sulfuric acid, and finally buffing lightly to allow slight oxidation to remain. Jensen believed fully in the right of artists to sign their work, as he had been allowed to do as a designer with Mogens Ballin, and many pieces of holloware bear artists' monograms.

Art Deco designs were also produced by Count Sigvard Bernadotte (1907–2002), a member of the Swedish royal family and devoted Modernist who favored geometric designs, and Harald Nielsen (1892–1977), Georg Jensen's brother-in-law (through his third wife). The latter joined the firm as a young apprentice in 1909 and designed several classic Art Deco models, including the popular Pyramid flatware pattern. After Jensen's death, Nielsen took a greater role in the company.

silversmiths made inferior copies of the famous Cactus and Acorn flatware patterns. The best modern reproductions are made, of course, by the modern Jensen Silversmithy, which still operates in Copenhagen, though with a greatly reduced workforce and output compared with the boom period from World War I to the 1950s.

POPULAR STYLE

Around 1935, Jensen produced over 1,200 patterns of holloware, including candelabras, wine coolers, and mounted elaborate pieces with amber, amethyst, garnet, lapis, malachite, opal, and quartz. His style was widely copied throughout Scandinavia, continental Europe, and the United States, where several

Silver cigar case of rectangular form designed by Sigvard Bernadotte with thin block feet and blocks of ribbing to the front and sides. c. 1935 6½ in (16.5 cm) high **$4,000–7,000 SF**

Hemispherical silver bowl (design number 823) raised on a fluted domed foot. Designed by Sigvard Bernadotte, it also features a large rosette at the bottom of the bowl. *1930s*

6¼ in (16 cm) wide

$1,500–2,200   **SF**

Three-piece silver coffee set (plus tray) comprising a sugar bowl, double-spouted milk bowl, and coffee pot. The handles and the finial on the pot lid have ebony insulators. *1930s*

Tray: 14¾ in (37.5 cm) wide

$18,000–22,000   **SF**

Footed silver centerpiece bowl by Johan Rohde (design number 625), of oval form with twin loop handles modeled as stalks with berries. *c. 1925*

11½ in (29 cm) wide

$900–1,500   **SF**

Pyramid-pattern silver bowl by Harald Nielsen (design number 600), of footed, hemispherical form. It has a domed lid with a ball-grape finial. *1930s*

4½ in (11.5 cm) high

$2,000–3,000   **SF**

Silver cream jug by Johan Rohde (design number 321), with a plain, spreading foot and simple scrolling-stem handle. This model is a more decoratively minimal version of Rohde's design number 235, in which the bowl is raised above the foot on a network of tendrils. *1920s*

4 in (10 cm) high

$3,000–5,000   **SF**

Jug-shaped silver cocktail shaker by Sigvard Bernadotte (design number 7542), with a banded cap and D-shaped handle, trellis-pattern engraving to the body, and a capped spout. *1937–38*

5¾ in (14.5 cm) high

$7,000–9,000   **SF**

Silver pillbox of discoid form with a curved and elongated clasp and a stepped lid in the form of slightly offset concentric circles resonant of Jensen's Pyramid-pattern lids. *c. 1930*

1¾ in (4.5 cm) wide

$1,500–2,000   **SF**

Pyramid-pattern silver tureen by Harald Nielsen (design number 547). It has stepped twin handles with ebony insulators, and the handle of its stepped cover is modeled as leaves and berries. *c. 1925*

10¾ in (27.5 cm) wide

$9,000–12,000 SF

Silver caviar dish by Harald Nielsen (design number 499a). Its hemispherical bowl is raised on a circular foot with a rolled edge, and its slightly domed lid has a plant-form handle. *c. 1925*

4 in (10.5 cm) high

$4,000–6,000 SF

Silver salt and pepper pots in the Cactus pattern (design number 629) by Gundolph Albertus. Their slender ovoid bodies rest on plain, circular feet and are topped with ball finials. *1930s*

2¾ in (7 cm) high

$10,000–15,000 SF

Standard five-piece silver place setting in the Pyramid pattern, designed by Harald Nielsen, with stepped and ball-grape finial terminals to the handles. *1920s*

Knife: 8¾ in (22 cm) long

$700–900 SF

Pyramid-pattern circular silver tray by Harald Nielsen (design number 600), with twin stepped handles and a stepped rim. *1920s*

7 in (18 cm) wide

$4,000–6,000 SF

A CLOSER LOOK

Sterling-silver condiment set by Jorgen Jensen (design number 793) comprising salt and pepper cruets and a lidded mustard pot with spoon. All are of cylindrical form and mounted on square, stepped bases. *c. 1935. Cruets: 4¾ in (12 cm) high* **$10,000–15,000** SF

Jorgen Jensen's functionalist aesthetic is reflected in the design of the salt cruet, where the dispenser holes are an integral part of the decoration

Jorgen Jensen's preference for linear forms during the 1930s is clearly evident in the exceptionally slender cylindrical bodies of the cruets

Stylistic similarities between Jorgen Jensen's designs and those of Sigvard Bernadotte include their use of cylindrical forms and, as on the cover and spoon handles, incised parallel lines

Minimal geometric-pattern decoration is characteristic of Jensen's designs in the 1930s, evident here in the simple two-tone chevron pattern around the bases

Hood Ornaments

The earliest hood ornaments were made before World War I, most famously the Rolls-Royce Spirit of Ecstasy, modeled by Charles Sykes in 1911. The fashion peaked by 1930, when long-hooded automobiles sported prominent chrome radiator caps.

The popularity of hood ornaments rose and fell with the sleek automobile style fashionable from about 1925 to the early 1930s.

Most Art Deco ornaments are French and modeled anonymously, typically in realistic or whimsical taste. The best are distinctively Art Deco, embracing the aerodynamic streamlining demanded by the purpose and spirit of the age. Collectors typically focus on themes, with lots to choose from—female or mythological figures, animals of all types, birds, airplanes, cars and drivers, Egyptian, African, or American cultures are all popular. Most are white metal, with bronzed or silvered finishes, frequently worn. Better examples are bronze or nickel-silvered brass, both indicating French origin. Most American ornaments are streamlined chrome

and postwar, with little value. Rarity and provenance are important. Look for signatures, but be aware that many unsigned ornaments are still attributable. Art Deco modelers include brothers Jan and Joel Martel, Max le Verrier, Edouard Sandoz, C. Brau, a horse specialist, and Frederick Bazin (1897–1956), best known for his graceful stork used on Hispano-Suizas from 1920. Some famous metal ornaments have been recast.

The best glass ornaments were made by Lalique; others were by Sabino, Etling, and, in England, Red Ashay. Original mountings, especially illuminating fixtures made for Lalique by Breves of Knightsbridge, are rare and may be more valuable than ornaments. Mounts featuring pressure meters or "dog bone" twists are of less interest.

Butterfly Girl ornament in frosted glass and chromed spelter by Red Ashay. *c. 1930 7½ in (19 cm) high* **$3,000–5,000 FFA**

Unsigned chrome-plated ornament modeled as a young nude female kneeling with outstretched arms. *1930s. 6¼ in (16 cm) high* **$500–700 PSI**

American Indian ornament with snake and hatchet, designed by Frederick Bazin. *1920 5½ in (14 cm) high* **$4,000–6,000 FFA**

Nickel-plated ornament modeled as a scantily draped nude female leaning into the wind. *1920s. 6½ in (16.5 cm) high* **$500–700 WW**

Large, rare, and exceptionally beautiful horse ornament designed by Casimir Brau and originally retailed by Hermès. *1925. 8¼ in (21 cm) long* **$6,000–9,000 FFA**

Leaping-lion ornament designed by Casimir Brau in heavy chromed bronze. *c. 1920 8¼ in (21 cm) long* **$12,000–18,000 FFA**

Large Bentley "B" ornament with two wings, more common than one-wing examples. *1930s 5¼ in (13.5 cm) long* **$1,000–1,800 CARS**

Rare chrome-plated Latil Elephant ornament by Frederick Bazin. *c. 1920 6¾ in (17.5 cm) long* **$3,000–5,000 FFA**

Chrome-plated Rolls-Royce Spirit of Ecstasy ornament from the Phantom II and Silver Dawn models. *1930s. 5¾ in (14.5 cm) high* **$1,000–1,800 CARS**

Superb Hispano-Suiza ornament in silvered bronze, designed by Frederick Bazin. *1919 5¼ in (13.5 cm) high* **$5,000–7,000 FFA**

European Silver and Metalware

There are vast quantities of Art Deco metalware on the market; the majority, however, is very affordable. Silver items usually fare better than other metals, but there are exceptions. Copper or enameled metal by Jean Dunand or Claudius Linossier, for example, is more valuable than most silver, as are signed compacts or cigarette cases.

Items such as candlesticks or boxes are more commercial than tea or coffee services and most holloware, unless these are very stylish and by a good maker. French pieces tend to be more popular than other continental ware, and British metal has little appeal overseas. Commemorative engravings or monograms tend to diminish value.

Silver marks vary—from full hallmarks on British pieces to a simple impressed "800" on some continental ware and "925" or "Sterling" on North American silver. The best marks include the conjoined "WW" of the Wiener Werkstätte, particularly if accompanied by a designer's monogram. Plated and brass ware with this mark may be equally valuable.

Hexagonal-sided tin jug designed by Arnold Stockmann, with a hinged lid and a patinated bronze handle in the form of a bearded man wearing a loincloth. *1924*

6¼ in (16 cm) high

$400–700 VZ

Silver coffee set made by Hermann Bauer of Schwäbisch Gmünd, Germany. The coffee pot, creamer, and sugar bowl have black bakelite handles; the tray is made of wood. *c. 1930*

8¼ in (21 cm) high

$3,000–4,000 VZ

Rectangular silver compact case by Cartier. It has an all-over chased sunburst motif and an 18-carat-gold catch. *c. 1945*

4¼ in (11 cm) wide

$1,800–2,200 DOR

Lidded and footed hemispherical container designed by Josef Hillerbrand and made in silver plate and black bakelite. *c. 1930*

4 in (10 cm) high

$500–900 HERR

French wrought-iron magazine rack with an arched central divider and sides, the latter with heart-shaped scrolls and curlicues. *c. 1925*

26 in (66 cm) high

$1,200–1,800 MOD

English cylindrical silver caster by Edward Barnard & Sons, on a spreading circular foot and with a stepped and pierced cover. *1934*

5¾ in (14.5 cm) high

$200–300 DN

English kettle and urn of angular pyramidal form. It is made in chromed metal with light-brown bakelite finial, handles, buttresses, and feet. Marked "Regd. 849217." *1940s*

16½ in (42 cm) high

$600–900 WW

French silver-plated box of rectangular form with a stepped lid and raised on end supports. The latter, like the handle, are partly composed of cream-colored bakelite. *1930s*

10¾ in (27.5 cm) wide

$5,000–7,000   **SF**

Unsigned continental silver pillbox of circular form. It has a wide band of green enamel encompassing a geometric motif of inlaid black enamel on the lid. *c. 1920*

1¾ in (4.5 cm) wide

$400–500   **JBS**

Ovoid copper vase made by L. Gerfaux of Paris with a mottled brown patina and further decorated in silver with a network of angular geometric forms. *c. 1925*

7½ in (19 cm) high

$1,000–1,500   **HERR**

Nickel-plated brass candlestick made by the Hagenauer Werkstätte of Vienna. It features inverted bell-shaped candle sockets raised on a footed, semicircular frame pierced with angular, stylized animal forms. *1925*

9¼ in (23.5 cm) high

$5,000–7,000   **QU**

Pair of silver candelabra made in Belgium, each with twin sockets supported on shallow C-scroll branches flanking a faceted baluster stem rising from an octagonal stepped base. *1930s*

5¾ in (14.5 cm) wide

$10,000–12,000   **SF**

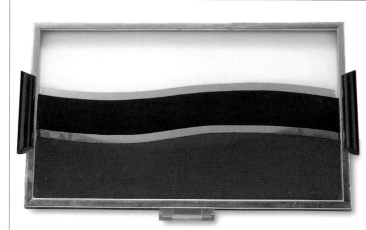

Metal, wood, foil, and glass tray probably made by the Deutsche Werkstätten. Its chrome frame has black enameled wooden handles and encloses a chipboard base covered with polychrome tin foils in a geometric pattern set under glass. *1930s*

14¾ in (37.5 cm) wide

$150–300 QU

Brass cigar box designed by Josef Hoffmann and made by the Wiener Werkstätte. The sides of its cofferlike form are ribbed and chased with star motifs; the inside is lined with black-stained wood. *c. 1920*

5¼ in (13.5 cm) long

$3,000–5,000 DOR

Unusual table lighter modeled by Saunders & Shepherd Ltd. of London in the form of a hexagonal gas pump with a domed top surmounted in turn by a Rolls-Royce Spirit of Ecstasy figure. *1934*

6 in (15 cm) high

$9,000–12,000 DN

Lidded silver vase made in Birmingham. Its cone-shaped body is raised on a short stem with an annular knop above a stepped and spreading circular foot. The lid is topped with an ivory finial. *1936*

12¼ in (31 cm) high

$900–1,200 WW

Circular lidded silver tin made by Hermann Behrnd in Stuttgart. Slightly tapering at the base and on the lid, it is hammered and chased into convex vertical segments. Its handle is turned and carved from amber-colored phenolic. *c. 1930*

7 in (18 cm) high

$1,200–1,800 VZ

Hungarian silver sugar bowl with a circular foot, a slightly domed lid, and an inverted bell-shaped finial. The body and lid are chased with a zigzag geometric pattern. *1930s*

4¼ in (11 cm) wide

$300–500 BMN

Four-piece tea and coffee set designed in silver-plated pewter by Pierre du Mont. The sides of the tea and coffee pots, sugar bowl, and creamer are hammered and chased into convex vertical segments; all the handles are made of hardwood. *1930s*

Coffee pot: 7¼ in (18.5 cm) high

$1,000–1,500   HERR

Pair of silver candlesticks made by Heinrich Eggs of Zurich. Their rope-twist stems rise from hexagonal bell-shaped bases and split into three leafy branches, each supporting a candle socket in the form of a stylized flowerhead. *c. 1930*

17¾ in (45 cm) high

$5,000–7,000   VZ

Silver tea service by Wolfers Frères of Brussels. The ball-shaped teapot, milk jug, and sugar bowl have vertically and horizontally segmented sides, and the pot and bowl have domed lids with finials made, like the handles, from stained ebony. *c. 1925*

Teapot: 6¼ in (16 cm) high

$1,800–3,000   QU

Pair of silver candelabra designed by Harold Stabler and made by Adie Brothers. Rising from spreading circular bases with stepped rims, they have fluted, spindlelike stems branching into three candle sockets. *1936*

11¾ in (30 cm) high

$9,000–12,000   VDB

Pair of footed ovoid Ikora vases made by W.M.F. Their verdigris patination contrasts with craquelure-like, copper-bronze deposits. *c. 1925*

12½ in (32 cm) high

$4,000–6,000   MOD

Silver-plated lidded chalice made by Charles Boyton for King George VI's coronation. The bowl has foliate handles with shield-holding lions; the lid has a crown finial. *1936*

10½ in (27 cm) high

$700–1,000   DN

Silver tapered candlestick made by Peter Bruckmann & Sons with a graduated four-part telescopic stem rising from a spreading circular foot to a simple candle socket. *c. 1925*

6¼ in (16 cm) high

$900–1,500   VZ

Cocktail and Barware

Even today, the distinctive outline of a cocktail glass evokes a peculiar Art Deco spirit, the kind championed in Harry Craddock's classic *Savoy Cocktail Book* of 1937. Collecting Craddock's legacy is highly entertaining.

American cocktail table with a mahogany top and end-support, and chrome banding, post, and stretcher. *c. 1935. 36 in (91.5 cm) wide* **$7,000–9,000 HSD**

Cocktails became fashionable among the newly liberated after the horrors of World War I. Some have argued that their popularity was aided by the American Prohibition (1920–33), which effectively encouraged the consumption of more potent drinks in clandestine speakeasies.

Today's collectors will find a wealth of American and European bar-related collectibles, from cocktail cabinets to ashtrays. Most drinking vessels are made from inexpensive glass or chrome, but look for marked silver or American glasses by Steuben attributable to designer Walter Dorwin Teague. The lamp-worked novelty glasses made by Bimini of Vienna from 1923 to 1938 are widely collected, especially those with colorful figurines.

Cocktail shakers are by far the largest and most rewarding area of barware collecting. This is a growing field offering extraordinary variety, as well as the opportunity to use your find. Glass and metal shakers tend to be inexpensive, as are plain or common chrome shakers, but silver examples by Asprey or better American makers do well. Design and condition are the key points. Look for very stylish or novel designs, and ensure that all the elements are present and in working order. In general, the use of bakelite indicates a 1930s or 1940s date. Complexity in a shaker is valued, as is handcraftsmanship in modern taste. The sense of humor reflected in the more playful designs is also attractive.

Other collectible areas include "swizzle sticks" or stirrers for champagne cocktails presented in boxed sets, cocktail trays, ashtrays, cigarette or match holders, and cocktail menus.

American chrome cocktail shaker with butterscotch phenolic finial and stopper, by the Revere Copper & Brass Co. *1930s 11 in (28 cm) high* **$1,000–1,500 SDR**

Danish circular solid-silver ashtray by Georg Jensen with cutouts to the rim. *1930s 5 in (12.5 cm) wide* **$1,800–2,500 SF**

Chrome and bakelite Empire cocktail cups (set of four) by William A. Weldon. *1938 3¾ in (9.5 cm) high* **$600–800 MI**

American rectangular cocktail tray with a chromed brass frame and a red, black, and cream geometric-pattern glass base. *1930s 18 in (45.75 cm) wide* **$500–700 DETC**

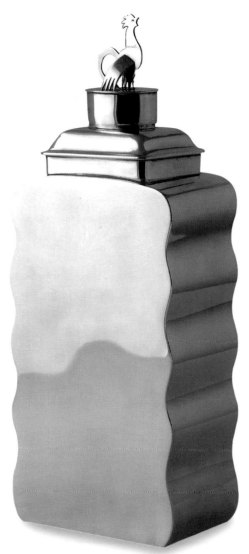

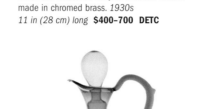

American dumbbell-shaped cocktail shaker made in chromed brass. *1930s* *11 in (28 cm) long* **$400–700 DETC**

Silver cocktail shaker by Arnold Bung with rippled sides and a rooster finial. *1930s* *8 in (20.25 cm) high* **$8,000–12,000 SF**

Glass cocktail decanter and matching glasses (two of six) by Fritz Lampl for the Bimini Glass Co. *c. 1930. Decanter: 9¾ in (24.5 cm) high* **$1,200–1,800 (the set) AL**

American chrome and acid-etched glass cocktail shaker with matching glasses (two of seven). *1930s. Cocktail shaker: 10½ in (26.5 cm) high* **$200–300 (the set) DETC**

Mixit cut-glass and silver-plated cocktail shaker with a revolving cocktail menu lid, including Martini and Kicking Horse. *c. 1935* *9½ in (24 cm)* **$1,000–1,500 TAG**

English silver-plated cocktail shaker with gilt highlights and a twist sleeve exposing ingredients for various cocktails. *c. 1935. 11 in (28 cm) high* **$1,800–2,500 TAG**

Cocktail shaker in the form of a suited man by Yona Original, Shafford, Japan. He wears a top-hat stopper. *1930s. 9 in (23 cm) high* **$200–350 DETC**

Silver-plated cocktail shaker in the form of a bowling pin with a contrasting hardwood neck and stopper. *c. 1935. 15½ in (39.5 cm) high* **$1,200–1,800 TAG**

Connoisseur cocktail shaker by The Manning Bowman Co. in chrome and with a yellow phenolic and chrome lid. *1936. 12 in (30.5 cm) high* **$300–500 MI**

KEY FACTS

Bel Geddes began his career as a theater-set designer in the 1920s.

He coined the term "industrial design" and opened the first industrial design studio in America in 1927.

Bel Geddes designed 17 models for the Revere Copper & Brass Co. from 1935 to World War II.

He designed metal furniture for Simmons in the 1930s.

Bel Geddes achieved household-name status in the United States through his contributions to the New York World's Fair in 1939.

Norman Bel Geddes

Few designers were as prolific or influential in their time as Norman Bel Geddes. His style and vision steered American design through the Depression era into a modern age, touching everything—from architecture to kitchenware.

Norman Bel Geddes (1893–1958) learned the value of economy and versatility as a theater-set designer, and he applied his experience to an extraordinary range of American design. By the late 1920s, his studio accepted commissions for furniture, lighting, and all manner of products, including newly popular electrical appliances.

Bel Geddes worked consistently in bold, American Art Deco style, evolving into streamlined form by World War II. For the 1939 World's Fair he created the popular Futurama exhibit for General Motors, showing concept cars apparently able to defy gravity.

His Art Deco metal is mostly limited to the 1930s, specifically the designs created for the

Revere Copper & Brass Co. These were mostly in chrome and include the Manhattan drink service and Skyscraper cocktail shaker, introduced shortly after the repeal of Prohibition, and the classic *Normandie* water pitcher. This was modeled as the French liner's looming prow, a tourist attraction in New York Harbor from its maiden voyage in 1936.

Bel Geddes's least-known but most successful design, however, may be Revere's streamlined saucepan line, which is still in common use.

Above: Aluminum candlestick (one of a pair) designed with triple sockets on scrolled and undulating bases for the Kensington Co. *c. 1935. 7 in (18 cm) wide* **$600–900 (the pair) HSD**

REVERSE OF PIECE

Silver-plated bronze medallion minted by the Medallic Art Co. to commemorate the 25th anniversary of General Motors. The relief decoration on both sides includes a wing and a futuristic, streamlined car. *1933*

3 in (7.5 cm) wide

$1,800–2,200   SDR

Manhattan chrome cocktail shaker designed for the Revere Copper & Brass Co. Its cylindrical body has vertical ribbing and shows a restrained linearity in keeping with the streamlined styles of 1930s American Art Deco. *c. 1940*

13 in (33 cm) high

$900–1,500   SDR

Russel Wright

An artist who delighted in all aspects of modernity, Russel Wright dropped out of law school and devoted his life to improving living standards in the ordinary American home with mass-produced, inexpensive everyday items.

Anyone who has ever watched an American TV show or movie set in the 1940s or 1950s is bound to have seen the work of Russel Wright (1904–76), evident in most kitchens of the era.

Along with industrial designers Norman Bel Geddes (*see opposite*) and Walter Dorwin Teague, Wright mastered modern materials and techniques, creating innovative household uses for a variety of them, especially aluminum. Spun aluminum was developed in the 1920s, mainly for the aircraft industry, and rapid technological advancements were made in its production during World War II.

Wright adapted this material for decorative tableware, plates, trays, and tumblers, used both domestically and in canteens to this day. This

ware was made by various manufacturers, the largest being West Bend Aluminum. It is very common, but some Art Deco designs are collected.

Wright was most successful with his American Modern ceramic line (*see p.147*), but he also designed houseware for the Chase Brass & Copper Co., metal furniture for Heywood-Wakefield, and radios for Wurlitzer. In the 1940s he worked with plastics, mainly melamine, retiring soon after the 1951 publication of his design philosophy *A Guide to Easier Living*.

Above: Very rare stylized elephant paperweight/doorstop from Russel Wright's Circus Animal range. *1930s* 12 in (30.5 cm) high **$18,000–22,000 SDR**

Chrome-plated liqueur set designed for the Chase Brass & Copper Co. and numbered 90046 in Chase's catalog. It comprises six cordial cups and a tray with a cobalt-blue glass liner. *1934*
Glasses: 2½ in (6.25 cm) high; Tray: 6 in (15.25 cm) wide

$500–900   **DD**

Pair of chrome-plated salt and pepper shakers of square shape. In a classic example of Machine Age design, decoration is linear and confined to the rows of functional dispensing holes. *1930*
1½ in (3.75 cm) square

$700–1,000   **DD**

Chrome-plated Pancake and Corn Set designed for the Chase Brass & Copper Co. and numbered 28003 in Chase's catalog. It comprises a butter-syrup pitcher, a salt shaker, and a sugar sifter, on a tray with a cobalt-blue liner. *1934*
Pitcher: 5¼ in (13.25 cm) high; Tray: 6 in (15.25 cm) wide

$500–900   **DD**

Chase Brass & Copper Co.

"Chase Chrome," as it is widely known in the United States, presents an affordable and stylish variety of collecting opportunities. Most items are practical and delightful, and many are simply irresistible to Art Deco fanciers.

Eastern Connecticut has been home to a thriving metalworking industry since the mid-19th century, although most large firms closed down following World War II. The armaments industry in World War I perfected the technique for making chrome, and this metal was widely made and used as a silver substitute after the Depression.

In the 1930s Chase embraced the Art Deco style, employing several outside designers. Among them were the German immigrant Walter von Nessen, who brought a Bauhaus influence to more than 60 Chase models, and Russel Wright (*see p.191*) and Lurelle Guild, who designed more than 30 models, mainly lamps. Other Art Deco designers employed by Chase included the husband-and-wife team of William and Ruth Gerth, and Harry Laylon, who worked from 1933

to 1939, when he retired as design director. Three Chase models—a cigarette box, a wine cooler, and a bottle stand—are attributed to the artist Rockwell Kent. All are decorated with a Bacchus image and are today's most valuable Chase items.

Chase Chrome was made widely available across the country through inexpensive Chase Stops in large stores, and it is plentiful today. Only attributed or elaborate pieces, including lighting and larger items, have more than decorative value. Original boxes add value to Chase, and model names add charm. Who could resist the Gaiety cocktail shaker, for example, designed by Howard Reichenbach? The Revere Copper & Brass Co., Chase's main rival, also named its creations as a marketing tool.

Above: Detail of a copper-and-brass bookend (below left), showing Chase's Orion brand mark. **HSD**

ALTERNATIVES TO SILVER

The term "poor man's silver" was applied to pewter in the 18th century, silver plate in the 19th, and chrome in the 20th. The Depression brought economic hardship to millions of Americans, and Chase chrome—especially the traditional holloware patterns, which resembled silver services—was largely made in response to this phenomenon. Even cheaper was aluminum ware, made mostly in Midwestern states from the late 1930s. Chrome and aluminum were as affordable as Depression glass and Midwestern dinnerware, which substituted respectively for crystal and imported porcelain in modest homes.

Circular bookend (one of a pair) designed by Walter von Nessen and comprising an outer copper and an inner brass ring on a rectangular brass base with three ball finials. *1930s* *5¼ in (13.5 cm) wide* **$700–900 (the pair) HSD**

Electric advertising wall clock manufactured for Chase by the Pan Clock Co. of New York with the company slogan, logo, numerals, and hands in red and black enamel. It is mounted in a brass frame. *1930s. 15¼ in (38.5 cm) high* **$350–450 SDR**

Taurex asymmetrical chromed brass candelabrum (one of a pair) designed by Walter von Nessen and mounted on fluted circular bases. *1930s*

9¾ in (25 cm) high

$70–150 (the pair)   **SDR**

Copper bud vase designed by Ruth and William Gerth. It has four asymmetrical tubes bound by a bakelite collar and mounted on a stepped, circular base. *1930s*

9 in (23 cm) high

$70–150   **FRE**

Rare architectural bookend (one of a pair) comprising three graduated arches of copper tubing mounted on a plain brass base. *1930s*

6½ in (16.5 cm) high

$400–700 (the pair)   **DETC**

Elegant water pitcher designed by Walter von Nessen. The copper cone-shaped body has a stepped rim and tapered spout. The base collar, handle, and ball finial are brass. *1930s*

10¼ in (26 cm) high

$300–400   **SDR**

Chrome breakfast set designed by Ruth and William Gerth. It comprises a tray and a hemispherical creamer and lidded sugar bowl, both with black bakelite handles. *1930s*

Sugar bowl: 4 in (10.25 cm) high

$100–300   **FRE**

$300–400

Diplomat copper coffee service designed by Walter von Nessen. The cylindrical coffee pot, creamer, and lidded sugar bowl have fluted sides and black bakelite handles and/or finials. *1932*

Coffee pot: 10½ in (26.75 cm) high

FRE

Golf-ball-shaped candlestick (one of a pair) fashioned in chromed brass and mounted on square and stepped blue glass on chrome bases. *1930s*

2½ in (6.5 cm) wide

$400–700 (the pair)   **HSD**

American Silver and Metalware

Interesting American Art Deco metalware includes commercial commissions by notable designers, such as Donald Deskey or Warren McArthur, and silver by the better manufacturers, which is usually stamped "Sterling" with a maker's mark. Small silversmiths of note include Robert Jarvie of Chicago and the artists at the Cranbrook Academy in Michigan. The better large firms are Tiffany & Co. and Gorham. Tiffany introduced modern design in 1935 and four years later received international acclaim at the New York World's Fair. The Fair brought fame to many designers, particularly Norman Bel Geddes, who conceived the remarkable Futurama exhibit for General Motors. His metalware includes the skyscraper-style Manhattan cocktail service and the looming Normandie water pitcher, designed for Revere Copper & Brass Co. Revere, founded in 1801 and still in operation, made a wide range of Art Deco chrome. Much affordable houseware is also available, produced in the Depression years, from the 1930s to the late 1940s.

Unsigned tabletop torchère (one of a pair), its stem comprising five graduated copper cones mounted on a circular stepped mahogany base. *1930s*

10¼ in (26 cm) high

$900–1,500 (the pair)   DETC

Iron-cast andiron (one of a pair) designed by Donald Deskey and made by Bennet. The stylized floral uprights have open brass centers, and the feet are also brass. *1930s*

17½ in (44.5 cm) high

$1,000–1,500 (the pair)   SDR

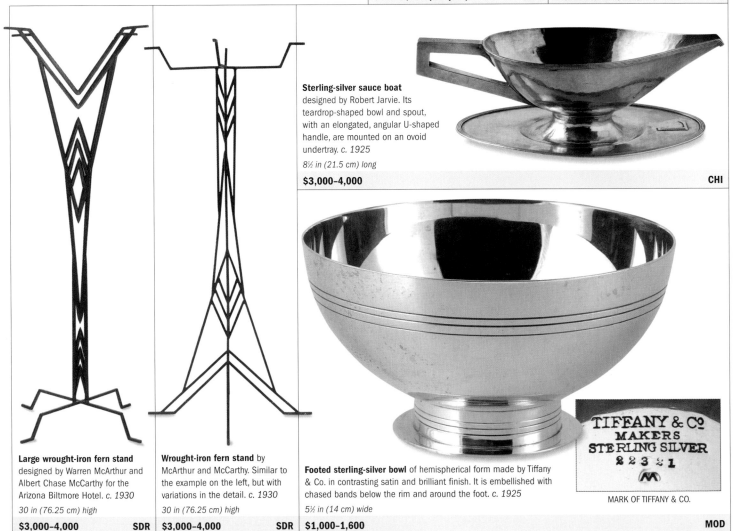

Large wrought-iron fern stand designed by Warren McArthur and Albert Chase McCarthy for the Arizona Biltmore Hotel. *c. 1930*

30 in (76.25 cm) high

$3,000–4,000   SDR

Wrought-iron fern stand by McArthur and McCarthy. Similar to the example on the left, but with variations in the detail. *c. 1930*

30 in (76.25 cm) high

$3,000–4,000   SDR

Sterling-silver sauce boat designed by Robert Jarvie. Its teardrop-shaped bowl and spout, with an elongated, angular U-shaped handle, are mounted on an ovoid undertray. *c. 1925*

8½ in (21.5 cm) long

$3,000–4,000   CHI

Footed sterling-silver bowl of hemispherical form made by Tiffany & Co. in contrasting satin and brilliant finish. It is embellished with chased bands below the rim and around the foot. *c. 1925*

5½ in (14 cm) wide

$1,000–1,600   MOD

TIFFANY & C?
MAKERS
STERLING SILVER
22321

MARK OF TIFFANY & CO.

Chromed coffee service designed by Michael W. McArdle for Sunbeam. It comprises a circular tray and cylindrical-bodied coffee pot, creamer, and sugar bowl. All have thin bands of black Bakelite inlay, and all but the sugar bowl feature black Bakelite handles. *1934*

Coffee pot: 9½ in (24 cm) high

$300–500   **FRE**

Chrome-plated Penguin ice bucket of hemispherical form with two brown Bakelite handles and a ball finial, made by the West Bend Aluminum Co. of Wisconsin. *1930s*

10¼ in (26 cm) wide

$100–250   **ANAA**

Unusual U-shaped chrome candlestick (one of a pair) on a stepped black bakelite base, made by the Dole Vale Co. of Chicago and exhibited at the World's Fair in 1939.

8 in (20.5 cm) wide

$1,500–2,000 (the pair)   **HSD**

International Silver

The International Silver Co. was founded in 1898 in Meriden, Connecticut, when a dozen local firms merged to make America's largest silver company, as it remains today. International Silver made vast quantities of silver and plate, mostly in traditional style. Examples are common and less sought-after than the work of Tiffany or Gorham. Art Deco pieces include designs by the Finnish architect Eliel Saarinen (*see p.53*), who designed flatware from 1929 and an outstanding spherical coffee urn in 1934, and Alfred G. Kintz, whose designs from 1928 include the Tropical Sunrise bowl. Most International Silver is clearly stamped. Marks include Meriden Silver Plate Co., Derby S.P. Co., and Rogers Bros.

Chrome face lamp (one of a pair) made by Revere and designed in the tribal-art style of Amedeo Modigliani, possibly by Helen Dreyfuss. *1930s*

10 in (25.5 cm) high

$700–1,000 (the pair)   **DETC**

Silver coffee pot made by the International Silver Co. Its gently flared cylindrical body rises from a circular stepped foot to a stepped and finialed lid. The latter, like the angular handle, is made of black Bakelite. *c. 1925*

8¾ in (22 cm) high

$400–700   **MOD**

Plastics

Plastic became the revolutionary material of the Art Deco period. Manufactured widely across Europe and the United States, it was inexpensive and easily molded into the new streamlined look.

Australian blue Bakelite kitchen canisters (set of six). Full sets in blue are very rare. *1930s. Largest: 9½ in (24 cm)* **$300–400 (the set) MA**

Celluloid-type plastics, often imitating expensive natural materials such as tortoiseshell, and black hard rubber were in common use by the early 20th century. However, most Art Deco plastics are the legacy of Dr. Leo Baekeland, who patented Bakelite, the world's first truly synthetic plastic, in 1907. Most Bakelite is found in black, cream, or mottled maroons or browns, and brighter colors such as red and blue are scarce.

The term "bakelite" is now generically applied to other early plastics that developed from this discovery. Among the most desirable of these is Catalin, a form of phenolic resin popular during the late 1920s and 1930s. It could be made in a rainbow of bright colors, such as red, orange, green, and yellow, and could also be cast into shapes and carved. Colored plastics such as

these ended the domination of brown woods, metal, and ceramics in the home, ushering in a new age of bright and modern style.

Many plastic items were affordable at the time, and so they were thrown away once they became unfashionable or damaged. Collectors today look for radios, lamps, clocks, dressing-table sets, picnic sets, and telephones. Brightly colored plain, marbled, or mottled pieces are popular, particularly if the styling is typical of the period. Look for clean, modern lines and stepped designs. Animal-shaped or novelty pieces, such as napkin rings, ashtrays, or perfume bottles, are also popular. Catalin radios from the 1930s offer some of the most stylish and valuable plastic items available. Notable makers include FADA, Emerson, Motorola, and EKCO.

Brown Bakelite photograph frame with a stepped base and arched and stepped sides. *1930s. 6¼ in (16 cm) high* **$50–90 JBC**

Rare cast phenolic Cleopatra box with a green lid and a black base, both with fan motifs. *1930s. 5¾ in (14.5 cm) wide* **$400–600 MI**

EKCO wireless (model number AC85) with a Bakelite case designed by Wells Coates. *c. 1935 23 in (58.5 cm) wide* **$300–500 LC**

Plastalite desk lamp designed by Wells Coates for E. K. Cole Ltd., of EKCO radio fame. *1930s. 14½ in (37 cm) high* **$300–500 MHC**

French Jumo desk lamp made in black and brown Bakelite for the Brevette company. *Early 1940s. 17¾ in (45 cm) high (extended)* **$1,000–1,500 ROS**

FADA Bullet radio (model number 189), in red, blue, and butterscotch Catalin. *Early 1940s 10¼ in (26 cm) wide* **$2,500–3,000 CAT**

Blue Bakelite owl case for a Bourgeois Evening in Paris glass perfume bottle. *c. 1930. 4 in (10 cm) high* **$180–220 LC**

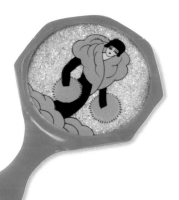

Green celluloid-framed hand mirror with painted decoration of a fashionable young woman. *c. 1930. 3¾ in (9.5 cm) high* **$200–300 TDG**

American mantel clock with a Catalin case and base in a desirable color combination. *1930s. 3½ in (9 cm) high* **$300–400 CBU**

Lidded box with a triangular finial and ribbed sides in mottled yellow-green Catalin. *1930s 3¼ in (8.25 cm) high* **$400–500 MI**

Promotional Michelin Man ashtray made in black and white Bakelite. *1930s. 5 in (12.75 cm) high* **$250–300 DH**

Sculpture

With the possible exception of photography, no other medium offers a more accurate glimpse into the Art Deco era than sculpture. The interwar years saw an explosion in demand for decorative sculpture, much of it accurate representations of contemporary figures in miniature. There was also continued respect for salon bronzes, which had been popular in France since the mid-19th century.

Art Deco sculpture can be classified in three principal categories: chryselephantine (normally made of bronze and ivory in combination), academic (made by trained sculptors as works of fine art), and decorative (made from more affordable materials).

INNOVATIVE SUBJECT MATTER

Bronze and ivory Art Deco statuary is among the most expensive—and the most widely faked. Most of it was produced in France or Germany during the 1930s, though the tradition began in earnest around the 1890s and is rooted in the European Middle Ages.

The beauty of this art is not simply the extremely high standard of ivory carving and casting, but also the modeling of elegant figures from contemporary life, an innovative concept rarely applied before the Art Deco years. Popular subjects were found mainly on the Parisian stage, the focus of the world's entertainment industry before the advent of Hollywood. Exotic dancers, frozen in mid-step from routines at the Folies Bergères or the Ballets Russes, were favorites.

Many have survived in remarkably good condition, considering the fragility of tiny ivory hands and the tendency of ivory to split as it dries and reforms over the decades. Collectors need to pay attention to exquisite carved elements, which may be replaced, and be aware of the extensive forgery, a problem since the 1970s. Reproductions are often complete with convincing marble bases and engraved signatures. Even among the earliest or best fakes, few capture the high quality of casting and carving found in the originals, and most modern examples are of poor quality and simply look new.

Bronze figure of a scantily clad female dancer mounted on a striated black marble base and modeled by Fayral, a pseudonym of the French sculptor Pierre Le Faguays. *c. 1925. 15 in (38 cm) high* **$700–1,000 ROS**

SOUGHT-AFTER IVORY SCULPTORS

The leading chryselephantine sculptors were Demêtre Chiparus (*see p.203*) and Ferdinand Preiss (*see p.202*). Other artists of note are Bruno Zach (1891–35), who sculpted erotic flapper girls; Claire Colinet, a Belgian sculptor who favored Russian dancers; Paul Phillipe, a Polish sculptor whose work is comparable to Colinet's; and Roland Paris, a Viennese sculptor who studied under Henry van de Velde. Paris made eccentric work, mostly in small scale, including bookends and lamp bases. Many of his pieces feature impish figures and some erotica, typically finished in colorful Austrian cold painting.

CHALLENGING THE FRENCH LEADERSHIP

Academic Art Deco sculpture is rare but varied and well worth exploring. Artists may be relatively obscure but highly prized if their work is stylish and innovative. Leading French names include Jean Lambert-Rucki (1888–1967), a Polish immigrant who worked in singular Art Deco style, mixing African and Cubist imagery.

Great sculpture was also produced outside France, including most continental European countries, Britain, Scandinavia, and the United States. Italian notables include Amadeo

Patinated bronze figure of a nude African woman kneeling by Karl Hagenauer of the Hagenauer Werkstätte. Mounted on an oval wooden plinth and wearing only a brass bangle, she combines elongated tapering limbs with flowing curves and clean angles. *1930s. 16¾ in (42.5 cm) high* **$4,000–5,000 HERR**

Gennarelli, whose large, allegorical sculptures represent the Age of Speed. British Art Deco sculpture is more reserved but is well illustrated in the work of Eric Gill. American Academics often trained in France, and many show European influence. The neoclassical work of Paul Manship (1885–1966), familiar to visitors to New York's Rockefeller Center, which is graced with his magnificent Prometheus, is unique and highly sought-after, though small statuary is rare.

THE DECORATIVE REALM

Most Art Deco sculpture is decorative, ranging from mass-produced, inexpensive, white-metal statuary to cleverly stylized items made and signed by leading sculptors. White metal, or spelter (an alloy composed mainly of zinc), was easily disguised as bronze with patination or cold painting. Many artists produced the same work in both materials at different prices.

Much decorative Art Deco sculpture is unsigned, but common signatures include Marcel Bouraine, whose style is similar to that of Josef Lorenzl (*see pp.204–05*); Jean (Joe) Descomps (1872–1948), who also made ivories; and Pierre Le Faguays, a popular French sculptor throughout the period. Le Faguays has been extensively reproduced since the 1960s and may be signed "Favral" or "Fayral." Also heavily reissued is work signed by the Parisian sculptor and founder Max Le Verrier, including figural lighting.

KEY POINTS

Young women are the favorite subject of Art Deco sculptors, and they are commonly depicted either erotically or in Jazz Age pursuits, such as dancing or athletic activities. Animal sculptures also figure large, especially of sleek and fast subjects such as panthers, gazelles, deer, dogs, cats, and birds. During the 1930s, figures became increasingly stylized. However, even the most naturalistic earlier Art Deco figures usually contain elements of stylization, notably in the elongation of limbs to enhance a sense of elegance.

Gilded-bronze Prometheus fountain sculpture by Paul Manship. It stands in front of the RCA Building at the Rockefeller Center in New York City. According to Greek mythology, Prometheus, the son of a Titan, brought fire to humankind. He "floats" above the basin below, rather than standing upon it. *c. 1930*

The Flame Leaper by Ferdinand Preiss, in the form of a female acrobat composed of cold-patinated bronze flames, clothing, and hair. She has an ivory torso, head, and limbs, and amber flaming torches, and is mounted on a stepped, black Brazilian-onyx base. *1920s. 13¾ in (35 cm) high* **$40,000–70,000 WW**

Miss Doris Humphrey demonstrates a dance move with a large hoop in 1925 in Seattle. Frowned upon during the Victorian era, athletic female pursuits such as this (and their practitioners) provided considerable inspiration for Art Deco sculptors.

Small sculptures, paperweights, and bookends by Edouard-Marcel Sandoz (1881–1971) are collectible, too. This Swiss artist worked in Paris and specialized in animals and birds, but he also modeled metalwork for Christofle (*see p.176*) and porcelain made in Limoges. Comparable to Sandoz's work is that of twin brothers Jan and Joel Martel (1896–1966), who always worked together. Their Paris residence was designed by the noted Art Deco architect Robert Mallet-Stevens.

Also in the decorative category is work by Hagenauer (*see pp.206–07*) and related sculpture, most of which is unsigned.

Pigeon Boulant figure cast in bronze and cold-patinated in mirror-black by the Valsuani foundry of Paris, from a sculpture by Charles Artus, who was much influenced by the famous animalier François Pompon. Like Pompon's, Artus's figures are very stylized—in this case, particularly elongated—but still display very lifelike postures. *Late 1930s 12½ in (32 cm) high* **$5,000–9,000 PIL**

Bird hood ornament cast by the Etling foundry of Paris in silvered bronze from a sculpture by Marcel Bouraine. Mounted on a stepped, octagonal bronze base, it has an ivory beak. The chryselephantine combination of bronze and ivory is, like the use of silvering or selective enameling, a recurring feature of Bouraine's work. *c. 1920. 7½ in (19 cm) high* **$5,000–7,000 FFA**

Ferdinand Preiss

Highly successful and prolific, Ferdinand Preiss was active throughout the Art Deco period. His early work is conventional, in the style of his mentor, Professor Poertzel, and of limited value. Art Deco Preiss consists of exquisitely carved ivory and bronze, unmistakable in the quality of execution.

The German artist Johann Phillipp Ferdinand Preiss (1882–1943) is best known as an Art Deco sculptor. He developed his style by 1930 and applied it to his favorite subjects: sporting figures (especially popular around the 1936 Berlin Olympics), children, and dancers. His best pieces are cold-painted contemporary characters in elegant poses, including a powerful figure of a woman pilot in a red flying suit, inspired by pioneer pilot Amy Johnson. Other sporting characters include tennis players, javelin throwers, skaters, fencers, golfers, and swimmers. Some dancers are depicted balancing with ivory or metal balls or hoops, and one celebrated model leaps a gilt-bronze fire while holding two flaming torches carved from ivory and amber (*see p.201*).

Figures from contemporary life are among the most charming. They include a striding male flute player and a series of young girls in various stages of undress, several gazing into mirrors.

Preiss depicted some figures in neoclassical garb and also designed ivory figures as mounts for clocks, boxes, and table centerpieces. Over 90 bronze and ivory models are recorded, including clocks. Most are signed, with a full signature or "PK" for Preiss & Kassler.

Patinated bronze and ivory figure entitled Stile. Mounted on onyx, it depicts a young woman dressed in a stylishly casual short-sleeved blouse and pair of slacks. *c. 1930*

12 in (30.5 cm) high

$20,000–35,000   **L&T**

Bronze and ivory figure of a young woman entitled Champagne Dancer. Mounted on a marble base and with selective black enameling to the costume, her ivory face and hands are typically finely carved. *c. 1930*

16¼ in (41.5 cm) high

$12,000–18,000   **DOR**

Patinated bronze and ivory figure entitled The Mandolin Player. It depicts a bare-legged, daringly clad female musician mounted on a stepped onyx and marble base. *c. 1930*

23¼ in (59 cm) high

$20,000–35,000   **WW**

Demêtre Chiparus

Chiparus was as prolific as Preiss, with over 100 attributable sculptures. His wide range of conventional or religious subjects is of limited interest, but his powerful dancers are among the most compelling and valuable of all 20th-century sculpture, plucked from the Art Deco stage and frozen in time.

Unlike Preiss's production (*see opposite*), the works of Demêtre Chiparus (1888–1950) are often all bronze, though the most popular do combine bronze and ivory.

Not all Chiparus figures are of high value. For example, his early work, which consists largely of religious or historical statuary and small bronzes of children, has some charm but little collector interest. His best pieces feature dancers from the Parisian stage in elegant poses and costumes. Popular models include the vertically posed Starfish Dancer, her catsuit adorned with starfish in relief. This model was made in at least two sizes, as were several others. The ultimate is The Girls, a chorus line of five dancers on pointe.

Although Chiparus's casting is generally less fine and his ivory faces less expressive than Preiss's, his figures tend to be larger and more impressive. Unlike Preiss, who delighted in folded satin, Chiparus adorned most of his figures with tight, relief-molded costumes, many finished in cold painting and gilt highlights.

Most pieces are engraved "D. H. Chiparus" on the base, which is typically large and composed of at least two colored marbles. The same signature may appear on fakes, made since the 1980s, the best of which are quite convincing.

Gilt and patinated bronze figure of Vedette, a young female dancer on pointe with arms aloft, wearing a diaphanous dress, and mounted on a stepped marble base. *1920s*
31½ in (80 cm) high

$25,000–35,000   **WW**

Gilded bronze figure on a stone socle, called La Bourrasque (The Gust of Wind). A young woman with an ivory face, wearing a hat, stole, and winter coat, braces herself against the wind. *c. 1930*
12¼ in (31 cm) high

$9,000–12,000   **DOR**

Chryselephantine (bronze and ivory) figure of a young female, the Dancer of Kapurthala, wearing a headscarf and bodysuit. She is posed on one leg with arms aloft above a stepped brown and green onyx base. *c. 1925*
21¾ in (55 cm) high

$30,000–40,000   **L&T**

Josef Lorenzl

During the interwar years, Josef Lorenzl was a popular and prolific sculptor, and dozens of models are signed by or attributed to him. His style is highly distinctive, and figures are always depicted in animated pose.

Austrian-born Josef Lorenzl (1892–1950) is a well-known name in the world of Art Deco statuary, but little is known of his life. His first pieces, dating from the early 1920s, usually depict naturalistic, fully clothed women in conventional poses. By the end of that decade, however, his style had evolved into an almost Mannerist version of Art Deco.

Almost all of Lorenzl's subjects are lithe female dancers depicted nude or dressed in scanty clothes. Their limbs and bodies are elongated and unnaturally slim, which emphasizes the elegance of their posture. This fragility is further enhanced by posing the figures on tiptoe and raising them on a plinth. This makes most Lorenzl figures vulnerable at the balancing point, and it is wise to check here for repairs.

Very few Lorenzl pieces include more than one figure, or even single figures with other elements, though some dancers hold scarves or symbols, which are cast integrally. Among his best and most ambitious designs is a figure of Diana the Huntress, depicted holding a bow aloft and with two hounds flanking her.

Together with statuettes, which vary in size from about 5 in (13 cm) to over 30 in (75 cm), bookends, figural clocks, and hood ornaments are also recorded, although they are quite rare. Many models of the statuettes were made in several sizes and varying materials.

Josef Lorenzl's work is typically signed with an impressed signature at the base but no foundry mark. Pieces may also be signed simply "Lor" or "Enzl."

Above: Female dancer with a diaphanous skirt cast in bronze with a gilt finish and mounted on an onyx waisted block base. *c. 1930. 7¼ in (18.5 cm) high* **$800–1,200 DN**

SCULPTURAL MATERIALS

Lorenzl worked with several materials, all widely used in the realm of Art Deco statuary. Most common is patinated bronze, usually with a silvered or gilt finish; conventional nut-brown or green patinas are less common. Many clothed figures were cold-painted in a manner popularized by Viennese foundries in the 19th century and shaded in an airbrush effect. This surface treatment is easily chipped or rubbed. Lorenzl also used carved ivory for hands and faces but not for other elements. Bases are typically green Brazilian onyx, sometimes in combination with hard stones of contrasting color. Spelter (white metal) or synthetic ivory were used in reproductions and some inferior period models.

Large figure of a nude female dancer cast in bronze patinated with a silver finish. Mounted on a columnar onyx base, she is holding a bronze clock face with silvered numerals. *c. 1930. 21¼ in (54 cm) high* **$7,000–10,000 WW**

Female dancer cast in bronze patinated with a gilt finish. She stands on an angular onyx and black slate pedestal. The ivory head has some damage; it would otherwise be worth around $2,500. *c. 1930. 8¾ in (22 cm) high* **$1,000–1,500 DN**

Female figure in Egyptian-dance pose cast in silvered bronze, with floral enameling to her dress. Mounted on an oval onyx plinth. *c. 1930*

9½ in (24 cm) high

$4,000–5,000   **DN**

Prancing figure of a nude female dancer cast in bronze patinated with a gilt finish and mounted on a green onyx base. *c. 1930*

13½ in (34 cm) high

$7,000–10,000   **RG**

Bronze and ivory figure of a dancing girl wearing a pleated dress and gloves, mounted on a stepped columnar onyx base. *c.1930*

11 in (28 cm) high

$2,000–3,000   **WW**

Figure of a nude female cast in bronze as Victory, holding two laurel wreaths aloft. Mounted on a stepped, square green onyx pedestal, the figure has a gilt finish, while the wreaths have selective green enameling. *c.1930*

11½ in (29.5 cm) high

$1,800–2,200   **WW**

Particularly stylized figure of a nude female dancer cast in bronze patinated with a silver finish and mounted on a conical green onyx base. *c.1930*

15 in (38 cm) high

$3,000–4,000   **WW**

Hagenauer Werkstätte was founded in Vienna, Austria, in 1898 by Carl Hagenauer (1872–1928).

Art Deco–style pieces were made under the direction of Karl Hagenauer (1898–1956), the founder's son, after he joined the company in 1919. Karl's brother Franz also became a designer with the company. Karl assumed the role of manager on the death of his father.

Modern, semiabstract, or Cubist designs date from around 1925–30.

Most prewar and postwar Hagenauer is fairly similar.

Recent reproductions are easily confused with originals.

The workshops closed in 1956.

Hagenauer Werkstätte

Hagenauer's singular style found mass appeal in the Art Deco period, particularly in the United States, where it is still popular. Hagenauer is not especially rare, and most pieces are affordable. Only virtuoso designs command high prices.

The Austrian firm Hagenauer produced a wide range of inexpensive, ornamental metal sculptures that can be divided broadly into two categories—African and Western inspiration.

At the lower end of the value scale are African animals or figurines modeled as stick figures and finished in black enamel. These are typically in tribal costume and may be carrying metal or wood implements. Mostly produced in the 1930s and post–World War II, they reflect the popular fascination with colonialism.

More desirable are larger wood or metal African and other figures with stylized bodies and sculptural poses, which echo the sophistication of some contemporary French furniture. Such figures include a metal element, loosely fitted, which is often replaced. Of even greater interest are the more developed Art Deco designs of African inspiration, including masks, some on a scale comparable to actual African ritual masks. The better examples consist of multiple elements and materials and evoke Picasso.

Hagenauer designs with Western subjects are less common. These include figures in stylish costume, mostly in sheet metal. Often of large scale, they were sometimes used as store displays or standing receptacles.

Most Hagenauer sculpture is signed with a stamped monogram "WHW," a mark that was used before and after World War II, as well as on modern reproductions.

Above: Large, polished-chrome sculpture of a woman's head in profile, with stylized features and a beaded choker. *1920s 21 in (53.5 cm) high* **$10,000–15,000 SDR**

PLAYFUL DESIGNS

Hagenauer used a variety of metals but rarely silver. Most common is silver plate, chrome, brass, and patinated or silvered bronze. Wood, in natural finish or stained, is also common, normally in smaller, less expensive figures. These include whimsical models of bellhops, sailors, and athletes made as bookends and other utilitarian desk items, or as ornaments. Long considered kitsch, this area of Hagenauer is full of delight and growing in value. Such pieces were originally designed to provide a charming distraction and, despite rising prices, they are currently still attainable for many collectors.

Figures of male and female tennis players by Franz Hagenauer. They are highly stylized, modeled in sheet-metal brass, and mounted on flat, circular bases. *c. 1930. 13¼ in (33.5 cm) high* **$3,000–5,000 DOR**

Unusual pair of muscleman figures made from polished chrome and black enameled wood. One is smoking a cigarette and the other a pipe. *c. 1930 17½ in (44.5 cm) high* **$4,000–6,000 SDR**

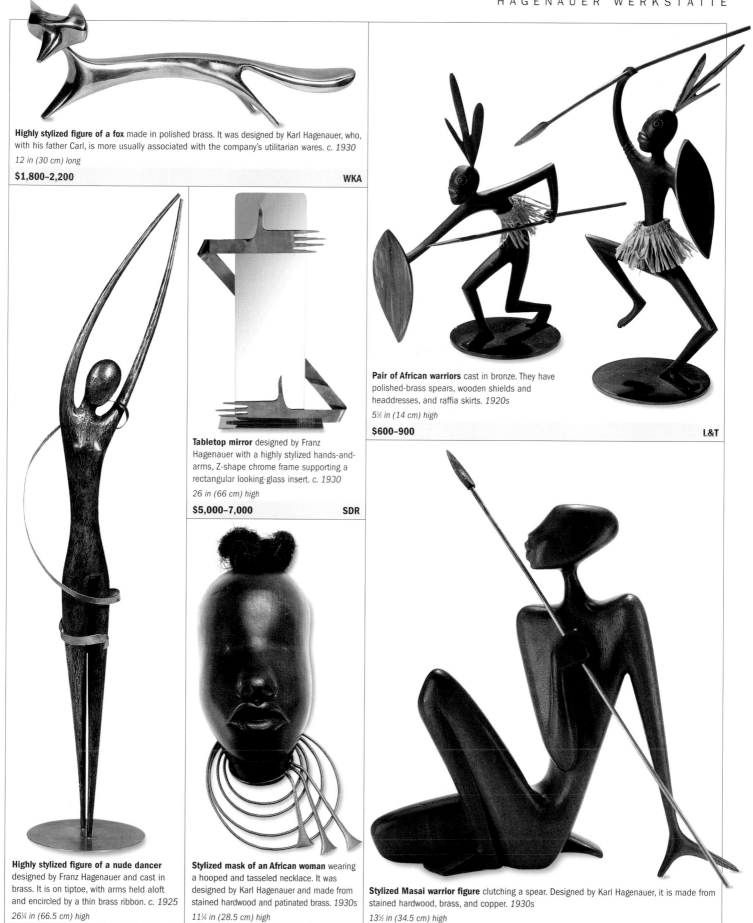

Highly stylized figure of a fox made in polished brass. It was designed by Karl Hagenauer, who, with his father Carl, is more usually associated with the company's utilitarian wares. *c. 1930*

12 in (30 cm) long

$1,800–2,200   WKA

Tabletop mirror designed by Franz Hagenauer with a highly stylized hands-and-arms, Z-shape chrome frame supporting a rectangular looking-glass insert. *c. 1930*

26 in (66 cm) high

$5,000–7,000   SDR

Pair of African warriors cast in bronze. They have polished-brass spears, wooden shields and headdresses, and raffia skirts. *1920s*

5½ in (14 cm) high

$600–900   L&T

Highly stylized figure of a nude dancer designed by Franz Hagenauer and cast in brass. It is on tiptoe, with arms held aloft and encircled by a thin brass ribbon. *c. 1925*

26¼ in (66.5 cm) high

$5,000–7,000   WKA

Stylized mask of an African woman wearing a hooped and tasseled necklace. It was designed by Karl Hagenauer and made from stained hardwood and patinated brass. *1930s*

11¼ in (28.5 cm) high

$1,200–2,000   HERR

Stylized Masai warrior figure clutching a spear. Designed by Karl Hagenauer, it is made from stained hardwood, brass, and copper. *1930s*

13½ in (34.5 cm) high

$700–1,000   HERR

Clocks

Art Deco clocks were made to suit every taste and budget, representing the whole spectrum of modern design. They exist in wind-up, electric, or battery movement, but most collectors are more concerned with how clocks look than how (or if) they work.

Clocks designed to sit on the mantel, desk, and dressing table during the interwar years are widely available today, and most are relatively affordable. At the upper level are French clocks signed by leading jewelers and designers, notably Cartier, Albert Cheuret, or René Lalique, or attributable to an *artiste décorateur* such as Süe et Mare.

Clocks made "in the style of" these designers are more widely available, but they are not of as good quality and are less valuable. There are also many timepieces manufactured by specialist clockmakers, such as Le Coultre, Omega, or ATO of Paris, which made its own designs and sold movements in cases designed by Lalique and others. There are more than 20 ATO Art Deco clock models, all typically made in glass, metal,

and plastic, with battery movement; they are all highly stylized. Because hands are often replaced, original ones are more valued.

Large but inexpensive figural clocks, made of hard stone and mounted with spelter figures, are usually of low to modest value, as are American clocks from the 1930s and 1940s in a streamlined, sleek style. These usually feature chrome and Bakelite elements and are more likely to be electric movement. Those attributable to leading designers are the exception and remain highly popular.

French mantel clock with a patinated brass frame on a marble stand and base. *c. 1925 13¾ in (35 cm) high* **$3,000–4,000 DOR**

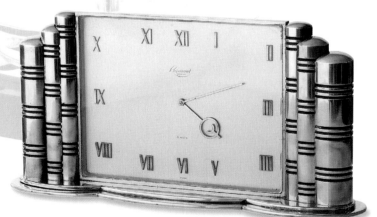

Mantel clock with an Egyptianesque stepped columnar frame in enameled brass; marked "Rosemont." *1920s 14 in (35.5 cm) wide* **$800–1,200 TDG**

Tabletop clock with a stepped, variegated marble case surmounted by two spelter German shepherds. *1930s 26¾ in (68 cm) wide* **$400–600 DN**

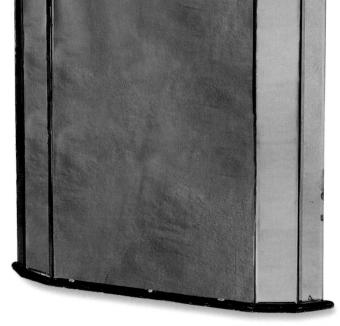

Large mantel clock with a stepped, arch-topped mount made from smoked-gray and pink beveled-edge plates of mirror glass. *c. 1930. 40½ in (103 cm) high* **$400–600 L&T**

Zephyr electric table clock in brass, bronze, plastic, and enamel by Lawson Time, Inc. *1930. 7¾ in (20 cm) wide* **$500–900 HERR**

Electric clock probably by Gilbert Rohde for Herman Miller. It has a burr-walnut case, square face, and three applied chrome bands. *1930s 13 in (33 cm) wide* **$300–400 DN**

French mantel clock by Blangy with a stepped square case molded from Bakelite. *1930s. 5 in (13 cm) high* **$300–400 MHC**

Electric carriage clock with a Telechron mechanism and a wood and chrome pyramidal case by the Revere Clock Co. of Cincinnati. *c. 1925. 13½ in (34.5 cm) wide* **$700–1,000 DETC**

French table clock with a chromed case on a Bakelite base, by JAZ of Paris. *1930s 4¼ in (11 cm) high* **$100–200 JBC**

German mantel clock by Kienzle, with an enameled bronze case on a ribbed base. *1930s. 7½ in (19.5 cm) high* **$400–700 DN**

Chromed and green-enameled table clock with a Jaeger Le Coultre movement. *c. 1925 10 in (25.5 cm) high* **$1,200–2,000 TDG**

German ATO-movement mantel clock with a cast silver face and a Bakelite base. *c. 1925 7½ in (19 cm) wide* **$2,000–3,000 MOD**

European Sculpture

Decorative statuary was a hugely popular art form during the interwar years and much has survived in fine condition. Most Art Deco sculpture was made in continental Europe but widely exported. France and Austria had well-established metal foundries and produced good-quality work by sculptors from all over the continent. French work tends to be particularly elegant.

In many ways, foundry marks are as important to the value of the piece as the artist's signature. They are a cachet of quality and only appear on better work, usually in the form of a seal and/or the foundry name spelled out. Most models were made in a variety of scales and standards of manufacture to suit all budgets. The lower end includes all spelter (a white metal alloy composed mainly of zinc) and most unsigned pieces, as well as smaller or later casts by lesser foundries. Many artists, including Fayral and Bruno Zach, have been widely reproduced in modern Art Deco revival *surmoulages*, or recasts.

Swimming fish sculpture designed by Georges Lavroff and cast in patinated bronze, possibly by the Marcelle Guillemard foundry. Russian-born Lavroff worked in Paris 1927–35 and is best known for his animal sculptures. *Late 1920s*

15½ in (39.5 cm) high

$3,000–4,000   TDG

Dynamic bronze figure of an American Indian on horseback by Bruno Zach, cast by Argentor of Vienna. Cold painted in gray-green enamel, it is mounted on an onyx base. *c. 1930*

18¾ in (47.5 cm) high

$3,000–5,000   DOR

Seated nude female cast in bronze by Emile de Bisschop of Brussels. Clasping a cascade of blossoms, the figure, Flora, is cold-patinated in a pale brown and mounted on an octagonal base. *c. 1925*

11½ in (29.5 cm) high

$1,000–1,500   VZ

Pair of unmarked bookends modeled as athletic, nude young females with fashionably cropped hair. They are cast in bronze with green metallic patination and mounted on rectangular onyx bases. *c. 1925*

6¾ in (17.25 cm) high

$900–1,500   TDG

Female discus thrower by Fayral, a pseudonym of Pierre Le Faguays. It is cast in silvered spelter and mounted on a striated-marble base. *c. 1925*

8 in (20.5 cm) high

$600–900   ROS

Figure of a nude female dancer by Paul Phillipe for Goldscheider. It is cast in gilt bronze and mounted on an hexagonal marble base. *c. 1925*

16¼ in (41 cm) high

$1,500–2,000   DN

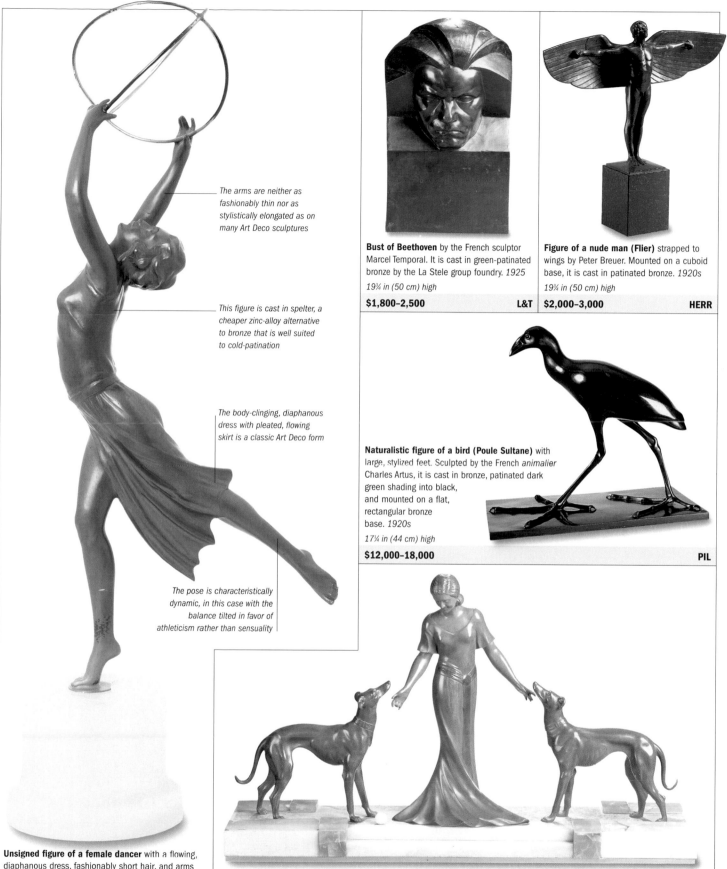

The arms are neither as fashionably thin nor as stylistically elongated as on many Art Deco sculptures

This figure is cast in spelter, a cheaper zinc-alloy alternative to bronze that is well suited to cold-patination

The body-clinging, diaphanous dress with pleated, flowing skirt is a classic Art Deco form

The pose is characteristically dynamic, in this case with the balance tilted in favor of athleticism rather than sensuality

Bust of Beethoven by the French sculptor Marcel Temporal. It is cast in green-patinated bronze by the La Stele group foundry. *1925*
19¾ in (50 cm) high

$1,800–2,500   L&T

Figure of a nude man (Flier) strapped to wings by Peter Breuer. Mounted on a cuboid base, it is cast in patinated bronze. *1920s*
19¾ in (50 cm) high

$2,000–3,000   HERR

Naturalistic figure of a bird (Poule Sultane) with large, stylized feet. Sculpted by the French *animalier* Charles Artus, it is cast in bronze, patinated dark green shading into black, and mounted on a flat, rectangular bronze base. *1920s*

17¼ in (44 cm) high

$12,000–18,000   PIL

Unsigned figure of a female dancer with a flowing, diaphanous dress, fashionably short hair, and arms aloft holding hoops. Cast in gold-patinated spelter, she is mounted on a columnar white-marble base. *c. 1925*

19¾ in (50 cm) high

$900–1,200   TDG

Unattributed group sculpture comprising a young lady in a form-hugging, flowing gown, flanked by a pair of hounds. They are cast in green-patinated bronze and mounted on a rectangular and stepped green-and-white onyx base. *1920s*

17¾ in (45 cm) high

$4,000–7,000   L&T

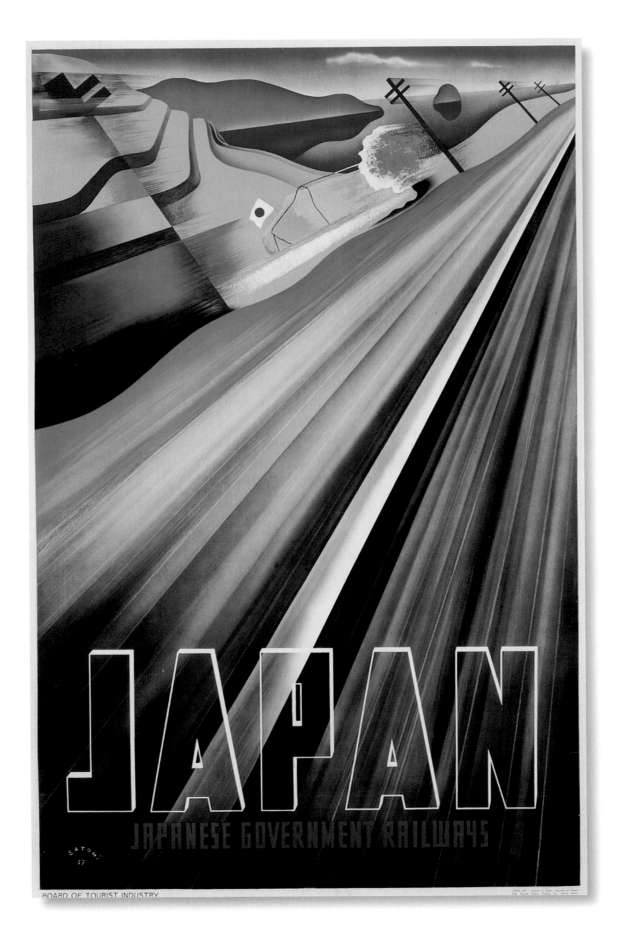

Posters and Graphics

Commercial graphic designers were almost nonexistent at the beginning of the 20th century. By 1925, thousands were employed, some working independently and others well organized in associations. Advertising had begun its attack in earnest. Though high-style Art Deco posters are relatively scarce, they provide an open window on to a remarkable era.

The increased popularity of posters was due in part to advancements in printing techniques, pioneered in Paris by Jules Cheret (1836–1932). Cheret's process facilitated economical production of large-scale, high-quality images using color lithography. The best French Art Deco posters were made in this way from metal plates, allowing a matt finish, strong depth of color, and sharp contrast and outlines. Some later Art Deco posters use photographic reproduction, commonplace since World War I but widely considered inferior to plate lithographic work.

Modern collectors are faced with a wealth of variety and may even look to Art Deco work made in Japan, China, or South America. In Europe, regional styles evolved in Britain, the Germanic countries, the Netherlands, and Italy. However, as with most Art Deco, it was France that led the way.

UNDERSTANDING POSTER ART

Poster design allowed individual expression, and as a result, there are few discernible schools. Many commercial artists who pursued careers as illustrators or graphic designers saw poster art as a sideline. Others were principally fine artists who designed the occasional poster, a tradition dating from the days of Henri de Toulouse-Lautrec.

In order to appreciate Art Deco poster design, one must first understand the unique cultural developments that precipitated it. This knowledge will in turn permit a justifiable view of Art Deco posters as a legacy of interwar social trends, fashions, entertainment, recreation, and politics, and may even inspire investigation of our recent history. The poster's original intent was to attract viewers to a particular opportunity, and it still serves this function.

Japanese Tourist Board poster designed by Munetsugu Satomi, with a blurred view from a speeding train of a rural landscape of lakes, hills, telegraph poles, and a cherry tree in blossom. *1937. 38½ in (97.5 cm) high* **$6,000–8,000 SWA**

A VARIETY OF SUBJECTS

The typical consumers of three generations ago were rather conservative in outlook, and most of their posters were fairly conventional. It is only striking images—ranging from strangely avant-garde or overtly sexy to simply beautiful in composition and color balance—that have monetary value today. The majority of Art Deco posters fall into one of five categories: travel, recreation, events (including sporting events, movies, and theater), product, and propaganda.

This 1922 photograph shows a bus passing a large advertising billboard in London. All the posters on the billboard promote The Nation's Food Exhibition to be held at Olympia and are indicative of the growing presence of advertising posters after World War I.

Chicago World's Fair poster designed by Weimer Pursell and printed by the Neely Printing Co. The most dramatic of Pursell's Chicago Fair posters, it depicts the three towers of the Federal Building, which represent the three branches of government in the United States. *1933. 41½ in (105.5 cm) high* **$2,000–3,000 SWA**

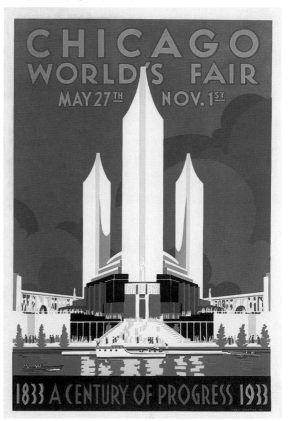

ADVERTISING A LUXURY LIFESTYLE

Travel posters are the most common and collectible, and they often promote sporting or recreational themes, too—such as railroad posters enticing you to sail, ski, or play golf. Some—for example, those featuring ocean liners or trains—simply encourage use of the travel facility, while others advertise a resort. After World War I, Europeans discovered leisure in travel, and any railroad company fortunate enough to serve exotic destinations commissioned graphic artists to promote them. In general, summery travel posters fare better than wintry ones, and well-known destinations are preferable. Even London Underground touted suburban beauty spots for day trips,

while British Railways lured people to English resorts such as Skegness and Cornwall.

The leading British poster and graphic artist was Edward McKnight Kauffer (1890–1954), but many British poster designs were commissioned from European artists, including the Swiss Frederick Schneider Manner (1889–1961) and Frenchman Roger Broders (1883–1953), who also designed for French Railways.

The finest French Art Deco rail posters are by Adolf Mouron Cassandre (1901–68), who also created classic images promoting transatlantic crossing on the *Normandie*. Cassandre founded the Alliance Graphique in Paris in 1927 as an early advertising agency and publisher, helping establish a cohesive French style.

Left: Travel poster depicting the Royal Mail Line's ship *Rotterdam Lloyd*, with its cruise itinerary to the Mediterranean, Egypt, Ceylon, Malaysia, the Dutch East Indies, Australia, Indochina, China, and Japan. *1930s 27½ in (70 cm) high* **$3,000–5,000 LOZ**

Right: Cover of the American magazine *Vanity Fair* with artwork by an artist named Benito. It depicts the occupants of a box at the theater in highly stylized form. *1927 12¾ in (32.5 cm) high* **$90–180 DD**

EVENTS PROMOTION

One of Cassandre's colleagues at the Alliance Graphique was Charles Loupot (1892–1971), best known for his landmark poster advertising the 1925 Paris Exposition. This poster influenced a series of images promoting international fairs, including Paris again in 1931 and 1937, Chicago in 1933, London in 1935, and New York in 1939.

Other notable French graphic artists include Jean Dupas (*see p.216*), Jean Chassaing (*see p.217*), Georges Lepape (1887–1971), Robert Bonfils (1886–1971), and Paul Colin (1892–1985), who designed more than 500 posters in the Art Deco period, many for Parisian performing arts, including the Moulin Rouge, Josephine Baker, and La Revue Nègre.

Event posters, not used for extended periods, tended to be smaller in both format and print run. This was especially true of movie posters, produced mainly in the United States but printed in several countries. Few movie posters are in Art Deco style, and value is related more to rarity and celebrity than design. Classic period movies command the strongest prices, especially anything for Fritz Lang's visionary *Metropolis*. Many British movie theaters changed the marquee twice a week in the 1930s, so few posters were commissioned. An event's historical significance helps determine value, and obscurity rarely attracts. Sporting events to look for are the Monaco Grand Prix and notable tennis tournaments. Annual events provide the opportunity to collect series.

PRODUCT MARKETING

From the mid-1920s, posters were increasingly being used to advertise products and services. The Empire Marketing Board commissioned hundreds of posters to promote British goods and services abroad, and larger companies such as Shell Oil or fashionable department stores ran their own national or local campaigns. European product posters are mainly from automobile or alcoholic-beverage companies.

Themes endowed with a strong collector interest—for instance, posters featuring perfume bottles (which many people collect)—fare much better than obscure or uninviting products. Exceptions include the classic Pianos Daudé of around 1930, perennially popular despite the fact that few people collect pianos, and French toothpaste posters designed by Jean Carlu (1900–97) in the 1930s with a Surrealist influence.

Propaganda posters from Russia, Eastern Europe, or Italy are among the most avant-garde, with bold Futurist colors and composition. Most are only of academic interest, however, and are typically of inferior quality in manufacture.

Metropolis **poster** designed by Werner Graul, printed by Eckert, of Berlin, and advertising Fritz Lang's famous science-fiction movie showing at the Ufa-Pavillon in Nollendorfplatz, Berlin. It depicts the film's central character, Maria, as a robot in a hypnotic image of stylized realism. *1927 26¾ in (68 cm) high* **$40,000–50,000 SWA**

Linen-mounted, polychrome advertising poster for Pianos Daudé, a Parisian piano manufacturer, with a stylized, bird's-eye view of a piano player, and a grand piano in the background. *c. 1930. 62½ in (159 cm) high* **$1,800–2,500 VZ**

Unique poster by Paul Colin advertising *Black Birds*, a musical revue at the Moulin Rouge. It depicts three of the show's performers: two men and Adelaide Hall in the center wearing a pink dress and flowered hat. *1929. 62 in (157.5 cm) high* **$180,000–250,000 SWA**

KEY FACTS

Jean Dupas began exhibiting at the Salon des Artistes Français in 1909, following his studies in Bordeaux and Rome.

He triumphed at the 1925 Paris Exposition with a mural in Jacques-Emile Ruhlmann's pavilion.

Dupas designed posters from the mid-1920s until after World War II.

He also designed interior glass panels for French liners, including *Ile de France* (1930) and *Normandie* (1935).

At the end of his career, Dupas taught painting at the Ecole des Beaux-Arts in Paris (1942-54).

Jean Dupas

One of the most respected artists of the Art Deco era, Jean Dupas developed a unique style intended for large-scale paintings and murals that proved ideally suited to poster design and earned him international commissions.

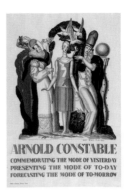

ARNOLD CONSTABLE
COMMEMORATING THE MODE OF YESTERDAY
PRESENTING THE MODE OF TO-DAY
FORECASTING THE MODE OF TO-MORROW

The work of Jean Dupas (1882–1964) is unmistakable. All his images feature elegant female beauties, dressed in fashionable costume or provocatively nude, their statuesque bodies sculpted with just the right degree of geometry into "a re-creation of nature according to my own temperament," as Dupas explained it. Each image is a feast for the eye—one ought to stare at a Dupas for some time to take it all in.

Dupas studied in Bordeaux and in Rome and developed his style under the tutorship of Albert Besnard. In 1922 Dupas's painting *Les Pigeons Blancs* took a gold medal at the Salon des Artistes Français, and birds, juxtaposed with figures, featured in most of his later images.

Posters by Dupas are scarce and all highly desirable. His best known, for the fashionable Arnold Constable department store in New York, features mannequins posed as the Three Graces. In 1937 he designed an exceptional poster for a World's Fair in Bordeaux (*see below left*), widely available in modern reproductions.

Dupas's poster commissions included several luxury retailers and the London Underground.

Above: Arnold Constable New York department store poster depicting stylized mannequins dressed in past, present, and future fashions. *1928. 45¾ in (116 cm) high* **$5,000–6,000 SWA**

EDITÉ PAR LA MUNICIPALITÉ DE BORDEAUX   ROUSSEAU FRÈRES, IMPRIMEURS A BORDEAUX

BORDEAUX
SON PORT · SES MONUMENTS · SES VINS

SAKS FIFTH AVENUE

Original drawing on paper in gouache, pen, and ink over pencil, for one of a series of fashion posters for the American department store Saks Fifth Avenue. *c. 1930*
23½ in (59.75 cm) high

$25,000–40,000	CHR

Bordeaux poster commissioned to promote the port, wine, and monuments of Dupas's birthplace. The aquiline nose and rouged cheeks of the model, the robust representations of architecture, the understated colors, and the separation of the slogan from the picture are all typically Dupas. *1937*
38¼ in (97.5 cm) high

$4,000–6,000	SWA

Jean Chassaing

During his life, Jean Chassaing collected posters by the leading Art Deco designers. When the collection was sold, 65 years after his death, several of his own designs were seen in public for the first time.

Jean Chassaing (1905–38) began his career in design at age 21 as an intern in the Parisian studio of Adolphe Mouron Cassandre (1901–68). Following the publication of his first poster in 1923, Cassandre had rapidly become the era's most respected artist. After he established the Alliance Graphique in 1930, several of his other interns forged independent careers, including Raymond Gid and Raymond Savignac. Chassaing clearly learned about composition and technique, such as the use of the airbrush, from Cassandre.

Another mentor was Paul Colin (1892–1986), founder of a school of poster design in 1933. Colin's influence is evident in Chassaing's facial images and some subject matter.

Only 11 Chassaing designs are recorded: Pilotes d'Avion and Bernay, both aeronautical images dating to c. 1927; Janie Marèse (1928); Casino de la Mediterranée and Sardines (for which only maquettes are recorded, c. 1928); La Regia, Kerlor, C'Est un Amour Qui Passe, featuring a gramophone, Le Blanc de Boka, and La Ligne Aurore (all c. 1930); and Chassaing's final work, Josephine Baker, of 1931. The exotic star of the Casino de Paris was enormously popular by 1931, promoted mostly through posters by Chassaing's own mentor Paul Colin.

Above: Caricature-style poster depicting French actor La Regia rendered with Cubist touches and in a bold, stylized palette. *c. 1930. 62 in (157.5 cm) high* **$1,200–1,800 SWA**

KEY FACTS

Jean Chassaing probably worked for Adolphe Mouron Cassandre as a graphic designer from about 1925.

Paul Colin had a strong influence on Chassaing from about 1927.

Chassaing poster designs date from 1927 to 1931.

His best-known image of Josephine Baker was designed in 1931.

Chassaing collected Art Deco posters from 1925 until 1932. Swann Galleries in New York ultimately sold his collection of 72 works at auction in 2003.

Jean Chassaing died prematurely and in poverty in 1938.

Advertising poster for the La Ligne Aurore shoe range. In well-balanced light and dark colors, it includes the stylized silhouette of a woman as chic and aerodynamic as the shoes themselves. *c. 1930*
63 in (160 cm) high

$1,800–2,200 SWA

Early and unique poster portrait of the French actress Janie Marèse, who died tragically in 1931 in a car crash near St Tropez, just after filming Jean Renoir's *La Chienne*. *1928*
63 in (160 cm) high

$7,000–9,000 SWA

Poster portrait of the actress Josephine Baker with excellent stylization of her hair and eyes, effective use of color, and clever use of the underlying white paper for the eyes and mouth. This is Chassaing's most striking and best poster, and the one of which he was most proud. *c. 1930*
61½ in (156 cm) high

$18,000–22,000 SWA

European Posters

French Art Deco posters by Cassandre were widely copied in continental Europe, but individual national identities are also evident. Among the best Dutch work are posters for the Holland-America Line by Wilhelm Gispen (1890–1981) and Willem Ten Broek (1905–93). Many show Jugendstijl roots in their symmetrical composition, or the avant-garde taste of De Stijl. Most Belgian Art Deco posters were designed by Leo Marfurt (1894–1977) through his advertising agency, Les Créations Publicitaires. German posters represent all themes, including films. Ludwig Hohlwein (1874–1949) was the most prolific German artist, producing thousands of posters before the late 1930s, when German and Italian art became overshadowed by Fascist propaganda. Italian Art Deco is colorful and chic. Images for Italian products such as Olivetti or Fiat are growing in popularity outside Italy. Other names of note include Marcello Nizzoli (1887–1960) and Severo Pozzati (1895–1983), who was born in Italy but worked in France, signing his work "Sepo."

Holland-America Line shipping poster by Willem Ten Broek. The stylized, fish-eye view of the liner is Cassandre-esque. This poster is corporate advertising—it doesn't portray a specific vessel but promotes the company and the concept of sea travel in general. *1936*
38½ in (97.75 cm) high

$7,000–9,000 SWA

Adriatica Line shipping poster plotting the route of a ship on the horizon using an arched arrow above the national flags of the countries along the coasts of the Adriatic and the eastern Mediterranean. The poster for the Venice-based company is Cassandre-esque in style. *c. 1940*
39 in (99 cm) high

$1,000–1,500 SWA

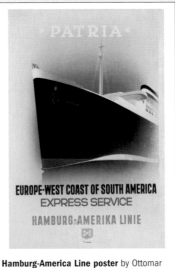

Hamburg-America Line poster by Ottomar Anton showing the vessel *Patria* cutting a wave on its Europe-to-South-America route. *1930s*
39½ in (100.25 cm) high

$1,500–2,000 SWA

Adriatica Line poster advertising exotic destinations represented by the Parthenon in Athens and Hagia Sophia in Istanbul. *c. 1940*
39½ in (100.25 cm) high

$1,200–2,000 SWA

COMPAGNIE GÉNÉRALE
TRANSATLANTIQUE

JAN AUVIGNE

AMÉRIQUE DU NORD SPITZBERG BALTIQUE

AMÉRIQUE CENTRALE

AMÉRIQUE DU SUD

ANTILLES MAROC ALGÉRIE TUNISIE

ÉDITIONS L'ATLANTIQUE · Printed in France

Very rare *Normandie* poster by Jan Auvigne. The famous liner is depicted at the center of a compass circled by its various destinations. This is almost certainly a pre-text version of a poster designed by Auvigne for the 1937 Exposition Internationale Paris.

40 in (101.5 cm) high

$5,000–6,000   SWA

Paris–Havre–New York poster by Albert Sebille, advertising the ease of traveling from Paris to New York by boat and train. *c. 1930*

39¼ in (99.75 cm) high

$2,000–3,000   SWA

A Pleasant Trip to Germany poster by Jupp Wiertz, showing a zeppelin, a plane, a ship, and the skyline from Manhattan to Munich. *c. 1935*

39¾ in (101 cm) high

$7,000–9,000   SWA

Automoto bicycle company poster by Marton Lajos with a close-up of front forks and wheel in gray on a vivid red-and-black ground. *1930*

37¼ in (94.5 cm) high

$1,500–2,000   SWA

Classic Delahaye automobile poster by Roger Perot. The typography mirroring the angle of the car adds to the sense of movement. *1935*

61 in (155 cm) high

$5,000–7,000   SWA

Palais de la Nouveauté poster by Sepo (Severo Pozzati) advertising the French department store. The Cubist-style train set against hills and the ocean symbolizes the summer escape from the city to the country and seaside, for which the bourgeoisie would need new outfits. *1928*

63 in (160 cm) wide

$10,000–15,000   SWA

CAMPAGNE
BAINS DE MER SPORTS

PALAIS DE LA NOUVEAUTÉ

IMP. DE L'AFFICHAGE NATIONAL DUFRESL. PARIS   CRÉATION DORLAND. PARIS

23 JUILLET 1938

KURHAUS SCHEVENINGEN

BAL DE FILM MONDIAL

Bal de Film Mondial poster by Mes & Bronhorst, promoting both a film festival and the luxury Kurhaus hotel in Scheveningen, Holland. *1938*

33½ in (85 cm) high

$1,500–2,000   SWA

Champagne Veuve A. Devaux poster by Dryden and printed by Joseph Charles of Paris. Fashion illustrator and poster and costume designer Dryden was born Ernst Deutsch in 1887 in Vienna. *1938*

61 in (155 cm) high

$3,000–5,000   **SWA**

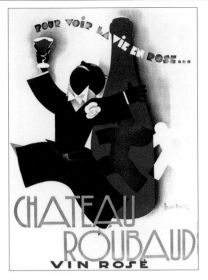

Château Roubaud wine poster by Leon Dupin, printed by Joseph Charles of Paris. It depicts a celebratory image toasting the good life. With some damage. *1931*

56 in (142.25 cm) high

$1,800–2,500   **LOZ**

Vins Camp Romain wine poster designed by L. Gadoud and printed by Camis of Paris. In graduated shades of red to white on a black ground. *1930s*

64 in (162.5 cm) high

$1,500–2,000   **LOZ**

Plate of a Dentrifice Gellé (toothpaste) poster from a series of 15 graphic-design portfolios entitled *L'Art International d'Au-jourd'hui*. Other subjects include architecture, furniture, sculpture, and interior design. *c. 1930*

13 in (33 cm) high

$3,000–4,000   **SWA**

Josephine Baker poster by the Russian artist Georges de Pogedaieff. Many posters promoting both the actress and her revues were produced in Paris during the 1920s and 30s. Both highly realistic and a caricature, this portrait is rendered in black and white and skin tones, encloses white text, and is set against a vivid-green ground. *1931*

63¼ in (160.5 cm) high

$10,000–15,000   **SWA**

Drawing for promotional caviar posters by Alexey Brodovitch (one of two). Both are in black and white and this one depicts a sturgeon, while the other (not shown) is of caviar in an open tin. Brodovitch started his career in Paris, but in 1930 he emigrated to the United States. *1924*

11¾ in (29.75 cm) wide

$15,000–20,000 (the pair)   **SWA**

Festa Major poster by J. Vilarrasa promoting a series of fiestas in July. In black and the yellow and red of the Catalan flag. *1932*

46¾ in (118.75 cm) high

$1,500–2,000   **SWA**

Jaarbeurs Utrecht poster by Henri C. Pieck for an international fair. The typography is an integral part of the industrial architecture shown. *1935*

39¼ in (99.75 cm) high

$2,000–3,000   **SWA**

Jaarbeurs Utrecht poster designed by Franz Ter Gast and printed by Lankhout. This poster bridges the gap between Dutch Art Nouveau and Dutch Art Deco: the former is still evident in the style of the typography and the formal layout, while latter is apparent in the stylized, commercial ziggurat emerging from an old, green forest. *1920*

46¼ in (117.5 cm) high

$1,000–1,500   **SWA**

Goldina chocolate bar poster designed by Louis Oppenheim and printed by W. Kulemann of Hanover with the bar, typography, and Renaissance pageboy in shades of red and gold against a black ground. *c. 1925*

47½ in (120.5 cm) high

$2,000–3,000   **VZ**

British Posters

The best of British Art Deco may be found in posters designed by a small group of artists active between the wars, many from abroad. Great Britain's leading designer was Edward McKnight Kauffer, who was associated with the Bloomsbury Group of London intellectuals. He also designed book jackets and carpets. His best Art Deco work is found in posters for British patrons such as London Transport, British regional railroads, British Petroleum, and Shell Oil. Other artists of note include Austin Cooper (1890–1964), Fred Taylor (1875–1963), and Charles Pears (1873–1958).

Most collectors focus on one patron, rather than one artist. London Underground posters are especially compelling for British collectors, as are Art Deco images advertising Wimbledon tennis tournaments in the 1930s. Travel posters are most common, with luxury liners highest in demand, especially anything related to the *Normandie*, followed by automobile subjects. Railroad posters were made in two standard sizes, the larger being horizontal.

Shell For Go study in gouache designed by Tom Eckersley and Eric Lombers for a poster that was actually never put into print. Rendered in yellow, brown, orange, black, and blue, and containing silhouettes of an oil can and a car above a splash, it represents a particularly fluid and lyrical interpretation of Art Deco style. *1935*

24½ in (62 cm) high

$3,000–5,000   **SWA**

Rare London & North Eastern Railway poster by Simon Bussy, printed by McCorquodale of Glasgow. It promotes the East Coast Line from London to Scotland. Printed in reddish-brown, tan, and black, it depicts a fawn leaping through ferns. Bussy is best known for his connections with the Bloomsbury Group and the woodcut designs he contributed to the Omega Workshop. *1927*

50½ in (128.25 cm) wide

$4,000–6,000   **SWA**

Imperial Airways calendar poster by Tom Purvis, whose style lends itself perfectly to the image of technical proficiency, efficient service, and luxury the airline wanted to convey. *1935*

30 in (76.25 cm) high

$3,000–4,000 **SWA**

Anonymous French Line lithographic poster printed by Hill, Stiffken & Co. of London. It elegantly depicts the luxury cruise liner *Normandie* at night. *1939*

39¾ in (101 cm) high

$15,000–20,000 **SWA**

Nelson Steam Navigation Company (NSNC) promotional poster showing a phalanx of stylized steamers rendered in black, yellow, and white above blue and green waves. *1930s*

40¼ in (102 cm) high

$1,000–1,800 **ON**

Edward McKnight Kauffer

Born in the United States, Edward Kauffer (1890–1954) was urged to travel by a professor in Chicago named McKnight. Out of respect, he later assumed the professor's name. Kauffer moved to London in 1914, returning to the United States in 1940. He is best known for his provocative London Underground posters, notably Power (1930), which depicts a fist, a train wheel, and a lightning flash. Influenced by Cubism and Futurism, Kauffer also designed for Shell Oil, British Petroleum, and Eastman & Sons. After 1940 he designed for numerous American patrons, including the New York City subway. Kauffer was married to the carpet designer Marion Dorn.

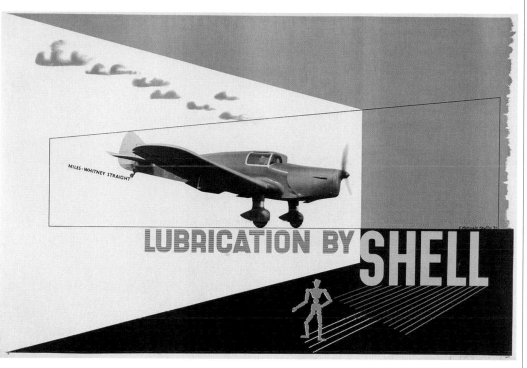

Edward McKnight Kauffer's Lubrication By Shell poster showing a Miles M-11 Whitney Straight airplane within a geometric layout of intersecting planes above a heavily stylized human figure. The main typography is cleverly positioned to serve the purpose of a runway. *1937*

44 in (112 cm) high

$7,000–8,000 **SWA**

Edward McKnight Kauffer poster promoting an exhibition at the New Burlington Galleries in London. Printed in three colors, it combines asymmetrical typography with post-Cubist forms. *1938*

30 in (76.25 cm) high

$3,000–4,000 **SWA**

Edward McKnight Kauffer's first-edition dust jacket for *The Green Toad* by Walter Masterman. Printed in two colors, blue and brown, the image was also used for a promotional poster. *1928*

8¼ in (21 cm) high

$900–1,500 **BLO**

Edward McKnight Kauffer two-color poster advertising an exhibition of modern art by The London Group. It includes stylized figures and abstract evocations of fine art. Printed by Dangerfield of London. *1919*

29¾ in (75.5 cm) high

$3,000–4,000 **SWA**

American Posters

Due to the popularity of magazine advertising, which had no impact in Europe until after World War II, there are relatively few American posters in Art Deco taste. Most date to the 1930s, the main exception being the 1920s works of Boris Lovet-Lorski. The majority of posters are travel-related, commissioned by the New York Central Railroad and other such companies. Among the best examples is a poster by Leslie Ragan (1897–1972) featuring the landmark Rockefeller Center complex in New York. Travel posters were also designed by the Vienna-born artist Gustav Krollman.

In 1935 President Franklin D. Roosevelt initiated the Works Progress Administration (WPA) as part of his post-Depression New Deal. The WPA sponsored thousands of struggling American artists and printed more than 2,000 poster designs by 1943, mostly for patriotic causes. Most reflect the optimism of the age in stylized Art Deco imagery but are of limited value. American posters promoting World's Fairs are more collectible.

Macy's in-store advertising poster (from a set of seven) promoting sales such as, as here, a Rosebush and Garden Sale. *1938*

33 in (83.75 cm) high

$1,500–2,000 (the set)　　　SWA

Restored National and State Parks poster from a series by Dorothy Waugh produced by the US Government Printing Office. *c. 1935*

40 in (101.5 cm) high

$1,500–2,000　　　SWA

New York Central Lines bird's-eye-view poster of the Rockefeller Center. Designed by Leslie Ragan, this poster was printed by the Latham Litho & Printing Co. of Long Island. *c. 1935*

40½ in (102.75 cm) high

$15,000–20,000　　　SWA

Hamburg-American Line poster by Albert Fuss depicting four cruise liners steaming for New York. Fuss designed several other similarly bold and stylized posters for the company. *c. 1930*

39½ in (100.25 cm) high

$1,500–2,000　　　SWA

Chicago World's Fair poster (one of several) by Weimer Pursell, printed by the Neely Printing Co. of Chicago in vivid colors. This example depicts the Hall of Science. *1933*

41½ in (105.5 cm) high

$5,000–7,000 SWA

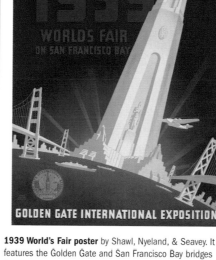

1939 World's Fair poster by Shawl, Nyeland, & Seavey. It features the Golden Gate and San Francisco Bay bridges flanking the Inca-inspired Tower of the Sun. *1937*

34½ in (87.5 cm) high

$5,000–7,000 SWA

1939 New York World's Fair bird's-eye-view poster by architect Nembhard N. Culin showing images of the futuristic Perisphere, Trylon, and Helicline buildings. *1937*

29 in (73.5 cm) high

$5,000–7,000 SWA

Polychrome Meet Me in St. Louis poster for the International Aircraft Exposition of 1930 (which later moved to New York). *1930*

26¼ in (67 cm) high

$4,000–5,000 SWA

Speed to Winter Playgrounds poster from a rare series by William P. Welsh for the Pullman Railway Co. With some damage. *1935*

26½ in (67.25 cm) high

$2,000–3,000 SWA

Boris Lovet-Lorski

Born in Lithuania, Boris Lovet-Lorski (1894–1973) emigrated to the United States in 1920, after completing studies in modeling at the Imperial Academy in St. Petersburg. Best known as a sculptor in bronze, he fashioned powerful, angular figures during the interwar years. Most of his subjects were female nudes. Posters by Lovet-Lorski are rare, but they show the strong influence of Constructivism and Futurism that he learned in Russia. They are among the most valuable of all American Art Deco posters. Lovet-Lorski's posters were produced by Hegeman, a specialty printer best known for World War I propaganda. After World War II Lovet-Lorski continued to create posters and public sculpture commissions, notably a statue of the young Abraham Lincoln outside the courthouse in Decatur, Illinois, completed in 1946.

New York Central Building poster by Chesley Bonestell showing the lit-up building at night framed by buildings on Park Avenue. *1930*

40½ in (103 cm) high

$6,000–8,000 SWA

Empire State Express poster by Leslie Ragan showing the train steaming through an autumnal landscape. *1941*

41 in (104.25 cm) high

$18,000–25,000 SWA

Boris Lovet-Lorski poster of the Russian dancer Mme. Anna Robénne, in black, gray, and white. She is depicted nude under translucent veils and Cubist abstract shafts of light. Printed by The Hegemen Print, New York. *c. 1925*

80 in (203.25 cm) high

$10,000–15,000 SWA

Glossary

Acid-etched A glass technique originally developed to create a matt or frosted finish by immersion in hydrofluoric acid. Areas not to be etched are protected with wax or varnish. Also used to remove areas of overlaid glass to create designs in relief on cameo-glass vessels.

Amboina-wood Sometimes spelled Amboyna, this is a decorative hardwood, varying in color from light reddish brown to orange, with a mottled figure and tightly curled grain.

Annealing A treatment of a metal that makes it malleable: it is heated and then quickly cooled so it can be manipulated into shape. In glassware, the term refers to slow cooling, which avoids cracking.

Annular Shaped like or forming a ring.

Atomizer A dispenser that transforms liquid, usually perfume, into a fine spray.

Aubusson The renowned French town that became a center for high-quality textile production from the mid-17th century.

Avant-garde A term used to describe an artist, design, object, or body of work that stands at the forefront of a movement. The work is often experimental, challenging established ideas and traditions.

Aventurine A translucent glass given a sparkling appearance by the incorporation of golden or copper flecks of oxidized metal. Can also be used as a glaze. The name probably derives from a quartz known in Italian as *avventurina*, which has a similar appearance.

Baguette cut A gem, often a diamond, cut to a long rectangular shape. It has a shape similar to the eponymous French bread stick.

Bakelite A synthetic plastic invented by L. H. Baekeland in 1907. This robust, versatile, non-flammable, and attractive plastic became popular in the 1920s and 1930s. It was used for domestic items, jewelry, and electrical fixtures. The term may also sometimes be used as a blanket term for early plastic.

Baluster form A bulbous shape similar to a vase or pear. It is a double-curved form that swells at the base and rises in a concave curve to a narrow neck. It is common on posts such as chair legs.

Banding A decorative strip of veneer in a contrasting wood. The technique is often used on the edges of drawer fronts, tabletops, and panels.

Baroque An ornate style that originated in 17th-century Italy and influenced architecture as well as furniture and the decorative arts. It is characterized by rich, heavy ornamentation with curves and scrolls.

Bauhaus The German design school founded by Modernist Walter Gropius in 1919 in Weimar. Its functional, geometric, and austere style focused on designs for industrial production. It greatly influenced the Art Deco style. The school was closed in 1933 by the German National Socialists, and many of the artists moved to the US to continue their work.

Bergère chair An informal, easy chair of generous proportions.

Bohemia The historical region in central Europe that occupies the western part of the Czech Republic. The area is particularly renowned for its glassware.

Book-matched Wooden veneer produced by slicing a single piece of wood into two (or more) pieces

so that the grain and figuring of each is identical. When folded open like the pages of a book, the two facing halves will display a mirror image of each other.

Brilliant cut Gemstones cut with 58 facets to produce a sparkling, light-reflecting effect.

Burr Also known as a burl, a burr is a growth that appears on a tree trunk. The wood inside is elaborately patterned and used for its decorative effect in veneering.

Cabriole leg A furniture leg with two curves forming an attenuated "S" shape.

Caliber cut Small stones cut into special shapes that are intended for use in commonly used designs. These stones usually have step-cut facets and are generally rectangular.

Cameo glass Glass made up of two or more separate, colored-glass layers. The top layer(s) is wheel-carved or acid-etched to produce a relief image and reveal the different-colored glass beneath.

Cantilever chair A chair with no back legs. The weight is supported by the base and the front legs of the chair. The style was popular with Modernist designers, who made examples from tubular steel.

Cased glass Where a piece of glass is covered with a further layer of glass, often of a contrasting color. In some instances, the casing will be further worked with cutting or etching to reveal the layer beneath.

Castellated A form of decoration similar in appearance to the indented battlements often seen on the top of castle walls.

Celadon Distinctive gray-green or blue-green glaze; the technique

imitates nephrite jade and has been used in China for over 2,000 years.

Chamfered A term for a surface that has been cut with a slanted edge for decorative effect or to protect a corner from damage.

Chasing A method of improving the detail on an embossed metal object. The surface is carefully engraved with a chasing tool, which resembles a small chisel, to add texture and pattern without removing any metal.

Chaton cut A circular gem with eight facets. Often used on rhinestones.

Chrome/chromium A shiny, silvery metal popular in the Art Deco period. It is made by smelting lead chromates and is usually plated on a base metal over nickel.

Chryselephantine A sculptural technique developed in ancient Greece, where wooden statues were covered with a layer of ivory and decorated with gold. In common usage, the term refers to a combination of bronze and ivory.

Cloisonné A method of applying enamel. Strips of metal are soldered on to the surface of an object to form individual cells arranged in a decorative design. The cells are filled with powdered colored enamels and fired. The resulting pattern is then highly polished.

Cold-patinated Metallic artifacts, most notably bronze statues, that change their surface color to, for example, green, brown, blue, or black once they have cooled after firing and after receiving a chemical coating.

Coquille d'oeuf A French term meaning "crushed eggshells." It refers to a decorative technique in which tiny pieces of eggshell are arranged on a surface and then covered with lacquer.

Cornice A decorated projection used as a crowning feature on tall pieces of furniture, such as cupboards.

Craquelure The deliberate crazing of a glazed surface achieved by firing ceramics to a precise temperature. The term also refers to a crackled effect on a glass or wooden surface.

Cubism An artistic movement often associated with painting. It was characterized by the use of two-dimensional, angular, and geometric forms. The style developed in the early 20th century and was highly influential on the work of Art Deco designers.

Cuerda seca A decorative technique originating in 15th-century southern Spain that translates roughly as "dry string" or "dry rope." It involves drawing the outline of a design onto a ceramic surface with a mixture of manganese and grease or wax. The spaces created by the outline are filled with colored glaze. When the ceramic is fired, the outlining prevents the colored areas from running into each other.

Curlicues Decorative devices that form fancy twists or curls.

Dentil pattern A design comprising a series of small rectangular blocks resembling teeth running beneath a band. The style comes from Classical architecture, where the ornamental device runs beneath a cornice. Since the 17th century it has also been used as a decorative molding on furniture and a painted border on ceramics.

Diaper A decorative motif that features a repeated pattern. The pattern incorporates geometric shapes such as diamonds, squares, or lozenges.

Dowel-jointed Two component parts fastened to one another by the insertion of one or more dowels—small headless pins of circular section—into directly aligned holes drilled into each of the components. Dowels are also often used to reinforce other traditional types of joints, such as the mortise-and-tenon.

Drop-in seat A removable, usually upholstered, chair seat made separately and then "dropped in" to the frame of the seat.

Drum table A writing table with a round top on a central column. The top is often leather-covered, with drawers beneath.

Earthenware Low-fired pottery made of a porous clay body. The piece is waterproofed with a coating glaze.

Ebonized Wood or furniture with a black stained or polished surface to resemble a species of hardwood.

Enameled A piece in which ename—a colored, opaque composition derived from glass—is used as decoration.

Etruscan A style used in the decorative arts and interior decoration that uses Classical motifs and was inspired by the 18th-century discovery of Etruscan and Greek artifacts. It is characterized by the use of terra cotta, red, black, and white, and motifs such as lions, birds, sphinxes, festoons, and urns.

Faience The French name for tin-glazed earthenware of a buff or pale-red color covered with white enamel or glaze, which gives it the appearance of porcelain.

Faux-marbre Translates from the French as "false marble," a type of decoration imitating marble, usually with paint.

Filigree Decorative arrangement of twisted gold or silver wire soldered into openwork forms or onto a flat panel. It is mostly associated with small objects and jewelry.

Finial A decorative feature that terminates the apex of a piece. It may form the pinnacle of a piece of furniture or appear on the cover of a vessel and also act as a handle.

Flapper An emancipated young woman of the 1920s who reveled in the new-found freedoms in fashion and leisure during the Jazz Age.

Flashed Method of decorating clear glass by covering it with one or more thin layers of colored glass.

Fluting A vertical pattern of shallow, concave, parallel grooves.

Free-blown Where a gather of molten glass is taken from the furnace using a blowing rod and then inflated by the glass-blower to form a shape.

Frieze A decorative band, as along the upper part of a wall in a room. This term derives from architecture and is sometimes used to describe furniture decoration.

Frosted glass Glass that has been given a matt, near-opaque finish similar to frost by the application of acid, sandblasting, or mechanical etching.

Fruit salads Also known as tutti frutti. Multicolored Indian gemstones carved to resemble flowers, fruits, or leaves. First used in the West by Cartier, they were copied for costume jewelry in pressed or molded colored glass.

Gilded A decorative finish in which gold leaf or powdered gold is applied to materials such as wood, leather, glass, ceramics, and silver.

Gilt Describes a surface that has been coated in gold, usually gold leaf or plate.

Gouache A quick-drying, water-based paint.

Half-doll A half-length figurine that became very popular in the 1930s. Half-dolls were typically made from porcelain and represented fashionable, elegant ladies.

Harlequinesque A style associated with a pattern of brightly colored diamond shapes. Derived from the costume of Harlequin, a character from the Italian theater style known as the *Commedia dell'Arte.*

Haute couture A French term that translates as "high fashion" and refers to innovative, well-made, exclusive, and expensive clothing designed by leading fashion houses.

Incised A pattern scratched into the body of a ceramic or glass vessel with a sharp instrument, such as a metal point, as decoration or to record an inscription, date, or name.

In relief A form of decoration in which a pattern or motif stands out from the surface.

Intaglio cut An image that is cut into the surface of a piece of glass or a gemstone.

Intercalaire A form of decoration applied between layers of glass.

Iridescence A surface effect that creates the appearance of rainbow colors caused by differential refraction of light waves, as sometimes observed on an oil spill on a wet surface. It is produced by spraying a mist of metallic salts on to the hot glass vessel.

Knop A protruding shape. The term can refer to a handle on a lid, the finial on the end of a spoon handle, or the protrusion found on the middle of a wine-glass stem.

Lacquer Natural resin of the *Rhus vernicifera* tree, native to China. It is colored with pigment, usually black, red, or with gold flecks, and applied, primarily to wooden surfaces, in layers that are polished to produce a hard, high-gloss finish.

Lamp work Delicate ornamental technique used to make glass pieces fashioned from thin rods. The rods are heated over a small burner and then shaped, bent, and attached to each other. These designs are sometimes embedded in paperweights and glass spheres.

Lathe-turned A term used to describe a piece of wood or metal that has been shaped using a lathe. The lathe turns the piece on a horizontal axis against a fixed tool, which shapes the piece of wood or metal.

Lead crystal A type of glass with a high red-lead content. It is a hard glass, ideal for producing successful cut-glass designs. However, it cools quickly, so it is not good for manipulating into complex shapes. It is sometimes known as "crystal" or "quartz crystal."

Lens cutting A glass-cutting pattern comprising a series of circular or oval cuts, each of a shape similar to eyeglass lenses and also concave or convex in profile, thereby causing minor distortions in the path of light passing through it.

Lithography Black-and-white or color printing process in which a design is drawn with a greasy crayon on a stone block or metal plate. Water and then ink are poured over the surface, and the crayon repels the water but retains the ink, which then transfers the design to another medium (such as paper) when the block or plate is applied under pressure.

Lozenge A diamond-shaped motif that forms a diaper pattern, or can be the base for other patterns.

Luster Iridescent metallic finish applied to the surface of ceramics or glass, mostly by the application of metallic pigments.

Luting Method of joining separate ceramic components using slip (liquid clay) as an adhesive.

Macassar ebony A variety of the expensive hardwood ebony, with streaked golden brown and black figuring. Also known as calamander or marblewood.

Machine-molded glass A form of glassware shaped by being mechanically blown into a mold.

Marquetry Decorative veneer work applied to furniture. Patterns or motifs are formed by contrasting grained or colored shapes of wooden veneer and/or other material such as metals, ivory, and mother-of-pearl.

Marquise cut A stone cut in the brilliant style with the exception that the outline is boat-shaped instead of circular. Also known as navette cut.

Medallion Flat or in-relief decorative motif of circular or oval outline used in most mediums and, in jewelry, worn as a pendant or brooch.

Mesoamerican A term that refers to objects or artwork from or inspired by Mesoamerica, a region that extends south and east from central Mexico and includes parts of Guatemala, Belize, Honduras, and Nicaragua.

Minaudière A small decorative case for carrying items such as makeup or jewelry.

Miter cut A type of cut decoration used on glass, made with a

V-edged grinding wheel to produce a deep groove.

Modern movement A vocabulary of architecture and design prevalent between the world wars. In theory, it shunned unnecessary ornament and emphasized the industrial origins of modern materials and methods of manufacture. Much of it was informed by Le Corbusier's desire to render the home "a machine for living in."

Moiré An irregular wavy finish or pattern.

Navette cut *See* Marquise cut.

Opalescent glass A form of glass with a milky blue appearance similar to the color of opals. It also displays an amber tint under certain lighting conditions.

Optic glass Hollow glass vessels dipped in a mold (in many cases prior to blowing) to create a very subtle ribbed or undulating wave-like pattern on their exterior or, more usually, interior surface. In both cases, this causes distortions— an "optical effect"— in the appearance of the glass when viewed from the outside.

Palisander Species of hardwood also known as rosewood, widely used for veneering and banding. It ranges in color from orange-yellow to orange-red and is streaked with black- or violet-colored figuring.

Parian An unglazed porcelain with a semi-matt finish, also called "statuary porcelain." It is known as parian because of its similarity to the white marble found on the Greek island of Paros.

Parquetry Decorative veneering technique applied to floors and furniture. It is similar to marquetry but restricted to geometric patterns.

Pâte-de-cristal Translates from the French as "paste glass" and is

a translucent form of glassware made by mixing ground glass with a liquid to form a paste. It is then either applied in layers to a preblown body or, more usually, pressed into a mold to form the required shape.

Pâte-de-verre *See Pâte de cristal.*

Patina Mellow and/or lustrous surface sheen on furniture or metalware acquired gradually over time through exposure to a combination of polishing, dirt, handling, and the atmosphere.

Pavé-set A discreet setting for diamonds or gems that places or "paves in" stones closely together. The effect is one of a continuous jeweled surface.

Pewter An alloy of tin and lead with other metals. It has been used as a more affordable and durable alternative to silver since the Middle Ages.

Phenolic An early type of plastic made from phenol and formaldehyde, produced in a range of bright colors. It was often used for jewelry and radios during the late Art Deco period.

Pillow-form vase A type of vase with a pillow-shaped body— usually a slightly bulbous ovoid form, but squarer versions were also produced.

Plastics A collective term for synthetic or semisynthetic substances that are moldable under heat or pressure. During the Art Deco period, phenolics and Bakelite came into widespread use.

Plywood An inexpensive form of wooden boarding first popularized in the early 20th century. It is used in the manufacture of furniture and architectural elements and is made from two or more thin layers of wood glued together. The woods are joined with the grains set alternately at right angles for strength.

Poincons The French term for marks of manufacture or brand.

Porcelain A translucent white ceramic body twice fired at high temperature in either hard- or soft-paste form. Hard porcelain is also known as true porcelain and includes china clay (kaolin) and china stone (petuntse). Soft porcelain excludes kaolin and is more brittle.

Powdered-enamel inclusions A form of decoration in which colored enamel in powder form is added to the body of a glass object, either within the body of the glass or between layers of glass.

Precious stones A set of gems treasured for their value and rarity. They have intrinsic value regardless of use or setting. The best-known examples include diamonds, emeralds, rubies, and sapphires.

Pulled-feather decoration A motif used in glassmaking, in which the colors are manipulated to resemble a feather.

Reeding Narrow parallel strips of convex molding.

Repoussé/reposse Translates from the French as "pushed out" and is the process of chasing metal that has been embossed to refine or further define the design.

Rose cut Form of gemstone cut, not as reflective as a brilliant cut. It is characterized by triangular facets (usually 24) above a flat base.

Saber legs Furniture legs of outward-pointing, gentle concave shape similar to the curved blade of a sabre (a form of sword).

Sabot French term for a metal "shoe" fitted to the bottom of furniture legs.

Semiprecious stones Stones that have intrinsic value but are not as valuable as precious stones, due to factors such as greater abundance. Examples include amethyst, garnet, opal, and tourmaline.

Sgraffito Decorative technique for ceramics that translates from the Italian as "little scratch." It involves cutting a pattern into an overlaid slip to reveal the contrasting ground beneath.

Shagreen Strictly, the skin of a shark or stingray, but also untanned leather with a coarse granular finish and usually dyed green; in both cases, used as a decorative veneer or for items such as handbags or purses.

Slipcast Forming technique for ceramics in which liquid clay (slip) is poured into water-absorbent plaster-of-Paris molds. After any excess is poured away, and as it dries, the slip forms an even layer on the interior surface of the molds. Following slight shrinkage of the slip, the molds are removed to reveal the undecorated cast.

Slip-glaze A ceramic finish containing both glaze and slip (liquid clay) that serves as both a decorative coating and a seal for a porous underbody.

Spinel Mineral stone that is often used in jewelry and found in numerous colors ranging from yellow to purple and including a rubylike red.

Split cut A cut-glass pattern consisting of leaflike elongated ovoid forms.

Sponged paint A decorative finish, mainly used on ceramics, in which a mottled effect with subtle gradations of color is created either by dabbing on paint with a wet sponge or by partially dabbing off already-applied wet paint with a sponge.

Squab A removable, stuffed chair cushion. The term can also be used to describe a large padded seat.

Star cut A cut-glass pattern in which a series of cut lines radiate out from a central point to form the shape of a star.

Streamlined Originally an engineering-design concept in which smooth, clean shapes are used to increase the speed of an object by reducing its resistance to the flow of air. This aesthetic was adopted in the decorative arts during the 1930s and used to create shapes and forms denoting speed and dynamism.

Stuffed over A form of upholstered seating in which, for comfort, the underlying stuffing and the seat cover are carried over the leading edge or front rail of the seat frame.

Surmoulages Copies of objects that have been cast in molds made from the original objects. Used to make, for example, recasts of sculptures or medallions.

Tabouret A French term for a low upholstered stool.

Tortoiseshell Semitranslucent hornlike material of mottled brown (or black) and yellow coloration, originally fashioned from the shell of the rare hawksbill turtle. The hawksbill is now a protected species, so most tortoiseshell is simulated in plastic.

Transom A crosspiece or lintel over a door, a small window above a door, or a component dividing a window horizontally.

Trellis pattern A geometric crisscross design similar in appearance to trelliswork supports for cultivated plants; often used as a background pattern for other decorative motifs.

Triptych Three separate panels hinged together to form one work of art or decorative artifact.

Tuja root Pale-colored root wood from the tuja tree (also known as thuja, thuya, or white cedar).

Uranium glass A type of glass tinted yellow by the addition of a small quantity of uranium; it appears fluorescent under ultraviolet light.

Veneer A thin layer of decorative wood (or a material such as ivory or tortoiseshell) glued to the surface of a coarser, blander, cheaper wood.

Vinyl Short for polyvinyl chloride, vinyl is a type of plastic that came into widespread use in the late 1930s.

Vitrified The hard, glasslike composition of enamels once they have been fired (on, for example, ceramics).

Wheel-carved Glassware with a decorative pattern or motif that has been carved (or cut or engraved) with a rotating wheel (or wheels) of metal or stone. The cutting edges of the wheels have different profiles to produce different effects.

Wrought iron A malleable form of iron containing, unlike cast iron, little cementite or graphite, which makes it suitable for fashioning into shapes.

Ziggurat Pyramidal temple towers originally built by Mesopotamian religious cultures and comprising a series of receding tiers rising from a rectangular, oval, or square base.

Directory of Dealers and Auction Houses and their Source Codes

Each Art Deco piece shown in this book has an accompanying letter code that identifies the dealer or auction house that either is selling or has sold it, or the museum or picture agency where the piece or image is held. It should be noted that inclusion in this book in no way constitutes or implies a contract or a binding offer on the part of any contributing dealer or auction house to supply or sell the pieces illustrated, or similar items, at the price stated.

AAC
Sanford Alderfer Auction Company
501 Fairgrounds Road
Hatfield, PA 19440
Tel: (215) 393-3000
E-mail: info@alderferauction.com
www.alderferauction.com

ABAA
No longer trading

ADE
Art Deco Etc
73 Upper Gloucester Road
Brighton, Sussex BN1 3LQ, UK
Tel: 011 44 1273 202 937
E-mail: johnclark@artdecoetc.co.uk

AG
Antique Glass @ Frank Dux Antiques
33 Belvedere, Lansdown Road
Bath, Somerset BA1 5HR, UK
Tel: 011 44 1225 312 367
Fax: 011 44 1225 312 367
E-mail: m.hopkins@antique-glass.co.uk
www.antique-glass.co.uk

AHL
Andrea Hall Levy
PO Box 1243, Riverdale, NY 10471
Tel: (646) 441-1726
E-mail: barangrill@aol.com

AL
Andrew Lineham Fine Glass
PO Box 465, Chichester
West Sussex PO18 8WZ, UK
Tel: 011 44 1243 576 241
Fax: 011 44 1243 576 241
Cell: 011 44 7767 702 722
E-mail: andrew@antiquecoloured glass.com
www.antiquecolouredglass.info

AMO
Alan Moss
436 Lafayette Street
New York, NY 10003
Tel: (212) 47-1310
Fax: (212) 387-9493

ANAA
Anastacia's Antiques
617 Bainbridge Street
Philadelphia, PA 19147

AS&S
Andrew Smith & Son Auctions
The Auction Rooms, Manor Farm
Itchen Stoke, Winchester
Hampshire SO24 0QT, UK
Tel: 011 44 1962 735 988
Fax: 011 44 1962 738 879
E-mail: auctions@andrewsmith andson.com

ATL
Antique Textiles and Lighting
34 Belvedere
Lansdown Road
Bath, Somerset BA1 5HR, UK
Tel: 011 44 1225 310 795
www.antiquetextilesandlighting.co.uk

BAD
Beth
Unit GO43/4, Alfie's Antique Market
13 Church Street
Marylebone
London NW8 8DT, UK
Cell: 011 44 7776 136 003

BB
Barbara Blau
c/o South Street Antiques Market
615 South 6th Street
Philadelphia, PA 19147
Tel: (215) 739-4995/(215) 592-0256
E-mail: bbjools@msn.com

BEA
Beaussant Lefèvre
32 Rue Drouot, 75009 Paris, France
Tel: 011 33 1 4770 4000
Fax: 011 33 1 4770 6240
E-mail: beaussant-lefevre@auction.fr
www.beaussant-lefevre.auction.fr

BEL
Belhorn Auction Services LLC
PO Box 20211
Columbus, OH 43220
Tel: (614) 921-9441
Fax: (614) 921-9447
www.belhorn.com

BEV
Beverley
30 Church Street
London NW8 8EP, UK
Tel: 011 44 20 7262 1576

BK
Bukowskis
Arsenalsgatan 4, Box 1754
11187 Stockholm, Sweden
Tel: 011 46 8 614 0800
Fax: 011 46 8 611 4674
E-mail: info@bukowskis.se
www.bukowskis.se

BLO
Bloomsbury Auctions
Bloomsbury House
24 Maddox Street
London W1S 1PP, UK
Tel: 011 44 20 7495 9494
Fax: 011 44 20 7495 9499
E-mail: info@bloomsburyauctions.com
www.bloomsburyauctions.com

BMN
Auktionshaus Bergmann
Möhrendorfestraße 4
91056 Erlangen, Germany
Tel: 011 49 9 131 450 666
E-mail: kontakt@auction-bergmann.de
www.auction-bergmann.de

BONBAY
Bonhams
101 New Bond Street
London W1S 1SR, UK
Tel: 011 44 20 7447 4447
Fax: 011 44 20 7447 7400
E-mail: info@bonhams.com
www.bonhams.com

BRI
Bridgeman Art Library
www.bridgeman.co.uk

BW
Biddle & Webb of Birmingham
Icknield Square
Ladywood
Middleway
Birmingham B16 0PP, UK
Tel: 011 44 121 455 8042
Fax: 011 44 121 454 9615
E-mail: info@biddleandwebb.com
www.biddleandwebb.co.uk

BY
Bonny Yankauer
bonnyy@aol.com

C
Cottees
The Market
East Street, Wareham
Dorset BH20 4NR, UK
Tel: 011 44 1929 552 826 /
01929 554 915
Fax: 011 44 1929 554 916
E-mail: auctions@cottees.fsnet.co.uk
www.auctionsatcottees.co.uk

CA
Chiswick Auctions
1-5 Colville Road
London W3 8BL, UK
Tel: 011 44 20 8992 4442
Fax: 011 44 20 8896 0541
www.chiswickauctions.co.uk

CALD
Calderwood Gallery
1622 Spruce Street
Philadelphia, PA 19103
Tel: (215) 546-5357
Fax: (215) 546-5234
E-mail: jc@calderwoodgallery.com
www.calderwoodgallery.com

CARS
C.A.R.S. of Brighton
4-4a Chapel Terrace Mews
Kemp Town, Brighton
Sussex BN2 1HU, UK
Tel: 011 44 1273 622 722
E-mail: cars@kemptown-
brighton.freeserve.co.uk
www.carsofbrighton.co.uk

CAT
CatalinRadio.com
5443 Schultz Drive
Sylvania, OH 43560
Tel: (419) 824-2469
E-mail: steve@catalinradio.com
www.catalinradio.com

CBU
Chèz Burnette
c/o South Street Antiques Market
615 South 6th Street
Philadelphia, PA 19147
Tel: (215) 592-0256

CHEF
Cheffins
Clifton House, 1&2 Clifton Road
Cambridge CB1 7EA, UK
Tel: 011 44 1223 213 343
E-mail: fine.art@cheffins.co.uk
www.cheffins.co.uk

CHI
Chicago Silver
E-mail: chicagosilver@charter.net
www.chicagosilver.com

CHR
Christie's Images
www.christiesimages.com

CHS
China Search
PO Box 1202, Kenilworth
Warwickshire, CV8 2WW, UK
Tel: 011 44 1926 512 402
Fax: 011 44 1926 859 311
E-mail: helen@chinasearch.co.uk
www.chinasearch.co.uk

CMG
Corning Museum of Glass
One Museum Way
Corning, NY 14830
Tel: (607) 937-5371
E-mail: info@cmog.org
www.cmog.org

COR
Corbis
www.corbis.com

CRIS
Cristobal
26 Church Street
London NW8 8EP, UK
Tel: 011 44 20 7724 7230
Fax: 011 44 20 7724 7230
E-mail: steven@cristobal.co.uk
www.cristobal.co.uk

CSB
Chenu Scrive Berard
Hôtel des Ventes Lyon Presqu'île
Groupe Ivoire
6 Rue Marcel Rivière
69002 Lyon, France
Tel: 011 33 4 7277 7801
Fax: 011 33 4 7256 3007
www.chenu-scrive.com

CUV
Cuvreau Expertises Enchères
6 Boulevard Saint-Vincent-de-Paul
40990 Saint-Paul-Les-Dax, France
Tel: 011 33 5 5835 4249
Fax: 011 33 5 5835 4247
E-mail: cuvreau.encheres@
wanadoo.fr

CWN
Cowan Museum
Rocky River Public Library
1600 Hampton Road
Rocky River, OH 44116
Tel: (440) 333-7610 (ext. 263)
www.rrpl.org

DA
Davies Antiques
c/o Cadogan Tate
Unit 6, 6-12 Ponton Road
London SW8 5BA, UK
Tel: 011 44 20 8947 1902
E-mail: hugh.davies@
btconnect.com
www.antique-meissen.com

DD
Decodame.com
853 Vanderbilt Beach Road
PMB 8, Naples, FL 34108
Tel: (239) 514-6797
info@decodame.com
www.decodame.com

DEL
DeLorenzo Gallery
956 Madison Avenue
New York NY 10021
Tel: (212) 249-7575
Fax: (212) 861-7507

DETC
Deco Etc
122 West 25th Street
(between 6th & 7th Aves)
New York, NY 10001
Tel: (212) 675-3326
Cell: (347) 423-6446
www.decoetc.net

DH
Huxtins
david@huxtins.com
www.huxtins.com

DN
Dreweatt Neate
Donnington Priory Salerooms
Donnington
Newbury
Berkshire RG14 2JE, UK
Tel: 011 44 1635 553 553
Fax: 011 44 1635 553 599
E-mail: donnington@dnfa.com
www.dnfa.com/donnington

DOR
Palais Dorotheum
Dorotheergasse 17
1010 Vienna, Austria
Tel: 011 43 1 515 600
Fax: 011 43 1 515 60443
E-mail: kundendienst@dorotheum.at
www.dorotheum.com

DRA
David Rago Auctions
333 North Main Street
Lambertville, NJ 08530
Tel: (609) 397-9374
Fax: (609) 397-9377
E-mail: info@ragoarts.com
www.ragoarts.com

DUK
HY Duke and Son
The Dorchester Fine Art Salerooms
Weymouth Avenue
Dorchester
Dorset DT1 1QS, UK
Tel: 011 44 1305 265 080
E-mail: enquiries@dukes-
auctions.com
www.dukes-auctions.com

ECLEC
Eclectica
2 Charlton Place
Islington
London N1 8AJ, UK
Tel: 011 44 20 7226 5625
E-mail: liz@eclectica.biz
www.eclectica.biz

EG
Edison Gallery
Tel: (617) 359-4678
E-mail: glastris@edisongallery.com
www.edisongallery.com

F
Fellows & Sons
Augusta House
19 Augusta Street
Hockley
Birmingham, B18 6JA, UK
Tel: 011 44 121 212 2131
Fax: 011 44 121 212 1249
E-mail: info@fellows.co.uk
www.fellows.co.uk

FFA
Finesse Fine Art
Empool Cottage, West Knighton
Dorset DT2 8PE, UK
Tel: 011 44 1305 854 286
Fax: 011 44 1305 852 888
Cell: 011 44 7973 886 937
E-mail: tony@finesse-fine-art.com
www.finesse-fine-art.com

FFM
Festival
London, UK

FIS
Auktionshaus Dr Fischer
Trappensee-Schlößchen
74074 Heilbronn, Germany
Tel: 011 49 71 3115 5570
Fax: 011 49 71 3115 55720
E-mail: info@auctions-fischer.de
www.auctions-fischer.de

FRE
Freeman's
1808 Chestnut Street
Philadelphia, PA 19103
Tel: (215) 563-9275
Fax: (215) 563-8236
E-mail: info@freemansauction.com
www.freemansauction.com

GCL
Claude Lee at The Ginnel
The Ginnel Antiques Centre
off Parliament Street, Harrogate
North Yorkshire HG1 2RB, UK
Tel: 011 44 1423 508 857
E-mail: info@theginnel.com
www.redhouseyork.co.uk

GHOU
Gardiner Houlgate
Bath Auction Rooms, 9 Leafield Way
Corsham, Wiltshire SN13 9SW, UK
Tel: 011 44 1225 812 912
Fax: 011 44 1225 817 777
E-mail: auctions@gardiner-houlgate.co.uk

GKA
Kismet Antiques
The Ginnel Antiques Centre
off Parliament Street, Harrogate
North Yorkshire HG1 2RB, UK
Tel: 011 44 1423 508 857
E-mail: info@theginnel.com
www.redhouseyork.co.uk

GYG
Galerie Yves Gastou
12 Rue Bonaparte
75006 Paris, France
Tel: 011 33 1 5373 0010
Fax: 011 33 1 5373 0012
E-mail: galeriegastou@noos.fr
www.galerieyvesgastou.com

HERR
WG Herr Art & Auction House
Friesenwall 35
50672 Cologne, Germany
Tel: 011 49 221 254 548
Fax: 011 49 221 270 6742
E-mail: kunst@herr-auktionen.de
www.herr-auktionen.de

HSD
High Style Deco
224 West 18th Street
New York, NY 10011
Tel: (212) 647-0035
Fax: (212) 647-0031
E-mail: howard@highstyledeco.com
www.highstyledeco.com

J&H
Jacobs and Hunt Fine Art Auctioneers Limited
26 Lavant Street
Petersfield
Hampshire GU32 3EF, UK
Tel: 011 44 1730 233 933
Fax: 011 44 1730 262 323
E-mail: auctions@jacobsandhunt.com
www.jacobsandhunt.com

JAZ
Jazzy Art Deco
34 Church Street
Marylebone
London, NW8 8EP, UK
Tel: 011 44 20 7724 0837
Fax: 011 44 20 7724 3727
Cell: 011 44 7904 262 591
E-mail: Jazzyartdeco321@aol.com
www.jazzyartdeco.com

JBC
James Bridges Collection
E-mail: james@jdbridges.fsnet.co.uk

JBS
John Bull (Antiques) Ltd
JB Silverware
139A New Bond St
London W1S 2TN, UK
Tel: 011 44 20 7629 1251
Fax: 011 44 20 7495 3001
E-mail: elliot@jbsilverware.co.uk
www.jbsilverware.co.uk
www.antique-silver.co.uk

JDJ
James D Julia Inc.
PO Box 830
Fairfield, Maine 04937
Tel: (207) 453-7125
Fax: (207) 453-2502
E-mail: jjulia@juliaauctions.com
www.juliaauctions.com

JES
John Jesse
160 Kensington Church Street
London W8 4BN, UK
Tel: 011 44 20 7229 0312
Fax: 011 44 20 7229 4732
E-mail: jj@johnjesse.com

JH
Jeanette Hayhurst Fine Glass
32a Kensington Church Street
London W8 4HA, UK
Tel: 011 44 20 7938 1539

JHB
Joseph Bonnar
72 Thistle Street
Edinburgh EH2 1EN, UK
Tel: 011 44 131 226 2811
Fax: 011 44 131 225 9438

JP
Juwelier Pütz
St Aspern Straße 17–21
50667 Cologne
Germany
Tel: 011 49 221 257 4995

JV
June Victor
Vintage Modes
Grays Antiques Market
1–7 Davies Mews
London W1Y 2PL, UK
Tel: 011 44 20 7629 7034
E-mail: info@vintagemodes.co.uk
www.vintagemodes.co.uk

K&R
Keller & Ross
PO Box 783
Melrose, MA 02716
Tel: (978) 988-1066
E-mail: kellerross@aol.com
http://members.aol.com/kellerross

KAU
Auktionshaus Kaupp
Schloss Sulzburg
Hauptstraße 62
79295 Sulzburg
Germany
Tel: 011 49 76 3450 380
Fax: 011 49 76 3450 3850
E-mail: auktionen@kaupp.de
www.kaupp.de

L&T
Lyon and Turnbull Ltd
33 Broughton Place
Edinburgh EH1 3RR, UK
Tel: 011 44 131 557 8844
Fax: 011 44 131 557 8668
E-mail: info@lyonandturnbull.com
www.lyonandturnbull.com

LANE
Eileen Lane Antiques
150 Thompson Street
New York, NY 10012
Tel: (212) 475-2988
E-mail: EileenLaneA@aol.com
www.eileenlaneantiques.com

LB
Linda Bee
Grays Antique Market
1–7 Davies Mews
London W1Y 2LP, UK
Tel: 011 44 20 7629 5921
E-mail: lindabee@grays.clara.net
www.graysantiques.com

LC
Lawrence's Auctioneers
The Linen Yard
South Street
Crewkerne
Somerset TA18 8AB, UK
Tel: 011 44 1460 73041
Fax: 011 44 1460 270 799
E-mail: enquiries@lawrences.co.uk
www.lawrences.co.uk

LH
Lucy
1118 Pine Street
Philadelphia, PA

LM
Lili Marleen Antiques
52 White Street
New York, NY 10013
Tel: (212) 219-0006
Fax: (212) 219-1246
E-mail: info@lilimarleen.net
www.lilimarleen.net

LN
Lillian Nassau Ltd
220 East 57th Street
New York, NY 10022
Tel: (212) 759-6062
Fax: (212) 832-9493
www.lilliannassau.com

LOZ
Frederic Lozada Expertises
10 Rue de Pomereu
75116 Paris, France
Tel: 011 33 1 5370 2370
Fax: 011 33 1 5370 9890
E-mail: fle@fredericlozada.com
www.fredericlozada.com

MA
Manic Attic
Stand S48/49
Alfie's Antiques Market
13 Church Street
London NW8 8DT, UK
Tel: 011 44 20 7723 6105
E-mail: manicattic@alfies.clara.net

MACK
Macklowe Gallery
667 Madison Avenue
New York, NY 10021
Tel: (212) 644-6400
Fax: (212) 755-6143
E-mail: email@macklowegallery.com
www.macklowegallery.com

MAL
Mallett Antiques
141 New Bond Street
London W1S 2BS, UK
Tel: 011 44 20 7499 7411
Fax: 011 44 20 7495 3179
www.mallettantiques.com

MARA
Marie Antiques
Unit G107
136–137 Alfie's Antique Market
13 Church Street, Marylebone
London NW8 8DT, UK
Tel: 011 44 20 7706 3727
E-mail: marie136@globalnet.co.uk
www.marieantiques.co.uk

MHC
Mark Hill Collection
Cell: 011 44 7798 915 474
E-mail: stylophile@btopenworld.com

MHT
Mum Had That
E-mail: info@mumhadthat.com
www.mumhadthat.com

MI
Mood Indigo
181 Prince Street
New York, NY 10012
Tel: (212) 254-1176
E-mail: info@moodindigo
newyork.com
www.moodindigonewyork.com

ML
Mark Laino
c/o South Street Antiques Market
615 South 6th Street
Philadelphia, PA 19147 USA

MOD
Moderne Gallery
111 North 3rd Street
Philadelphia, PA 19106
Tel: (215) 923-8536
E-mail: RAibel@aol.com
www.modernegallery.com

MSM
Modernism Gallery
800 Douglas Road, Suite 101
Coral Gables, FL 33134
Tel: (305) 442-8743
Fax: (305) 443-3074
E-mail: artdeco@modernism.com
www.modernism.com

NBLM
N. Bloom & Son (1912) Ltd
12 Piccadilly Arcade
London SW1Y 6NH, UK
Tel: 011 44 20 7629 5060
Fax: 011 44 20 7493 2528
E-mail: nbloom@nbloom.com
www.nbloom.com

OACC
Otford Antiques and Collectors Centre
26–28 High Street
Otford
Kent TN14 5PQ, UK
Tel: 011 44 1959 522 025
Fax: 011 44 1959 525 858
E-mail: info@otfordantiques.co.uk
www.otfordantiques.co.uk

OE
Galerie Olivia et Emmanuel
Le Village Suisse
78 Avenue de Suffren
75015 Paris, France
Tel/Fax: 011 33 1 4306 8530
E-mail: oliviasilver@aol.com

ON
Onslows
The Coach House, Manor Road
Stourpaine, Dorset DT11 8TQ, UK
Tel: 011 44 1258 488 838
Fax: 011 44 1258 488 838
E-mail: enquiries@onslows.co.uk
www.onslows.co.uk

PAC
Port Antiques Center
289 Main Street
Port Washington, NY 11050
Tel: (516) 767-3313
E-mail: visualedge2@aol.com

PBA
Pierre Bergé & Associés
12 Rue Drouot, 75009 Paris, France
Tel: 011 33 1 4949 9000
Fax: 011 33 1 4949 9001
www.pba-auctions.com

PC
Private Collection

PIL
Salle des Ventes Pillet
1 Rue de la Libération
27480 Lyons la Forêt, France
Tel: 011 33 2 3249 6064
www.pillet.auction.fr

PSA
Potteries Specialist Auctions
271 Waterloo Road, Cobridge
Stoke-on-Trent, Staffs ST6 3HR, UK
Tel: 011 44 1782 286 622
E-mail: enquiries@potteries
auctions.com
www.potteriesauctions.com

PSI
Paul Simons
5 Georgian Village, Islington
London N1, UK
Cell: 011 44 7733 326 574
E-mail: Pauliobanton@hotmail.com

QU
Quittenbaum Kunstauktionen München
Hohenstaufenstraße 1
80801 Munich, Germany
Tel: 011 49 89 3300 756
E-mail: info@quittenbaum.de
www.quittenbaum.de

RBRG
RBR Group at Grays
158/168 Grays Antique Market
58 Davies Street
London W1K 5LP, UK
Tel: 011 44 20 7629 4769
E-mail: rbr@grays.clara.net

RDL
David Rago/Nicholas Dawes Lalique Auctions
333 North Main Street
Lambertville, NJ 08530
Tel: (609) 397-9374
Fax: (609) 397-9377
E-mail: info@ragoarts.com
www.ragoarts.com

RG
Richard Gibbon
34/34a Islington Green
London N1 8DU, UK
Tel: 011 44 20 7354 2852
E-mail: neljeweluk@aol.com

RH
Rick Hubbard Art Deco
Cell: 011 44 7767 267 607
E-mail: rick@rickhubbard-
artdeco.co.uk
www.rickhubbard-artdeco.co.uk

RITZ
Ritzy
7 The Mall Antiques Arcade
359 Upper Street
London N1 0PD, UK
Tel: 011 44 20 7704 0127

RMN
Réunion des Musées Nationaux
www.photo.rmn.fr

ROS
Rosebery's
74–76 Knight's Hill, West Norwood
London SE27 0JD, UK
Tel: 011 44 20 8761 2522
Fax: 011 44 20 8761 2524
E-mail: auctions@roseberys.co.uk
www.roseberys.co.uk

ROX
Roxanne Stuart
Langhorne, PA
Tel: (215) 750-8868
E-mail: gemfairy@aol.com

RR
Red Roses at Vintage Modes
Grays Antiques Market
1–7 Davies Mews
London W1Y 2PL, UK
Tel: 011 44 20 7629 7034
E-mail: sallie_ead@lycos.com
www.vintagemodes.co.uk

RSS
Rossini SA
7 Rue Drouot
75009 Paris, France
Tel: 011 33 1 5334 5500
Fax: 011 33 1 4247 1026
E-mail: contact@rossini.fr
www.rossini.fr

RTC
Ritchies Auctioneers & Appraisers
288 King Street East
Toronto, Ontario M5A 1KA
Tel: (416) 364-1864
Fax: (416) 364-0704
E-mail: auction@ritchies.com
www.ritchies.com

S&K
Sloans & Kenyon
7034 Wisconsin Avenue
Chevy Chase, MD 20815
Tel: (301) 634-2330
Fax: (301) 656-7074
www.sloansandkenyon.com

S&T
Steinberg and Tolkien
193 King's Road
Chelsea
London SW3 5EB, UK
Tel: 011 44 20 7376 3660
Fax: 011 44 20 7376 3630

SCG
Susie Cooper Ceramics at
Gallery 1930
18 Church Street
Marylebone
London NW8 8EP, UK
Tel: 011 44 20 7723 1555
E-mail: gallery1930@aol.com
www.susiecooperceramics.com

SDR
Sollo:Rago Modern Auctions
333 North Main Street
Lambertville, NJ 08530
Tel: (609) 397-9374
Fax: (609) 397-9377
E-mail: info@ragoarts.com
www.ragoarts.com

SF
The Silver Fund
1 Duke of York Street
London SW1Y 6JP, UK
Tel: 011 44 20 7839 7664
Fax: 011 44 20 7839 8935
www.thesilverfund.com

SOM
Somlo Antiques
7 Piccadilly Arcade
London SW1Y 6NH, UK
Tel: 011 44 20 7499 6526
Fax: 011 44 20 7499 0603
E-mail: mail@somlo.com
www.somlo.com

SWA
Swann Galleries
104 East 25th Street
New York, NY 10010
Tel: (212) 254-4710
Fax: (212) 979-1017
E-mail: swann@swanngalleries.com
www.swanngalleries.com

SWO
Sworders
14 Cambridge Road
Stansted Mountfitchet
Essex CM24 8BZ, UK
Tel: 011 44 1279 817 778
E-mail: auctions@sworder.co.uk
www.sworder.co.uk

SWT
Swing Time
St Apern-Straße 66–68
50667 Cologne, Germany
Tel: 011 49 221 257 3181
Fax: 011 49 221 257 3184
E-mail: artdeco@swing-time.com
www.swing-time.com

TA
333 Auctions LLC
333 North Main Street
Lambertville, NJ 08530
Tel: (609) 397-9374
Fax: (609) 397-9377
E-mail: info@ragoarts.com
www.ragoarts.com

TAB
Take-A-Boo Emporium
1927 Avenue Road
Toronto, Ontario M5M 4A2
Tel: (416) 785-4555
Fax: (416) 785-4594
E-mail: swinton@takeaboo.com
www.takeaboo.com

TAG
Tagore Ltd
c/o The Silver Fund
1 Duke of York Street
London SW1Y 6JP, UK
Cell: 011 44 7989 953 452
E-mail: tagore@grays.clara.net

TC
Aux Trois Clefs
117 Boulevard Stalingrad
69100 Villeurbanne, France
Tel: 011 33 4 7244 2202

TDC
Thomas Dreiling Collection

TDG
The Design Gallery
5 The Green, Westerham
Kent TN16 1AS, UK
Tel: 011 44 1959 561 234
E-mail: sales@designgallery.co.uk
www.designgallery.co.uk

TEC
Tecta
Sohnreystraße 10
37697 Lauenförde
Germany
Tel: 011 49 52 733 7890
E-mail: museum@tecta.de
www.tecta.de

TEL
Galerie Telkamp
Maximilianstraße 6
80539 Munich
Germany
Tel: 011 49 89 226 283
Fax: 011 49 89 242 14652

TR
Terry Rodgers & Melody
(Antique and Vintage Jewellery)
30 Manhattan Art and
Antique Center
1050 2nd Avenue
New York, NY 10022
Tel: (212) 758-3164
E-mail: melodyjewelnyc@aol.com

TRIO
Trio
L24, Grays Antique Market
1–7 Davies Mews
London W1Y 5AB, UK
Tel: 011 44 20 7493 2736
Fax: 011 44 20 7493 9344
E-mail: info@trio-london
www.trio-london.fsnet.co.uk

V&A
Victoria & Albert Museum
http://images.vam.ac.uk

VDB
Van Den Bosch
Shop 1
Georgian Village
Camden Passage
Islington
London N1 8DU, UK
Tel: 011 44 20 7226 4550
E-mail: info@vandenbosch.co.uk
www.vandenbosch.co.uk

VGA
Village Green Antiques
Port Antiques Centre
289 Main Street
Port Washington, NY 11050
Tel: (516) 625-2946
E-mail: amysdish@optonline.net

VS
Glas Von Spaeth
Willhelm-Diess-Weg 13
81927 Munich
Germany
Tel & Fax: 011 49 89 280 9132
E-mail: info@glasvonspaeth.com
www.glasvonspaeth.com

VZ
Von Zezschwitz
Friedrichstraße 1a
80801 Munich, Germany
Tel: 011 49 89 3898 930
Fax: 011 49 89 3898 9325
E-mail: info@von-zezschwitz.de
www.von-zezschwitz.de

WAIN
William Wain at Antiquarius
Stand J6
Antiquarius, 135 King's Road
Chelsea, London SW3 4PW, UK
Tel: 011 44 20 7351 4905
E-mail: w.wain@btopenworld.com

WKA
im Kinsky Kunst Auktionen
GmbH,
Palais Kinsky Freyung 4
1010 Vienna, Austria
Tel: 011 43 15 324 200
Fax: 011 43 15 324 2009
E-mail: office@imkinsky.com
www.palais-kinsky.com

WRI
Wright
www.wright20.com

WROB
Junnaa & Thomi Wroblewski
78 Marylebone High Street
Box 39, London W1U 5AP, UK
Tel & Fax: 011 44 20 7499 7793
E-mail: junnaa@wroblewski.eu.com
thomi@wroblewski.eu.com

WW
Woolley and Wallis
51–61 Castle Street, Salisbury
Wiltshire SP1 3SU, UK
Tel: 011 44 1722 424 500
Fax: 011 44 1722 424 508
E-mail: enquiries@woolleyand
wallis.co.uk
www.woolleyandwallis.co.uk

Directory of Museums

US & CANADA

Charles Hosmer Morse Museum of American Art
445 North Park Avenue
Winter Park, FL 32789
Tel: (407) 645-5311
www.morsemuseum.org

Los Angeles County Museum of Art (LACMA)
5905 Wilshire Boulevard
Los Angeles, CA 90036
Tel: (323) 857-6000
www.lacma.org

Metropolitan Museum of Art
1000 Fifth Avenue
New York, NY 10028
Tel: (212) 535-7710
www.metmuseum.org

Minneapolis Institute of Arts
2400 Third Avenue South
Minneapolis, MN 55404
Tel: (612) 870-3200
www.artsmia.org

Museum of Modern Art
11 West 53rd Street
New York, NY 10019
Tel: (212) 708-9400
www.moma.org

Royal Ontario Museum
100 Queens Park
Toronto, Ontario M5S 2C6
Tel: (416) 586-5549
www.rom.on.ca

Virginia Museum of Fine Arts
200 N. Boulevard
Richmond, VA 23220
Tel: (804) 340-1400
www.vmfa.state.va.us

Wolfsonian at Florida International University
1001 Washington Avenue
Miami Beach, FL 33139
Tel: (305) 531-1001
www.wolfsonian.org

UK

Bakelite Museum
Orchard Mill
Williton TA4 4NS
Tel: 011 44 1984 632 133
www.bakelitemuseum.co.uk

Brighton Museum & Art Gallery
Royal Pavilion Gardens
Brighton BN1 1EE
Tel: 011 44 1273 290 900
www.brighton.virtualmuseum.info

Geffrye Museum
Kingsland Road
London E2 8EA
Tel: 011 44 20 7739 9893
www.geffrye-museum.org.uk

Manchester Art Gallery
Mosley Street
Manchester M2 3JL
Tel: 011 44 161 235 8888
www.manchestergalleries.org

National Museums of Scotland–Royal Museum
Chambers Street
Edinburgh EH1 1JF
Tel: 011 44 131 247 4422
www.nms.ac.uk

Victoria & Albert Museum
Cromwell Road, London SW7 2RL
Tel: 011 44 20 7942 2000
www.vam.ac.uk

SPAIN & PORTUGAL

Museo Art Nouveau y Art Deco
Calle Gibraltar 14
37008 Salamanca, Spain
Tel. 011 34 923 121 425
www.museocasalis.org

Museu Calouste Gulbenkian
Av. de Berna 45A
1067-001 Lisbon
Portugal
Tel: 011 21 782 3000
www.museu.gulbenkian.pt

Museu d'Art Modern (MNAC)
Parc de la Ciutadella
08003 Barcelona
Spain
Tel: 011 34 933 195 728

FRANCE & BELGIUM

Brangwyn Museum
Dijver 16, 8000 Brugge, Belgium

Clockarium Museum in Brussels
163 Reyers Boulevard
1030 Brussels, Schaerbeek
Belgium
Tel: 011 32 2 732 0828
www.clockarium.org

Musée d'Art et d'Industrie
23 Rue de l'Espérance
59100 Roubaix, France
Tel: 011 33 3 2069 2360

Musée de l'Ecole de Nancy
36–38 Rue du Sergent Blandan
54000 Nancy, France
Tel: 011 33 3 8340 1486
www.ecole-de-nancy.com

Musée des Arts Décoratifs,
105–107 Rue de Rivoli
75001 Paris, France
Tel: 011 33 1 4455 5750
www.ucad.fr

Musée des Beaux-Arts
3 Place Stanislas
54000 Nancy, France
Tel: 011 33 3 8385 3072

GERMANY & AUSTRIA

Bauhaus Archive-Museum für Gestaltung (Bauhaus Archive Design Museum)
Klingelhöferstraße 13–14
10785 Berlin, Germany
Tel: 011 49 30 254 0020
www.bauhaus.de

Bauhaus Dessau Foundation
Gropiusallee 38
06846 Dessau, Germany
Tel: 011 49 340 65080
www.bauhaus-dessau.de

Bröhan-Museum
(State Museum for Art Nouveau, Art Deco, and Functionalism)
Schloss-Straße 1a
14059 Berlin (Charlottenburg)
Germany
Tel: 011 49 30 3269 0600
www.broehan-museum.de

Kunstgewerbe Museum of Decorative Arts
Matthaikirchplatz Tiergartenstraße 6
10875 Berlin, Germany
Tel: 011 49 30 266 2902
www.smb.spk-berlin.de

MAK Austrian Museum of Applied Art/Contemporary Art
Stubenring 5
1010 Vienna, Austria
Tel: 011 43 1 711 360
www.mak.at

Museum beim Markt (Badisches Landesmuseum)
Karl Friedrich Straße 6
Karlsruhe, Germany
Tel: 011 49 721 6514
www.landesmuseum.de

Museum für Kunst und Gewerbe Hamburg
Steintorplatz
20099 Hamburg, Germany
Tel: 011 49 42 8134 2732
www.mkg-hamburg.de

ITALY

Fondazione Regionale Cristoforo Colombo
Palazzo Ducale, Piazza Matteotti 9
16123 Genova
Tel: 011 39 01 056 2046
www.fondazionecolombo.it

Museo del Bijou di Casalmaggiore
Via A. Porzio 9
Casalmaggiore
Tel: 011 39 03 7528 4424
www.museodelbijou.it

Museo Richard-Ginori della Manifattura di Doccia
Viale Pratese 31
50019 Sesto Fiorentino
Tel: 011 39 05 5420 7767
www.museodidoccia.it

RUSSIA

State Hermltage Museum
2 Dvortsovaya Ploshchad
190000 St Petersburg
Tel: 011 812 110 9625
www.hermitagemuseum.org

Index (Page numbers in *italics* refer to captions)

Acknowledgments

PUBLISHER'S ACKNOWLEDGMENTS

Dorling Kindersley would like to thank Neale Chamberlain and Richard Dabb for digital image coordination.

The Price Guide Company would like to thank the following for their contributions to the production of this book:

Photographer Graham Rae for his wonderful photography. Thanks also to Andy Johnson, John McKenzie, and Heike Löwenstein for additional photography.

All of the dealers, auction houses, and private collectors for kindly allowing us to photograph their collections and for providing a wealth of information about the pieces.

The teams at Sands and DK: David and Sylvia Tombesi-Walton, Simon Murrell, Paula Regan, and Mandy Earey for their dedication to the project.

Thanks to Susi Nichol for her help with planning U.S. photography.

Also special thanks to Claire Smith, Cathy Marriott, Dan Dunlavey, Sandra Lange, and Alexandra Barr at The Price Guide Company (U.K.) Ltd for their editorial contribution and help with sourcing information.

Thanks also to digital image coordinator Ellen Sinclair, workflow consultant Bob Bousfield, European consultants Martina Franke and Nicolas Tricaud de Montonnière, and consultants John Wainwright, Keith Baker, and John Mackie.

PACKAGER'S ACKNOWLEDGMENTS

Sands Publishing Solutions would like to thank Sarah Smithies for picture research, Pamela Ellis for compiling the index, Sam Spence for design assistance, and Luise Lorenz for editorial assistance. Many thanks also to the teams at Dorling Kindersley and The Price Guide Company.

PICTURE CREDITS

DK Picture Librarians: Richard Dabb, Neale Chamberlain

The publisher would like to thank the following for their kind permission to reproduce their photographs:
(Abbreviations key: t=top, r=right, l=left, c=center, a=above, b=below, f=far)
9: DK Images/Judith Miller/ADAGP Paris and DACS London 2005 (br); 10: DK Images/Judith Miller (tl); Judith Miller/ADAGP Paris and DACS London 2005 (cfl); 10: Getty Images/Topical Press Agency/Stringer (b); 11: Réunion des Musées Nationaux Agence Photographique/Chuzeville (tr); 12: Corbis/Hulton-Deutsch Collection (bl); 18–19: Getty Images/Image Bank (b); 19: Corbis/Nik Wheeler (tr); 20: DK Images/Judith Miller/DACS 2005 (tr), (bl); 21: DK Images/Judith Miller/FLC/ADAGP Paris and DACS London 2005 (br); 25: www.bridgeman.co.uk/Private Collection, The Stapleton Collection (tl); 25: Wright/ARS NY and DACS London 2005 (bl); 26: Rex Features/Roger-Viollet (br); 57: www.bridgeman.co.uk/Private Collection, The Fine Art Society, London, U.K. (br); 65: Alamy Images/Michael Booth (tl); 70: V&A Images/Victoria & Albert Museum/Given by Mr J.W.F. Morton (tr); 79: Rex Features/Roger-Viollet (tl); 80: DK Images/Judith Miller (tr); 80: Rex Features/Roger-Viollet (br); 81: DK Images/Judith Miller/ADAGP Paris and DACS London 2005 (tl), (bcr), (cfr); 82: DK Images/Judith Miller/ADAGP Paris and DACS London 2005 (tl), (tr), (bl), (br), (cfl), (tcl), (tcr); 83: DK Images/Judith Miller/ADAGP Paris and DACS London 2005 (tl), (tr), (cr), (bl), (br), (bcl), (bcr), (cfr); 100: Corning Inc. Archives/Corning.Inc.Archives (br); 109: Rex Features/Roger-Viollet (tl); 112: www.bridgeman.co.uk/Bibliothèque des Arts Décoratifs, Paris, France, Archives Charmet (br); 113: Corbis/Bettmann (cfr); 118: www.bridgeman.co.uk (br); 124: Stoke-on-Trent City Archives/Stoke-on-Trent City Council Libraries (br); 125: akg-images (cra); 125: The Art Archive/School of Art, Staffordshire University (tl); 128: Courtesy of Wedgwood/Wedgwood Museum Archives (br); 134: Alamy Images/Ace Stock Limited (br); 136: Courtesy of Wedgwood/Wedgwood Museum Archive (br); 150: Getty Images/Time Life Pictures (tr); 151: DK Images/Judith Miller/ADAGP Paris and DACS London 2005 (bl); 152: © Christie's Images Ltd: (br); 158: Mary Evans Picture Library/Anthony Lipmann (br); 159: www.hehishelo.co.uk/ Steve Sippitt (cra); 175: Claridges (tl); 178: Georg Jensen/ www.georgjensen.com (br); 179: Georg Jensen/www.georgjensen.com (cfr); 201: Corbis/Bettmann (tl); 202: DK Images/Judith Miller/ DACS 2005 (cb), (bl), (br); 203: DK Images/Judith Miller/ADAGP Paris and DACS London 2005 (cb), (bl), (br); 214: Getty Images (tr); 215: DK Images/Judith Miller/ADAGP Paris and DACS London 2005 (br); 216: © Christie's Images Ltd (br).

All other images © Dorling Kindersley and The Price Guide Company Ltd. For further information see: **www.dkimages.com**